THOMAS H. BRIGGS

OPERA
And Its
ENJOYMENT

BUREAU OF PUBLICATIONS

Teachers College, Columbia University, New York

FOR THOSE WHO KNOW LITTLE
ABOUT OPERA, BUT WISH TO
UNDERSTAND AND ENJOY IT

PREFACE

A GOOD many years ago I attended my first opera. I knew nothing about opera and only a little more about music. Why, then, did I go? For the same reason, no doubt, that thousands of others have gone for the first time or have hoped to go: because opera is reputed to be a high form of art enjoyed by men and women of culture. And all of us aspire in one way or another to be cultured.

My first opera was *Lohengrin*, with as great a cast as ever has sung that famous work: Nordica, Schumann-Heink, Jean de Reszke, and Edouard de Reszke. But I was bored, frankly and thoroughly bored, and disappointed. It is true that the music was enjoyable in a way: I liked the harmony, but I missed the melodies which up to that time had meant music to me. I had some pleasure in the scenic display; but I had not the slightest inkling of what it was all about. I had never read the libretto; the music was over my head; and I came away wondering how sane people could enjoy such an experience or could take seriously the swan and all the other artificialities. Though my seat had cost only two bits, I felt cheated.

Some months later I tried again. This time I selected *Il Trovatore*, because I was familiar with the "Miserere" and with "Home to Our Mountains." Again I made no preparation, and again I was bored and mystified while singers notable for adiposity as well as voices stalked about the stage and gave musical exclamations in a tongue with which I was not familiar. At last came the "Anvil Chorus" of the gypsies and then the two songs with which I had some acquaintance. I really thrilled to them, but much as I should have done had they been sung in a concert. All the rest meant almost nothing.

It was years before I got up courage to try again. In the meantime I had ridiculed opera and all its devotees. There is plenty for an ignoramus to ridicule in it, as there is in any other art the conventions of which he neither understands nor accepts. But gradually I came to realize that intelligent people would not spend their money and their time for experiences from which they did not get enjoyment. The opera devotees whom I knew I respected, and I wanted what they respected. So I resolved to try again.

With advice as to which operas are best for a beginner, I selected one and prepared for it. I read the libretto casually and familiarized myself with the more important musical numbers by playing them over several times on a reproducing machine. In the intervening years I had learned something of music—not much, it is true, but I had taken the first steps toward understanding the more important principles of composition; and I had heard much music, mostly symphonies and chamber concerts, which had gradually influenced my taste.

With such limited preparation I got from the performance at least an idea of the glories that are possible. I was not bored; I enjoyed the experience, from which I had occasional thrills, and I got a glimpse of the realms of enjoyment that I desired more fully to enter. But when I sought assistance from books I found nothing that exactly satisfied my need; and when I sought aid from those who know opera, I got little that was basic and nothing that aided me in understanding and enjoyment. Exclamations I got in plenty, and vague or picturesque phrases of evaluation, along with anecdotes that were more interesting than illuminating.

But I persisted. Each experience brought not only greater pleasure but also a better understanding of how to prepare

for the next one. Still an amateur; still, in the minds of friends
who are expert musicians, relatively an ignoramus, I have
learned to lose myself almost completely at a performance of
a good opera. I come away deeply moved both aesthetically
and emotionally, and with a feeling of enjoyment and gratification that makes me keen for another opera at the earliest
possible moment.

After I had heard many operas, I tried to help others who
wanted to know what the art form is, and in fact were just
where I was in the beginning. The experts whom I brought
before my students at informal teas knew too much; they
could not appreciate the complete ignorance of the beginner
and get his point of view, which is necessary for anyone who
is to be really helpful.

My own experience, mostly self-directed, gives me, I think,
an understanding of the attitude and the needs of the beginner
who wishes to find out what, if anything, opera holds for him.
And it brought a desire to help others as I should like to have
been helped when I stood with more than reluctant feet on
the threshold of a palace that I have found to contain many
exquisite pleasures, more of which I hope to learn to enjoy in
the future.

This little book is an introduction to opera for those who
know nothing or little about it, by one who knows only a
little more. After doing what is suggested in the following
pages, each one who is ambitious for greater knowledge will
himself find the means for getting it. The surest path of
progress is, of course, to hear and to see as many operas as
possible, preparing thoroughly for each one, and reflecting
afterward on each experience so as to learn what additional
knowledge is needed for greater and fuller enjoyment of the
next one. Both understanding and appreciation will be increased by a knowledge of the history of opera, perhaps beginning with the contrapuntal music of Orlando Lassus, Pales-
trina, and the other masters of the sixteenth century. An
acquaintance with Peri and Monteverdi and Scarlatti and

Gluck and Pergolesi will give new meaning to Mozart, Rossini, Meyerbeer, Berlioz, Weber, Wagner, and Verdi. And understanding of even an outline of the general historical development of opera will probably lead the curious into more intensive study of those composers whose works are still presented.

Not everything in this book is original by any means. Naturally, during my years of devotion to opera I have read widely in its literature, and the direct quotations that I have included do not indicate the extent to which I have been helped by others.

> When 'Omer smote 'is blooming lyre,
> He'd 'eared men sing by land and sea;
> An' what 'e thought 'e might require,
> 'E went an' took—the same as me!

Part I of this book gives a brief explanation of what opera is and prepares an amateur for his first experience. It also by way of illustration tells the story of *Carmen*, and comments on the contributions of the several elements that make the presentation effective. Part II, with some repetition, elaborates on the various elements which combine to make opera. In the Appendix is a list of books about opera and another of books that contain condensed versions of the stories.

T.H.B.

CONTENTS

PART ONE

Preparing to Enjoy Opera

Chapter One

INTRODUCTION

IF you don't like music, don't go to the opera. Although it is composed of many elements—story, drama, acting, dancing, and scenery, as well as vocal and instrumental music—each one alone is better exemplified elsewhere. One can read stories in books and magazines; see excellent drama acted on the stage or on the cinema or television screen; enjoy interpretative dancing at recitals, in musical shows, or at vaudeville performances; and find the most beautiful paintings in galleries, and architectural art in buildings, both private and public. But nowhere except at the opera can he get a fusion of all these arts to arouse his emotions and to please his complex aesthetic tastes. Opera is music embellished by all of these elements or by any combination of them. But first and last and fundamentally the opera is music, vocal and instrumental.

Those who know most about the techniques of music and who after long study appreciate subtleties which evade the amateur, may prefer "pure" or "absolute" music; that is, music unaffected by story, setting, or even personalities. Mendelssohn in one of his letters protested against the giving of titles such as "Consolation" and "Meditation" to his Songs without Words, contending that the music said more distinctly and exactly what he felt than words could do. That may be true for those who are highly trained to understand the techniques of musical language, but it certainly is not true for the great majority of music lovers.

Amateurs are likely to prefer some form of program music, music which tells a story or at least suggests or interprets a scene or situation or action. In reality, many musicians also prefer program music. This is evident from the fact that they give titles to their compositions and usually in performance endeavor to induce in their auditors a recall or an imaginary construction of experiences or situations that evokes appropriate feelings. The *Eroica* Symphony, the *Pastoral*, the *Symphony Pathetique*, *The Sea*, *Scheherazade*, *Danse Macabre*, *Till Eulenspiegel's Merry Pranks*, and the like would be titled merely Opus so and so if the composers had not desired to help the imagination of the hearer by suggesting beforehand the general idea that the music is intended to express. All songs are program music; and program notes for most orchestral and chamber music concerts attempt to help the audience in appreciation by suggesting a setting or a situation from which the music is derived or which it attempts to interpret.

Program music does not always convey to a hearer what the composer intended. The long representation of the flowing river at the beginning of *Rheingold* can hardly fail to be understood by everyone. But the Prelude to Act III of *Parsifal* gains immeasurably in meaning and in beauty when one knows what Wagner intended it to represent. He wrote:

> At the beginning, the clear blue air of Heaven seems to condense to a mysterious vision, scarce traceable by the eye of over-earthly yearning, yet holding the enraptured gaze with magic spell; in infinitely soft, but gradually distincter outline, appears the wonder-bringing host of angels, descending slowly from ethereal heights, and bearing in its midst the sacred vessel. As the vision waxes plainer still and plainer, and hovers down towards this vale of Earth, the sweetest fragrance wells out from its wings: entrancing vapors stream from it in clouds of gold, usurping every sense with hallowed awe, and thrust into the throbbing heart's profoundest depth. Now blissful pain, now

shuddering delight, transfix the breast; with power resistlessly all, its downtrod seeds of Love swell out to wondrous growth, awakened by the quickening charm: widen as it may, it seems that it must burst at last for vehemence of its desire, its self-surrender, its ardor to dissolve away, as never heart of man had felt before. But this feeling awakes again to highest, happiest bliss, as the holy sight draws ever nearer to the kindled senses; and when at last the Cup itself is bared to all the marvel of reality, and plainly set before the gaze of the elect, when the godlike fluid held within the Grail sends forth the sunbeams of sublimest Love, like the shining of a heavenly fire, and every heart is set a-quivering with its radiance: then swoon away the seer's senses; to his knees he sinks, in worship and annihilation. Yet o'er the Man thus lost in Love's delight the Grail now sheds its blessing, and consecrates him to its knightly service: the dazzling flames are softened down to gentler glory: like a breath of joy and ecstasy ineffable, it spreads across the earthly vale, and fills the suppliant's breast with happiness ne'er dreampt before. Then, smiling as it looks below, the angel-host wings back its flight to heaven in tender gladness: the fount of Love, run dry on Earth, it has brought into the world anew; it has left the Grail in keeping of pure mortals, whose hearts its very Content now has drenched with blessing. In the clearest light of Heaven's aether the radiant host melts into distance. . . .[1]

Opera is an extreme form of program music. From beginning to end it presents a story, the atmosphere of which is in large part created by the music, and the action of which is carried forward and interpreted by what the actors do, by what they sing, and by what the orchestra plays. Drama to a considerable extent takes the place of form, which is so important in absolute music. Drama is the foundation and the moving force of opera, but music is the essential element.

We have definite program music when it imitates the whinnying of the Valkyrie horses, when it goes with the fire that

---

[1] "One single motif wonderfully developed bears the whole burden; it symbolizes the Grail. This mysterious motif first appears in the upper regions of the divided violins, then passes to the woodwind thence to the violas, violoncellos, clarinets, horns, and bassoons, bursts forth on the trumpets and trombones, and then, after a tremendous crescendo, gradually fades away and dies in the glow of the muted violins, leaving behind a glimpse of supernatural radiance, which is like a foretaste of *Parsifal*." Lavignac, *The Musical Dramas of Wagner.*

Loge has kindled to protect Brünnhilde, in the 136 bars that suggest the calm flowing of the Rhine, in the forest murmurs in *Siegfried*, in the measures that tell the meanness of Mime, in the pompous chords that we hear with Wotan. In the first act of *Boheme*, harp and tinking triangle accompany Rudolph's crackling fire, and when Colline tumbles downstairs an organ point slides chromatically down every few measures until it is two octaves lower than when it started.

Some lovers of vocal music are content with the oratorio or the cantata, which without scenery, costumes, or action presents a story by means of song, solo and ensemble. The auditors are interested primarily in the music, especially that which is sung, but oratorio and cantata are epic approximations to dramatic opera, each attempting to interpret a story. What they fail to give in scenery, costumes, and acting the members of the audience in varying degrees supply from their imaginations—or lose much that opera gives. As a rule the oratorio presents drama of internal struggle, of the victory or defeat of man's spirit, rather than the drama of achievement of an overt sort. Some operas, like *Samson et Delilah* and *Four Saints in Three Acts*, have in them so little of external and acting drama that what they say can be presented in concert form or in oratorio with almost complete possible enjoyment by the audience, but usually the well-known dramatic situations make their contribution simultaneously. The fact that in the United States oratorio and cantata are rare and that opera is increasingly popular is evidence that audiences prefer the opera form. The great majority of music lovers enjoy music drama more with the help of scenery and action.

It must not be thought that program music does not have its requirements of form too. Today an opera overture or an aria or a chorus must follow rules of composition as truly as any piece of absolute music. Usually the rules are simpler, and in consequence the amateur has less difficulty in perceiving their application and in understanding the effects. The creation of any work of art, in music no less than in poetry or painting or sculpture or architecture, challenges the ingenuity of the artist to follow successfully the rules of composition in such a way that the effort will not be too obvious and intrusive and that the result will be pleasing and effective. Just as the sonnet must develop a dignified subject in fourteen lines of iambic pentameter with certain limitations as to rhyme, the conventional operatic aria, a solo set piece, must, if not the *da capo* form, express with rich orchestral accompaniment an emotion in a song of three parts, the third repeating, frequently with embellishments, the first. Similarly, every other piece of music has its requirements of form.

Just as following the rules in creation is satisfying, so is appreciation when one knows the rules and is able to discern how the creator has applied them. Even a beginner is thrilled when he learns to recognize the statement of a musical theme and its development. One gets a fillip, too, from discerning how the creator has concealed his art and occasionally has with intent violated the rules to improve the effect by audacity of inventing new ones. Beethoven did this when he substituted a scherzo for a minuet in a symphony and when he first used drums for melodic effects; Mozart when he used trombones with effectiveness in *Don Giovanni;* Gluck when he abandoned the conventional opera form to get greater dramatic unity; and Wagner when he created his peculiar form of music-drama. In *The Ring* Wagner broke with the traditional use of the distinct aria, which the operas of Rossini, Weber, Meyerbeer, and other composers had trained audiences to expect. Sometimes innovations are resented and hissed off the stage; sometimes they are so successful that, immediately or later, they are approved and become a part of conventional practice.

The more one knows of the rules of musical composition, the more intellectual pleasure he will have in listening to music. After a while he becomes so accustomed to the rules that an almost automatic appreciation of their successful application gives aesthetic pleasure too. The amateur can understand this better by recalling his own enjoyment of similar successful application of rules in other art fields with which he is more familiar—in poetry, painting, sculpture, or architecture.

To get enjoyment from appreciation of musical form one must have a good auditory memory. He can reread a poem or any part of it as many times as he pleases; he can return at will to see again and yet again a painting, an etching, a piece of sculpture, or a well-designed building. But a piece of performed music is evanescent. It is true that one can sometimes have it played or sung again, or, if he has the necessary knowledge, he can study the score; but the auditor wants to understand the structure as he hears music. To do this he must be able to hold in mind a musical theme, to recognize it when it appears again—often somewhat modified and usually in an orchestra expressed by another combination of instruments—and at the same time to combine it with other themes that have already been announced and developed.

It is easy to perceive form in such simple compositions as the familiar hymn "Nearer, My God, to Thee," in which the form may be expressed by the symbols *a b a* or *aa bb aa*, each letter representing the same, or approximately the same, musical phrase. But in complex musical compositions it becomes difficult.

There is more or less unconscious self-gratulation and consequent pleasure in perceiving form in any art composition. The more complex it is and the more the technique is concealed, the greater the challenge and the greater the pleasure in understanding appreciation. By studying simple musical compositions the veriest amateur can get the idea of form, and by practicing with gradually more complex pieces he will, if he has a good auditory memory, steadily increase his power. He should not feel unduly discouraged if involved forms like the fugue baffle him. They are challenges for still further growth in power. Even a recognition of the chief structural members gives pleasure.

As power grows to retain themes in memory and to see their relations to others subsequently announced and developed, one will get considerable pleasure from anticipating what is needed to complete a musical unity. Try the experiment of having some friend play or sing the first theme or part of a simple song and then imagine what is needed for contrast or to bring it to a conclusion. Comparison of one's own invention with that of the composer will be interestingly informative. The amateur will find it easier to appreciate the major structure of a musical composition and the rounded out conclusion than to understand the relations of all of the ornamental parts of a musical composition. The important thing in the beginning is for him to get the idea that music has definite structural form. Then he can develop his powers of appreciation as far as his interest sustains his effort.

But there is pleasure from music beyond, or before, understanding of the rules of composition. Most people begin their enjoyment of music with appreciation of rhythm, melody, and harmony beautifully expressed. This sensory enjoyment is natural to man and is developed by the normal experiences of almost everyone's life. But it can be greatly increased by the repeated hearing of the best music well performed, especially if one takes the trouble to listen with an attentive mind, attempting to perceive the subtler and more complex expressions of these elements and to explain to himself, so far as possible, the pleasure that he gets. The more good music one hears with active attention, the better he will learn to enjoy excellent music. It is a strength of the art that good music drives out music of an inferior kind. After one has become saturated with Mozart and Beethoven and Schubert and Wagner he can find little satisfaction in current popular music. When pleased by the sensuous elements of music one's emotions are more easily aroused by other appeals. That is why opera has certain advantages over the spoken drama and also why the latter often has introductory and incidental music.

In any kind of dramatic performance, music makes more

than a single contribution. It pleases in its own right with
rhythm, melody, and harmony, but it also expresses, interprets, and heightens the emotion felt and expressed by the
actors in the developing situation. We know from the story
that Manon feels sadness when she is leaving the room in
which she has been happy. But when she sings "Adieu, notre
petite table" the music interprets her words and makes us feel
keenly, as she does. We are ourselves almost the bereaved
Isolde in the last act of the opera, and when she sings the moving "Liebestod" her interpreted feelings become our feelings
deepened and intensified by the heard music. The expression
of a beautiful grief furnishes a catharsis, as it were, a purifica-
tion of our own emotions through vicariously sharing the
artistically presented experience of others. This is a function
that music serves everywhere in its contribution to the drama.
Especially in the opera, music, chiefly that performed by
the orchestra, creates in the hearers a mood that is appropriate
to the drama. The audience comes to the opera in a variety
of moods; like the instruments of the orchestra the listeners
must be tuned, as it were, for such receptive and interpretative
participation that they will share in the feelings expressed and
developed. The overture of any opera that one is likely to
hear today usually does no little to produce the proper an-
ticipatory mood, even if one is unfamiliar with the story of
the drama. This mood is still further developed by the music
of the early scenes. Compare the solemn, almost holy, beginning of *Parsifal*, for example, with the nervous gaiety of that
of *Carmen*, or with the romantic atmosphere created by the
early music of *Boheme*.

Contributing to the proper mood for appreciation is also
the setting or background of an opera. This is given partly by
the scenery used on the stage, but the scenery by itself is cold,
and alone it would give little stimulus to the emotions. It is
only when the music interprets it, gives life to the mechanical,
that one becomes ready for the drama that is to be developed.
When the curtain rises in *Otello* the scene is a seaport in a
storm. The music not only emphasizes the storm but also subtly

prepares the audience for the human tragedy that is to be developed. The prologue to *Pagliacci* does the same thing in a different way; and the beginning music of *Aïda* helps the scenery to transport us quickly from our workaday world to the glamour of Egypt.

And finally, music has an effective function of recalling to listeners previous experiences that have been highly charged with emotion. Everyone has had such experiences—personal sorrow, tragedy, joy, or amusement—and as music recalls or suggests them the hearer in some degree feels again what he has felt before. Thus at an opera he cooperates with the singers and the orchestra to produce in himself the emotions that are appropriate to the drama. As every person's experiences have been different from those had by anybody else and as everyone varies in the emotion originally felt or recalled, the resulting effect of an opera is highly individual. No two people will feel exactly the same or have emotions aroused to the same degree. The opera is all the more successful if it calls up the keen memory of similar experiences and evokes harmonious emotions.

Music unaided can seldom do this successfully. It needs the help of words and of drama. One expert in music has written:

> The function of music is expressing those sides of human emotion which lie too deep for verbal utterance, a function the gradual recognition of which led to the invention of opera . . . ; in it lies a power of appeal to feeling that no words can reach, and a very wonderful definiteness in conveying exact shades of emotional sensation. Not that it can of itself suggest the direction in which the emotions are to be worked upon; but this direction once given from outside, whether by a "program" read by the listener or by the action and accessories of the stage, the force of feeling can be conveyed with overwhelming power, and the whole gamut of emotion, from the subtlest hint or foreboding to the fury of inevitable passion, is at the command of him who knows how to wield the means by which expression is carried to the hearer's mind. And in this fact . . . lies the completest justification of opera as an art-form.[2]

[2] E. J. Dent, in the Introduction to R. A. Streatfeild's *The Opera*, Routledge.

OPERA DEFINED

Opera is a highly complex, difficult, and subtle appeal to human emotions. Dr. Johnson, who was aesthetically deficient, called it "an exotic and irrational entertainment." But perhaps more of the world's musical genius has gone into opera than into any other form of musical art. It is a reflection of natural culture at the time of its composition. When we recognize the breadth, the depth, and the persistence of its appeal, we too want to understand it, to appreciate it, and to enjoy the pleasure that an enviable part of our civilization gets from it. The opera may be a social event, as the newspapers emphasize every year in their "society columns"; it may have been subsidized by the rich; but it is attended and enjoyed by the elect, rich or poor, who have learned how to find pleasure in the combination of practically all the arts that man has developed. We too can find some of that pleasure if we take the trouble to hear the opera and to study it. When understood, it returns far richer enjoyment than the spoken drama or the cinema.

What, then, is the opera? Marco da Gagliano, in the Preface to *Dafne*, one of the earliest operas ever composed, says,

It [opera] is a princely spectacle, and delightful beyond all others, being one in which are combined all the most notable oblectations, such as contrivance and interest of plot, diction, style, mellifluous rhyme, musical art, the concert of voices and instruments, excellency in singing, grace in dancing and gesture; and it may also be said the painting therein plays a not unimportant part, in the matters of scenery and costume; so that the intellect and every noblest sentiment are fascinated at one and the same moment by the most delectable arts ever devised by human genius.

Opera is the interpretation by music, both vocal and instrumental, with the help of the contributing arts of scenery, acting, and dance, of the emotions aroused by a progressive and unified series of dramatic situations. All of the art factors must be fused in their effect—fused in the mind of the composer and impresario, and also fused in the minds and feelings of the audience. [Whenever song or instrumental music or ballet focuses attention exclusively on itself, opera in so far fails.] Too much emphasis cannot be given to the necessity of the fusion of all the contributing arts, a fusion that the audience has an important responsibility for achieving, in order that there may be opera.

One of the gravest mistakes that one can make when experiencing an opera is to assume that it should proceed according to his expectations of a drama on the speaking stage or on the screen. True, it is a play set to music, but always the action is subordinated to music, finding its chief reason for existence in the setting that produces the emotion-arousing melodies and harmonies. Music requires of an audience much closer and more continuous attention than need be given to ordinary speech, and no distractions from it can be allowed. In opera there cannot be a steady succession of sublime music, however, any more than in the spoken drama there can be an unbroken succession of sublime speech.

Edgar Allan Poe long ago pointed out the necessity of contrast in order that the beautiful may make its most effective appeal. In *Butterfly*, for instance, there are passages of music that are hardly more than harmonious sound accompanying the equally unemotional words used by Goro to explain the advantages of the house that he has provided. But such words and music both prepare for and serve as a contrast to the dramatic significance of what follows. Of course Wagner and Verdi and Beethoven and Mozart become prosaic in music less often and more briefly than do lesser composers, just as Shakespeare and Marlowe and Maeterlinck maintain the level of high diction more steadily than lesser dramatists. It is not fair to expect of opera more than we demand of other music and of other drama. Every part of opera should be experienced—seen and heard—as a fused part of a whole composition.

Of course opera has elements in common with the spoken

drama and with the cinema. Each of them presents a story with its exposition, conflicts, development, climax, and resolution. Each has characters which the authors attempt to make convincing and appealing. Each has its pictorial background and acting that interpret how the characters feel and develop. And each has its superiority in different elements.

But opera, as repeatedly emphasized, uses all of the elements of other drama and, adding both vocal and instrumental music, it fuses them into a unity of appeal. Opera condenses the basic story so that without previous knowledge of the libretto an auditor sometimes has difficulty in knowing what the background of the story is and how the plot develops. *Il Trovatore* is a mystery of music unless one is acquainted with the story beforehand. The condensation of the plot in a spoken drama is illustrated by the omission in *Traviata* of the second act of Dumas' *La Dame aux Camélias*, and it can be appreciated by comparing Verdi's *Otello*, *Falstaff*, and *Macbeth* with Shakespeare's plays from which the plots are drawn. "An operatic plot," says Henry Simon, "is not a vehicle for good music; rather, music is a help to the poignant expression of real feeling in a story that the composer takes with utter seriousness."

Opera emphasizes inner feelings that may be difficult if not impossible to express on the spoken stage. Simon well illustrates this in the following passage.

Spoken drama, because it deals in dialog and action only, must focus on those comparatively few moments in our lives when something important is happening, usually in the presence of others. Such moments, however dramatic they may be, are likely to be less intimately real—even less intense—than the much larger share of our emotional lives—the times when we feel strongly about something or other but can do nothing about it. It is the projection of emotion at such times, through words and music both, that makes certain passages of opera so real as to be almost unbearable.

Take, for example, the popular "Ridi, Pagliaccio" aria. Suppose that in a spoken play a simple and violently emotional Italian actor discovers that his adored and butterflyish wife is planning to elope with an unknown young man. In a little while, the player knows, he must go on the stage to act out a very similar situation with his own wife as leading lady. The play-within-the-play situation is common enough on the stage. But what could a modern realistic playwright do with such a situation? He could either rely on the actor to get across the conflict within himself through a gesture or two, or he could have him discuss it with a friend. Either device would give a distorted picture of what might be expected to happen in real life. For the most important, most moving, part of this man's experience would be the time he has to spend by himself before the evening's performance. Grand opera can, and does, paint this part of his experience as no other art can. It builds up to such scenes, just as spoken drama is likely to build up to scenes of action. Opera also has scenes of action quite as dramatic as these plays, but they fade into comparative insignificance beside the intense reality of the scenes of emotional climax. Few opera-goers remember the music played when Canio finally stabs Nedda in *Pagliacci*, when Rhadames surrenders his sword in *Aïda*, when Lohengrin slays Telramund in *Lohengrin*. In terms of spoken drama, these are important climaxes; but the great moments of grand opera come in rather more realistic, less stagey parts—when Rhadames lyrically longs to become a victorious general so that he may elevate his beloved to a throne ("Celeste Aïda"), when Violetta attempts to persuade herself that it is too late to hang on to hopes of seeing Alfredo again ("Addio del passata"), or when Faust, standing alone in Marguerite's garden, first senses the natural beauty that frames her innocence ("Salut! demeure").[3]

Furthermore, opera permits two or more characters singing in duets, trios, quartettes, or other ensembles to express simultaneously different and often conflicting emotions. Of the many illustrations may be cited the canon in *Fidelio* when Marzelline is ecstatic, Leonore worried, Rocco benevolent, and Jaquino frankly jealous of Fidelio, the trio in *Don Giovanni* when Leporello on the opposite side of the stage comments sardonically on what the Don and Donna Anna are singing, and the famous sextette in *Lucia di Lammermoor*. Opera also permits asides (Iago in *Otello* and Amneris in *Aïda*,

[3] Henry W. Simon, *Treasury of Grand Opera* (New York: Simon & Schuster, Inc., 1946).

I) and soliloquies ("Celeste Aïda," and Hans Sachs in *Die Meistersinger*, II), both effectively expressing feelings that are difficult to convey in spoken drama.

[Although operagoers seldom if ever weep at the presented tragedy, they do as a rule maintain a higher emotional level than is reached while experiencing any other dramatic entertainment. Moreover, they seldom tire of hearing the same opera over and over, each time perceiving from the music new understanding and new beauties that contribute to maintaining and increasing emotional responses.

Although the opera has been called the most aristocratic of all the arts, it is composed of elements that are in some form known and loved by people of all levels of society and wealth. There are no social or economic requirements for the love of story and drama, of instrumental and vocal music, of architecture and color in stage setting, of pantomime and dance. As one knows and enjoys any of these elements of aesthetic entertainment, he will learn to love the combination that we call opera. As a rule, for reasons that will be later presented, the dramatic story is not likely to be as good as that presented on the speaking stage, in the cinema, or in books and magazines; but the effects may be, and for many people undoubtedly are, heightened by the accompaniment of music and rhythmic movement. Music can be heard elsewhere, in the concert hall or at home, but its significance for most people is undoubtedly increased when it expresses emotion in a dramatic situation. Similarly, architectural settings such as we find on the opera stage, and color in scenery and costumes should be appreciated solely as contributing parts of the whole effect. The same may be said of pantomime or gesture and the dance, though the latter in the opera is often a harmonious episode rather than an essential part of the development of the emotion peculiar to the drama. No wonder that the opera is loved and attended by all sorts of people who have learned to respond to the combined appeal to their emotions.

As long as men will jubilate in their happiness, and laugh and sing, as long as they will cry and shout in the agony of pain and unhappiness, opera will be appreciated by many, because opera endeavors not merely to render the phenomena of life, but to give life itself, to depict man as he is, in the realm of passions that are intangible and inexpressible in mere words. It does not want to analyze characters by reasoning, but it places them before our eyes and ears in the making, in their acts.[4]

OPERA AS A FUSION OF ARTS

The ideal opera is, of course, a perfect fusion of all the contributing elements, each of those mentioned being capable of subdivision and still further supplementation. But a perfect fusion is never achieved in performance. Opera has seldom had one creator who is responsible for the harmonious combination of all the elements. It is true that someone—the composer in the case of Mozart, Weber, and Wagner, or an impresario, who should be an omniscient artist himself—is responsible for the blending of story and music and scenery and ballet; but there are many creating artists who contribute, and each one is, as a rule, thoroughly convinced that emphasis on his production will improve the general effect. By the very nature of genius, artists are more individualistic than cooperative, and for this reason it is difficult for a producer to get the perfect balance or fusion that the opera demands.

An opera used to be (and sometimes still is) initiated by someone who commissions its creation, often indicating its general character. The first step in the production is the libretto, the drama developed in words. The author, sometimes already notable as a poet or as a dramatist, has ideas of his art and ambitions that make against subordination for perfect cooperation. Then there is the composer, who with ideas and ambitions of his own creates the music for both instruments and voices. He is, of course, to a large extent limited by the libretto that has been written, but naturally he makes

4 P. H. Lang, *Music in Western Civilization* (New York: W. W. Norton).

or has made in it changes that he thinks are necessary or in the nature of improvements. It is easy to imagine the conflicts between these two artists, the composer having the final word. Verdi found a perfect cooperator and often a contributor of important musical ideas in Boïto, and Wagner wrote his own libretti. But most composers have been greatly handicapped by the poet, who, it must be recognized, writes under severe restrictions. And beyond librettist and composer are the designer of scenery and costumes, the conductor, the musicians in the orchestra, the singers, and the dancers in the ballet, especially when ballet is an integral part of the development of the drama. With so many competing ambitions it is marvelous that there is as much unity as is apparent in any opera.

The conflict and competition of the elements of the opera have been active ever since the first example of the new form of entertainment in 1594. At one time, in one city or country, one element became dominant; at another time or elsewhere it was subordinated. In the early Italian opera nothing was of much importance except the vocal music. In France the ballet has always been more highly esteemed and emphasized than anywhere else. In Beethoven's *Fidelio* the instrumental music blazes in such glory that the drama and the singers are sometimes in shadow.

The overemphasis on one element of the opera at the expense of an impression of a unified whole has several other explanations. First is the interest of the people for whom the opera is performed. It is true that their interest and taste are developed largely by what they are accustomed to hear and to see, but it must not be forgotten that they hear other music and see other drama and spectacle besides the opera, and if the opera is to be successful it must satisfy their developed expectations. A second explanation is the genius of the composer. Rossini and Verdi in their early days and Meyerbeer throughout his career gave audiences precisely what they were accustomed to and what they liked. On the other hand, Gluck, Mozart, Weber, Verdi in his later period, and Wagner gave audiences something new and made them like it. A third explanation is the conspicuous genius of the artists other than the composer. When Italy was full of brilliant coloratura singers, the aria flourished supreme. The Germans, whose language does not easily lend itself to coloratura, developed no such singers; however, they have produced notable composers of instrumental music and both comic and sentimental actors of high excellence. Each genius influences in his own way the emphasis in opera.

The degree of success in unity of an opera is determined by the effect produced on the audience. For this effect each auditor is himself largely responsible. Without knowledge of the necessity of a fused unity and intelligent effort to achieve it, each person naturally tends to give to one element or another an attention and emphasis influenced by his previous interest or by what happens to please, annoy, or amuse him at a time in the performance. The operagoer cannot afford to let himself concentrate disproportionately on the story, the scenery, the costumes, the personality of the singers, the acting, or even on the vocal or instrumental music, especially on the techniques of its composition and production. He must attend to the whole complex and make for himself a fused unity of it. He must concentrate on what is intended and, in order to get the maximum pleasure, he must respond emotionally with a minimum of restraint. He who hears an opera as a continuous critic, defying the production to make him enjoy greatly and feel deeply, makes a poor investment of his time and money.

There are records of eighteenth century Italian audiences who during the performance carried on audible conversations, sometimes calling loudly to friends across the house, played games or cracked jokes, and paid attention to only the arias, which was all they came to hear. We are told of audiences, especially in France, who were interested in only the ballets, and who praised or condemned operas solely on the basis of the amount, brilliance, or novelty of the spectacular element that they contained. They did not understand or enjoy opera, chiefly because they failed to appreciate that it is a balanced complex of several art elements. Amateur auditors sometimes are interested only in the dramatic story or in the personalities and the performance of individual artists, or in musical numbers with which they are familiar. No wonder they talk when they are not interested or hum the melodies that they know. Berlioz as a young man once exclaimed audibly during the performance of an opera, "The musicians around me make so much noise that I can't hear what the people on the stage are singing."

Chapter Two

THE CREATION OF AN OPERA

WHAT the elements of an opera are and what each one is intended to contribute may perhaps be better understood by considering the process of production. Each of these elements will be discussed more at length in Part II of this book.

THE LIBRETTO

The making of an opera begins, or should begin, with a dramatic story. The composer of the music, who is, of course, the most important of all the cooperating creators, cannot begin his composition until he has a plot expressed in words. A patron—in modern days probably an opera company—or an impresario may select or suggest a subject or even the outline of a story, or the composer may be attracted to a plot, perhaps in a piece of fiction or already in form for the spoken drama, that he thinks could be effectively expressed and interpreted in music. He may ask a dramatist to develop the story suitably for musical interpretation, an exceedingly difficult task, or, like Wagner, Leoncavallo, and Menotti, he may write his own libretto. Inevitably the composer must dominate, perhaps planning the construction in a general way and securing such revision as the requirements of music indicate.

A good plot should first of all be dramatic, capable of presentation so as to hold the interest and cumulatively to excite the emotions of an audience. But what is dramatically effective in another age and to other people may fail to move us today. There are fashions in drama as in everything else, and a play has to be in the fashion with which the audience is familiar or it is not likely to be successful with them. It is no wonder, therefore, that some operas that have been enjoyed and praised by people remote in time and place should fail to make the same appeal to us as it did to them. For the most part these operas are now interesting only as a commentary on other civilizations or as a historical explanation of how the opera has developed. Some old operas we enjoy in part, even if not as unified compositions; and some still retain their power to move audiences, thus proving their right to be called classic.

A good libretto is difficult to write, especially because it must move slowly enough to permit the development of music according to its own laws. A poet may be able to express quickly and in a few words a situation that is dramatically effective; but music takes time. It has to announce its theme and develop it by repetition, contrast, or other means that musicians have invented. This slowing up of the action, the reiteration of words in song that is necessary for the development of the emotions but not for conveying the sense, often amuses and even irritates auditors accustomed to the rapid movement of the spoken drama on stage or screen. And yet it is at times inevitable. It must be accepted as a necessity of the opera, in which music is supreme and must have the determining voice. "Poetry and music are not the loving sisters that the fancy of the literary man would make them out to be," says Ernest Newman. "They are rival goddesses, very jealous and intolerant of each other. . . . Good music often floats a poor poem, while the best of poems has never been able to float poor music."

Another important requirement of a libretto, a serious ob-

stacle to the ordinary literary development, is that it must permit a variety of music expression—solos, duets, and other ensembles, and even periods of silence, which are effectively used in *Boheme* and in *Pelléas et Mélisande*, and notably in *Tannhäuser*, when Venus turns away from the Grotto with a cry of dismay and buries her face in her hands:
Newman writes,

> The ideal text would be that in which the action was implicit in the emotion, that is to say, one in which there is no need for explanation, through the mouth of this or that actor, of events that were happening off the stage or that had occurred before the drama began. It is when the composer has to interrupt his purely emotional outpouring in order to allow the poet to become explanatory that he realizes the difficulty of making his opera musical throughout.

With such requirements it is no wonder that the libretti of operas by themselves are often disappointing. Some of the world's great literary artists—Rinuccini, Voltaire, Scribe, Molière, and Edna St. Vincent Millay—have tried their hands with indifferent success. Some of the libretti that have been set to glorious music are just plain absurdity as drama. The book for *The Magic Flute* probably deserves the prize as the worst in the history of opera that is still performed, and yet the opera is enjoyable because of the music that Mozart wrote. The fact that weak libretti have been used is additional evidence that the opera is primarily and basically music. Not all libretti, however, are bad from a literary point of view. In the books for Verdi's *Otello* and *Falstaff* Boïto achieved eminent literary success. In some respects, indeed, he improved on the dramas of Shakespeare which he adapted.

The earliest Italian opera used the classic stories of mythology, and it later drew from the historical tragedies. The use of these stories was probably a recognition of the difficulty of an audience's sufficiently understanding words when sung, even in a known language, to follow the plot. This difficulty makes felicities of diction less important than we realize when reading a libretto. An outline of the plot of an opera needs to be known by the audience, as it usually was in the Greek drama, and the chief task of the opera librettist is to sketch the development with broad strokes, so that the general movement by a series of big critical situations will be easily understood.

The chief reason why plots were drawn from myths or concerned remote situations and types of people not commonly known by the audience is that the former are likely to seem more seriously romantic or tragic than what is well known. It is easier to develop emotion for Iphigenia or for Brünnhilde, who are faraway personages, than to feel deeply about the prosaic consul friend of Lieutenant Benjamin Franklin Pinkerton. Butterfly is more easily made a romantic figure than Kate Pinkerton could ever be. *Traviata* failed when it was first presented as a contemporary play; it became a success when the story was pushed back to a setting a hundred years earlier.

It must not be thought, however, that librettists are always careless of felicities of phrase. Some of these that are well-nigh perfect in the language in which they were originally written suffer sadly in a translation, which has as its prime obligation the necessity of fitting the music that has already been composed for the original words. Illustrations can easily be found by anyone who, knowing the original language in which the best operas are written, compares the text with the English translations, often made by persons of no literary feeling, whose only felt obligation was to compose a text that would fit the music.

Debussy felt the diction of Maeterlinck's *Pelléas et Mélisande* to be so perfect that he invented a new form of opera music when setting it for presentation. But as a rule the words for an opera are merely a rough form to which music can be fitted to express, interpret, and convey the emotions that are inherent in the broad dramatic development. Often in the earlier opera the words were provided by the merest hacks, who were employed by the impresario to provide a book to which an engaged composer could write music. So supremely important was the music felt to be that the same general story has been used repeatedly by composers; Caccini and also Gluck even used for their *Euridice* and *Armide* the identical libretti previously used by Peri and by Lully.

As a rule, libretti of operas that are common in the current repertoire do present pretty well in outline the development of a dramatic story, but it was different until Gluck stressed the importance of a well-developed plot as a first essential of the reform that he attempted. Until Weber, in *Der Freischütz*, and Verdi, after he had found himself, and Wagner the libretto was not felt to be important. Verdi in his later work emphasized tense action well narrated leading to a dramatic climax; his *Rigoletto* is fine and moving as drama, regardless of music. And Wagner succeeded superbly in *The Ring* and in *Die Meistersinger*. Most other composers, however, have been less sensitive to the demands for dramatic effectiveness, especially in the unity of the whole leading to a climax. *Boheme* is merely four good scenes, episodes, as it were, any one of which could be presented separately without great loss. And *Manon Lescaut* is similarly a string of more or less detached scenes. The plots and dramatic development of *opera buffa* are usually more convincing than those of *opera seria*.

So much has been said about libretti because the amateur usually has more difficulty in accepting the plot and especially the diction than any other elements of the opera. Begin with an understanding that a libretto is merely a skeleton to be clad in the substantial and beautiful flesh of music, and it will be easier to ignore the ugliness of the bones or their imperfections and occasional failure to articulate perfectly. Keep in mind the difficulties and the obstacles with which the librettist has to contend, and it will not be hard to understand and to excuse the shortcomings of his work. If he makes possible the composition of moving music, he has done no poor service, whatever may be thought of his book in comparison with the drama written for action with speech.

In most situations, whether or not the audience understand

and appreciate the exact words makes less difference than is ordinarily imagined. It is absolutely necessary for the singer to have words so that he can know more precisely what he should express by his voice. In a very definite sense the words produce in him an illusion that he tries to convey by song. The essential thing is that the audience know what is going on at any point so that they too can understand the musical interpretation. But, as will be explained more clearly later, there are passages in which the exact words should be known or heard, or the intended effect will be lost.

Music seldom says exactly one thing, expresses one and only one emotion. Nearly a century ago an English critic expressed this idea, though too strongly some will think.

Music serves admirably to heighten the effect of a dramatic situation, or to give force and intensity to the expression of words; but the same music may often be allied with equal advantage to words of very different shades of meaning. Thus, the same melody will depict equally well the rage of a baffled conspirator, the jealousy of an injured and most respectable husband, and various other kinds of agitation; the grief of lovers about to part, the joy of lovers meeting again, and other emotions of a tender nature; the despondency of a man firmly bent on suicide, the calm devotion of a pious woman entering a convent, and other feelings of a solemn class. The signification we discover in music also depends much upon the circumstances under which it is heard, and to some extent also on the mood we are in when hearing it.[1]

The Music

Usually after the libretto has been prepared, at least in its first form, comes the composition of the music. Whatever musical ideas and themes a composer may have in his head, he has to begin writing the music of an opera for the plot that has been selected and perhaps already completely developed in a libretto. In some cases, no doubt, a composer will write a piece of music especially for a set piece such as an aria

[1] Sutherland Edwards, *History of the Opera*, II, 84.

or a chorus or a march, and then have the librettist compose words or provide a situation for it. But for the most part the procedure is quite the other way around: The composer invents music to fit the words of the libretto. Of course in many instances he will inform the librettist of changes needed for the more satisfactory development of the musical theme, which makes demands often not satisfied by the original words —changes in diction or in meter or even in the gross structure of the passage. He may even make the amendments himself for the improvement of the combined effect, if not to enhance the literary value of the text or the dramatic effect of the whole. Some opera composers have had a delicate feeling for words and a high sense of the dramatic; others, being deficient in these matters, have doubtless for the sake of the music weakened the literary and dramatic effect of the text. In any event, a librettist with some knowledge of music and appreciation for it, one who is a true cooperator and partner in the composition of the opera, will undoubtedly continue to make changes in his text as the music is written. We must think, then, of the composition of an opera as an adaptation of music and words, each to the other, continued until the final form is as satisfactory as it can be made.

So much the amateur can easily understand, and understanding should bring appreciation of the result and also a degree of charity for failure to achieve literary and dramatic perfection. But there is much of the work of the composer of music for an opera that the amateur can understand only in a general way, the technical requirements probably being beyond his appreciation.

The composer should have a keen feeling for the dramatic. Some excellent musicians have not had this in a marked degree. Beethoven was our greatest writer of symphonic music, but his one attempt at opera, *Fidelio*, is at times lacking in dramatic values; it is produced today almost solely for its exquisite music. Delibes, Tchaikovsky, von Flotow, and Thomas are other composers who lacked the dramatic sense.

On the other hand, Mozart, Rossini, Meyerbeer, Weber, Verdi, Wagner, Puccini, and many others had a fine feeling for the dramatic and also a knowledge of "theater," that is, of the tricks that give dramatic effects.

It should go without saying that the composer should have fertility of musical invention, the ability to think up new musical themes and novel means of developing them. Mozart, Rossini, and Verdi had this fertility in high degree. The amateur at first is not likely to be disturbed by the lack of freshness in musical theme or development, so long as they are both pleasing to his ear, but there will come a time, rather quickly if his memory is good, when he is satisfied only with the unusually skilled production of that with which he is fairly familiar or with new musical ideas pleasingly presented. One auditor at an imitative opera by a contemporary composer remarked in a bored voice at one point, "This is where we go from Gounod to Meyerbeer."

The composer must have the ability to write not only music that is appropriate to the story and to the several dramatic situations but also music that by elaboration deepens the effect by giving to feelings expression that is impossible to achieve in words. It must intensify the emotions that the auditor would have from putting himself into the dramatic situation presented by the words. The more nearly perfect the verbal or the musical presentation, the less either needs the other, but the effects of each are heightened by cooperation.

The composer must be a master of the technique of musical composition. But in addition to knowing musical theory, he must have the genius to apply it with results pleasing to an audience which includes amateurs as well as those who have professional knowledge. The amount of hard study necessary before one is competent to compose opera, whatever his native genius, is impressively great. The works of those composers who have depended on fertility of tune-making without sound technical knowledge do not, as a rule, last long. Enduring masters such as Mozart, Verdi, and Wagner have manifested growth at their trade possible only to geniuses who worked hard to apply known theories and techniques or to invent and develop new ones.

The composer of opera must learn how to give full musical development to musical forms such as the aria without unduly delaying the action and thus irritating the part of the audience who are eager for the progress of the plot. Many who attend the opera primarily for the music are not at all offended when King Mark sings for many minutes while hardly shifting his position, or when a coloratura soprano continues a syllable through a dozen bars or repeats the same words over and over in embellishing *fioriture* or roulade. Most music lovers, indeed, however amateur they are in opera, enjoy such music in set pieces, even though it does slow up the action. But the composer cannot safely go too far in this. While writing his music with due regard to the technical demands of form, he nowadays must constantly keep his attention on dramatic effects and dramatic progress. To become accustomed to the slowing up of the plot by the music is one of the difficulties of the amateur. But unless he learns to understand and to accept the necessity he will never become a wholehearted lover of the opera.

While producing a unity of atmosphere or tone for the opera the composer must provide sufficient variety in his music to appeal to wide differences in the audience and to keep the interest alert. The more important forms that he has at his disposal are overture; recitative or the equivalent; arias or other forms of solos; duets, trios, and other combinations of principal voices, culminating in the chorus and in the finale ensemble; intermezzi; music for ballets or marches, and accompaniments for spectacles. In the eighteenth century the number and the order of these forms were rather strictly determined by convention, but since then the composer has had an increasing amount of freedom.

Contrary to a common misconception, listening to an opera makes serious demands on the continuous intellectual and aesthetic attention of an auditor. With the best of intentions the amateur finds his attention frequently wandering. He and others more experienced as well need the help of variety in form to maintain the most continuous attention possible to the music itself in order that there may be understanding and appreciation of the combined effect and fitting emotional response.

The composer must know the possibilities of the instruments of the orchestra, singly and in combination, and of the human voice. If the amateur first realizes that there is an infinite number of possibilities before a composer when he has to decide what means to use to express a musical idea, he cannot but be filled with amazement and with admiration for the successes achieved. Strings, open or muted, alone and in combination with any other instruments of the orchestra, and the wood winds and the brasses similarly are capable of all sorts of different effects. Which, the composer has to ask himself, is best to arouse the listener's emotions in any situation? Try to answer this question for any theme in a given situation and you will in some degree appreciate the complexity of the composer's problem even after he knows what he wishes his music to say. He must have such knowledge of the instruments that he can decide in his study without hearing them which ones to use.

And he must know what are the limitations of instruments and of voices, so that he does not make on them demands that are impossible of satisfaction. Less now than earlier, when orchestras were not always uniform in their composition and the performers often lacked skill, the composer has to write with a knowledge of what resources of expression are available in the opera house for which the opera is intended. In Berlioz' autobiography we are told that when he was a guest conductor in various German cities he had to rewrite some of his music because the orchestra had no harp or no sufficiently skilled player of the oboe. Of course such obstacles no longer exist, but it has been recorded that more than one composer who did not know the limitations of certain instruments wrote unplayable music.

Similarly, we are told that composers at one time or another had to take into consideration the vanity and the limitations of certain singers. No important one could be safely neglected; and as a result there are songs in some operas that are far from necessary to the development of the drama. More than one composer has added an unnecessary aria so that a star could show his art. In one instance Mozart wrote an entire aria in monotone for a soubrette whose best note was B-flat! Some operas, *Norma* for example, are seldom produced nowadays because it is difficult to find singers who can do justice to the roles.

The composer must conceive the characters of the opera as individuals and gradually build them up with characteristic music so that the audience thoroughly know them. They should be as real as people whom we know, and not stock types on the stage. Faust and Canio and Iago and Osmin and Hagen are so clearly and consistently delineated that we can never confuse them or mistake their characteristic music. Nearly all early composers before Gluck conceived of their characters as types: they wrote characteristic love music, but one lover in an opera was not distinctively different from another. Since the beginning of the nineteenth century a greater attempt has been made to present every character with an individuality of his own. The composer must make clear through his music what that individuality is.

The composer must all the time keep in mind the unity of the whole opera. There is a unity of the drama, and that determines the unity of the music which expresses and interprets it. The composer should withstand the temptation, which he does not always do, to give a disproportionate emphasis to some musical number in which he sees unusual possibilities in music. He must set and continuously preserve a "tone" or emotional atmosphere that is appropriate to the drama and to the characters. No one who has once heard them can mistake the tone of *Parsifal* for that of *Die Meistersinger;* and the difference between the atmospheres of *Boheme* and *Pagliacci* or between those of *The Barber* and *Rigoletto* is unmistakable even to the beginner in opera. The way that Wagner kept in mind through the years when, with many and lengthy interruptions, he was composing *The Ring* not only a consistent plan for each opera but also a consistent atmosphere, though subtly varied for each opera, is one of the supreme feats in all artistry.

Finally, the composer should be a man of dominating and persistent personality. Inasmuch as the music, as before stated, is the basic and essential element in opera, its creator should be able to dominate all the other contributors to composition —the librettist, the impresario, the conductor of the orchestra and its players, the ballet master and the dancers, the designer of scenery and of costumes, and the stage director. When he cannot do that through his music, or, in the rare cases when his physical presence is possible, through his personality, the task devolves on the impresario. In order that there may be unity of the whole, each part contributing with due regard to importance and proportion, there should be someone who sees the production steadily as a whole and who is able to suppress inordinate personal ambitions and to weld the parts into the maximum of unity of impression.

The amount of labor that must be performed by a composer to create an opera with whatever degree of success is prodigious. Understanding of the challenges that he has to meet will enable an auditor to a large extent to increase his appreciation of the creation.

STAGE SETTINGS AND COSTUMES

After the librettist and the composer have done their work, the opera must be prepared for presentation. For this there must be designs for stage sets and for costumes. The librettist has already in a general way indicated the setting for each scene, often for economy as well as for dramatic effect using the same locale for two or more, and he has also indicated in the text action that makes necessary certain buildings, furniture, and other "properties," such as a table, moonlight, a statue, a fan, a letter. The period of the action and the characters themselves give some indication of the types of costumes required. All operagoers must use imagination, but it is made more active by the scenery, and it supplies additional details and idealizes to some extent the settings that are provided. The settings reveal and characterize the locale of each scene and suggest the atmosphere, romantic or tragic or comic, which the music still further interprets and develops.

The stage settings and the costumes, if artistically designed, in themselves give aesthetic pleasure to the eye, which subtly makes the ear more receptive. They make it seem right that lovers or conspirators or romancers be before the audience and sing the music that is provided. Although the Metropolitan Opera House is often criticized as being far from ideal, the excellence of its settings and costumes is appreciated when one sees a less artistic production. As all know from experience, opera music is ordinarily less effective in concert hall, unless the memory or the imagination is sufficient to create an appropriate setting. It is a strain on the imagination when Romeo's pleading or Cavaradossi's "E lucevan le stelle" or the Valkyries' cry is sung without contributing physical setting.

Stage settings and costume for the opera depend for their effectiveness on form and color. Because of the size of most opera houses and the consequent remoteness of most spectators from the stage, effects are sought from masses, bold line, and broad patches of color, small details being safely neglected. One of the most impressive effects in opera is the scene in which the knights, each clad in his red cape,* march in to the communion in *Parsifal;* gorgeousness is effectively displayed in the triumphal march in *Aïda;* and tragedy in the gloom of several scenes of *Rigoletto.* The modern stage has a great advantage over that of earlier days in the effects that can be

* In the 1956 Metropolitan production the capes were a lovely blue.

42721

produced by the skillful use of electric lighting. The same set can be mysteriously transformed by a change of lights, and by the same means colors can be given different shades and even different hues.

The first sight of the stage setting, which includes the costumes of the singers, serves to indicate the atmosphere in which the drama will develop. As the story unfolds, the setting is seen to provide places for entrances and exits, balconies, places for concealment, and other "practical" details demanded by the action. These all seem so natural as we experience the opera that seldom do we pause to appreciate the care that has been necessary to provide each one in its proper place for the need that will come. Even a slight incongruity will mar the effect by still further straining the credulity of the audience, already tensed, perhaps, by the libretto or by the personality of a singer who does not look the part.

There is constant temptation for the designer to attempt display for its own sake. The occasional applause by the audience before the opera begins is gratifying expression of appreciation for artistically pleasing settings; but if the settings should distract by their own intrinsic excellence from concentration on the opera as a complex whole, then they are in that respect a failure. Historical accuracy is usually sought in costumes, and fidelity in the reproduction of well-known places, like parts of the cathedral in *Le Jongleur de Notre Dame;* but accuracy and fidelity are less important than aesthetic appeal, contribution to the atmosphere, and practicality.

CASTING

Another important step in the production of an opera is the selection of the singers.* The first essential, of course, is that those selected shall be able to sing well the music of the parts that they are to represent. Certain roles require peculiar

---

* The difficulties of casting are well presented by Ernest Newman in *More Stories of Famous Operas,* pp. viii–ix.

technical skill, unusual range of voice, or distinctive timbre or tone color. Great care is exercised by the impresario when casting an opera to select singers who are as nearly as possible qualified to sing the several parts. Often he has to make compromises because no singer of perfect qualifications is available, because he must use all of the company, each of whom must earn his salary, or because of the necessity of keeping peace among those who are reputed to be abnormally sensitive and jealous.

A second desideratum is that the singer shall be a good actor. All singers who aspire to opera careers go through long and severe training in how to act, and to be engaged by any reputable opera company one must be at least acceptable histrionically. But many singers with great natural voices that have been highly cultivated are not by nature dramatic. Despite all training, even the intensive coaching by the director after the casting has been done, they remain mechanical and wooden. If their singing is good enough, they continue their roles anyway, the audience having to accept their music in lieu of the combination of music and acting that it has a right to expect. Other singers, by natural gifts and hard work become excellent actors. Such in recent times were Lawrence Tibbett, Laufkoetter, Lily Pons, and in her quiet way Kirsten Flagstad, who, Lawrence Gilman said, "has taught us that acting in opera need not be absurd, and that it can be infinitely suggestive through reticence and economy of means."

Acting in opera is not always the same as acting in the spoken drama. It has its peculiar art, its necessities imposed by opera itself. Modern audiences are so experienced with the acting of the spoken drama that they often have difficulty in appreciating the effectiveness, especially when the means are subtle, of the acting in the singing drama. In the last act of *Parsifal*, Flagstad as Kundry seemed to do next to nothing, but her prone remorse and her low note of anguish were among the most effective pieces of acting in modern stage history. Wagner set very severe restrictions on his singers as actors; he maneuvered them into position, usually making a fine stage picture, and then had them sing the divine music with scarcely a movement for long periods. Other composers, Rossini and Puccini for example, created situations and music that invite good acting.

A third desideratum in a singer is that he shall look the part and that he shall have a personality similar to the character whom he represents. Because of the requirements of the music and the limitations in the personnel of opera companies, this is often not possible of achievement. We are so accustomed to almost perfect casting for plays presented on the stage and on the screen that an audience is severely taxed to accept as the youthful Juliet or as Marguerite a singer of fifty whose avoirdupois evidences her years. But if she can sing the part better than one who merely looks it, she must be accepted nevertheless. We know that the house from which the lovely maiden comes is a mere illusion of canvas and paint, but we make no objection to accepting it as the dwelling in which she lives. We do not demand that the tinsel be real gold or that the glittering jewelry represent a real fortune. Similarly, the amateur must for the fullness of his own enjoyment accept whatever singer is selected for a role. He must help to make the illusion complete: that *is* Juliet or Marguerite or Mimi or Butterfly. He must sternly repress any inclination to dislike the personality of the singer, especially as not identical with his reasonable concept of what the character should be. Unless he can do these things he cannot fully enjoy opera. Like the stage setting, the actors are merely to help the music express and interpret the emotions that the auditor should feel. The auditor must cooperate by suppression of intellectual criticism and by actively supplying with his imagination whatever deficiencies there may be in the actors or in their acting.

Training in Stage Business

Singers must be trained not only in the general art of acting but also in the acting of the specific operas in which they are to appear. The traditions of no other form of drama are so firmly established and so rigidly followed. At the first production of an opera the director, with or without the advice of the singers, decides more or less precisely where they are to be and what they are to do at every moment in every scene, and singers in subsequent performances are trained to act in almost precisely the same way. Of course from time to time improvements are adopted, and occasionally genuine novelties are introduced in revivals, as illustrated in certain performances of *Coq d' Or* and *Cosi Fan Tutte* at the Metropolitan and of *Don Giovanni* in Paris. But as a rule an actor is taught to take so many steps to the right, to draw his sword at an exact point in the music, and to make his exit in a manner and at a time that suits the developing plot. This of course facilitates the transfer of a singer from one opera company to another. A singer is not expected to introduce action that had not been previously approved by the director.

This conformance to tradition is not so absurd as it may at first seem. The music is supreme, and nothing can be allowed which does not serve to promote its effects. In order that there may be a sustained unity in the entire opera, someone, usually the director, must see that all action and "business" are harmonious with the desired effects and contributory to them. To allow freedom to the singers to introduce such acting as may be spontaneous to them on the stage would be assurance usually of less unity of the whole. In the early opera, singers took liberty to improvise acting and even to "improve" the music, but not so now. The tradition carries on what numerous directors and actors have found to be the best ways of presenting the scenes of an opera. Every Tonio will stand just so and make precisely the same gestures when he sings the Prologue to *Pagliacci*, every Figaro will get lather into the eye of his victim and wave his razor essentially in the same way in *The Barber of Seville* because the combined genius of all directors and actors has found no better means of making each scene effective. There is usually more freedom given to actors in *opera buffa*, however, than in that which is more serious or tragic. Grand opera acting is for the most part frozen tradition.

[It must be remembered that no actor and no piece of music in any performance of any fairly modern opera is supposed to be seen and heard apart from the flow of the developing performance.] If several actors are on the stage at the same time, they must be so placed that the entire picture is pleasing and effective. In the old opera, the singer of a solo, or any ensemble when it had a special set piece, simply stepped toward the footlights, often out of the general picture, and sang. This gratified the vanity of the singers, and is sometimes done even today, but it did not make for a unified progression of the opera, and it tended to destroy any identification of the singers with the characters of the drama. Though the custom to a certain extent still persists, modern practice is to [subordinate individual singers and musical numbers to the whole effect, and this is done by making everything fit as naturally as possible into the general progress of the play].

The amateur at the opera is sometimes disturbed and mystified by what he considers meaningless gestures singers make with their arms. Some of them are merely an attempt to get those awkward appendages of the human body out of the way; it is hard, as all of us have found, to stand unembarrassed with arms dangling by one's side or with hands holding each other in front of the body. But most of the arm gestures of a singer are an attempt, more or less successful, to give physical expression to the emotions that are felt in the production of the song. They are the vestigial remains of pantomime, which once was an important medium of conveying dramatic feeling. Although some singers fall into the habit of waving their arms as they sing, without any conceivable dramatic purpose, the best singing actors do not do so; their every gesture is a visual counterpart of the auditory sensation communicated by the orchestra and voice.

SPECTACLES, MARCHES, AND BALLETS

Finally to be provided is the pageantry of the opera. Some of this is involved in the original plot development; some is merely decorative, and, though outside the unity of the whole, harmonious with it. For the first type the composer writes music in his original draft. The march in *Aïda*, the dance of the Flower Maidens in *Parsifal*, the dance of the people around the beach fire in *Otello*, and the two dances in *Don Giovanni* are component parts of the operas.

But often there are spectacles, marches, and ballets that are not required by the plot. Everyone likes rhythmic physical movement, which in the opera often not only pleases the eye but also serves as a vicarious expression of the emotions that the auditor has developed. In the early Italian and French opera much was made of spectacular pageantry; it began to be neglected for economy's sake when money came from the sale of tickets rather than from the treasury of royal patrons. France has always manifested a keener delight in pageantry, especially in the ballet, than other countries. The influence of France, which for many years was dominant because Paris was the capital of aesthetics and of wealth for the whole world, has led to more pageantry and to more ballets in many operas than otherwise might be found. In both composition and preparation for production, consideration is given to what spectacular elements are to be provided and to the means for making them as harmonious as possible with the opera as a whole.

The ballet has its rules for composition and its techniques of performance that are carefully worked out. The effects of ballet have been marvelously enhanced in these latter days by the invention of new dyes for costumes and by the development of wonderfully beautiful effects from the skillful manipulation of electric lighting. As a result a ballet is usually a gorgeous and aesthetically pleasing spectacle, whether or not it contributes vitally to the development of the dramatic action of the opera. Because spectators like ballets, they are often provided, even though sometimes they break the progress of the musical drama.

The pageantry of spectacle, in marches or in other form, is usually a more integral part of opera than the ballet. Consequently most spectacles are provided for in the original planning of an opera. The preparation for performance of spectacles gives opportunity for genuine artistry, and here as elsewhere in the opera it is important that art conceal art: the spectacle should seem entirely natural and, in the case of marches, folk dances, and mass movements, should give the impression of spontaneity. Some composers, Rossini and Meyerbeer for example, had a flair for the spectacular; others have had little of it.

SUMMARY

Story, music, stage setting and costume, casting, action and stage "business," and spectacle are the six constituent elements of opera. That the opera may be an effective unity of the arts each one must articulate unobtrusively with all of the others, must not draw attention to itself out of proportion to its importance for the whole. All must contribute to the effectiveness of the music. The composer and the impresario attempt to achieve this unity, but, as emphasized before, a great responsibility rests upon the auditor, who is at the same time a spectator, continuously from the opening bars of the overture to the drop of the final curtain, attempting to fuse everything heard and seen into a unified appeal to his emotions. It is hoped that this explanation of how an opera is composed and presented will help the amateur understandingly and sympathetically to do his part in achieving the maximum pleasure from an art that has conventions with which he has by other experiences not been made wholly familiar.

Chapter Three

CONVENTIONS OF OPERA

Conventions are symbols which people accept for reality. It is a convention that words stand for ideas: our *horse* by conventions of other people is *cheval*, *Pferd*, *caballo*, or *equus*. By convention *nag*, *charger*, *steed*, *plug*, *hackney*, and a dozen other synonyms make us think of as many specific kinds of horses. By convention a single word, like *yes* or *no*, may by intonation convey several different meanings. And by convention a facial expression such as lifting the eyebrows means the same thing to people of one country, while it may mean something different to those who live elsewhere. Our gesture of beckoning is in Mexico a salutation.

Our daily life is full of conventions or peculiar ways of doing things which are understood and used by everybody. They merge into mores, manners, fashions, and morals. Never formally adopted by legislative action, they develop slowly through the years until they have the power of laws. They can be successfully violated only by one who is strong enough to create and make acceptable to others conventions of his own. Conventions are meaningless unless understood.

Any art is possible only because its conventions are generally accepted by those who enjoy it. Painting and drawing

41

have only two dimensions, breadth and height, but conventionally we see the objects represented as having depth also. Subjects of diminished or of heroic size are acceptable. It was a convention of mediaeval painters to clothe the Virgin in blue and to indicate holy persons by halos. Sculpture in marble or bronze seldom has the color of what it models, but that disturbs us not at all if a statue brings vividly to our minds, say, Washington or Lincoln and interprets his character.

It is a convention that a certain combination of sounds and their rhythmic and melodic succession is music, and that music of different sorts is associated with emotions of various kinds. What we accept as harmony may be displeasing to people in other lands, and harmony today has conventions that our ancestors would have found unacceptable. Many of our contemporaries, indeed, reject the conventions of harmony that Schönberg, Berg, and other innovators have used. The native music of the North American Indian and of the Chinese sounds strange to us and may not move us emotionally because we neither understand nor accept its conventions.

Like the other arts, opera has its own conventions which we must understand and accept if we are to enjoy it. Many of these conventions it shares with other arts, especially those that it uses in presenting music drama; but a few are peculiar to opera alone.

Some conventions that opera shares with the spoken drama are the elevated open stage framed by a proscenium arch and by the tormentors, or wings; scenery made of painted canvas on frames; lights so manipulated as to represent bright daylight, night, or twilight; divisions into acts and scenes, each of which may have a different locale; the lapse of time between scenes; actors who for the time being are the characters of the drama; and curtain calls by characters who may have perished in the play. We are so accustomed to all of these conventions that we accept them without question, as a matter of fact without giving them a thought.

But opera has conventions of its own and also allows extravagances that have all but disappeared from the spoken drama. The aside and the soliloquy may be mentioned. In *Rigoletto* we see two characters in a room and at the same time two others outside watching, each pair singing harmoniously without the other pair supposedly hearing them; in *Aïda*, we see the interior of the temple of Vulcan and at the same time a dungeon below it; in *Das Rheingold* we see Wotan and Loge pass into a sulphurous passage whence on the same stage they emerge into Alberich's subterranean cave, and Alberich changes before our eyes into a not intellectually convincing dragon and toad. Erda and Kundry and Amor and the famous courtesans of antiquity miraculously appear in their several operas and as miraculously fade away. Why cavil at these things when we accept other conventions to which we are more accustomed as simulations of what they are intended to represent?

The one convention peculiar to grand opera is that everything must be sung. In lighter forms—*opera buffa* or *opéra comique* or the *Singspiel*—there may be some speech, but even in them, song is the most frequent means of expression. Even the passages formerly spoken—in *Carmen* for example —are nowadays usually set to music and sung. One does not go to the theater to enjoy normal speech or declamation, which are seldom the primary attraction in any drama, but he does go to opera to hear beautiful music that interprets and intensifies the emotions felt by the characters in the several developed situations. It is a challenge to the composer of opera to make the audience feel that music is the normal language of the characters in the drama. It is the obligation of the audience to accept song as normal expression.

An opera develops a dramatic story by music, both vocal and instrumental, that interprets, emphasizes, and intensifies the emotions that the characters feel, or should feel; it does this in such ways that the auditor has the same feelings himself. Authors of theater plays build up their characters by incidents; composers of opera build them up and make them real primarily by music. One should not expect opera to do what it has no intention of doing, present a story that is so novel and in its detail so effective that it will of itself keep the interest intense and satisfy by a succession of visual thrills or surprises. As emphasized elsewhere in this discussion, in order to get the greatest enjoyment from an opera one should know the story beforehand. Then he will more easily get the contributions that the music can make.

There is still another convention in which opera differs markedly from the spoken drama: the action is slow. Each musical form that is introduced must be developed according to the rules of music, and while it is developing, the story to a large extent stands aside. There are musical introductions, ritornelli, interludes between the stanzas, and sometimes a postlude, repetitions of words to fit with the music, and even repetition of an idea for the same purpose. The auditor must realize pleasure from the arousing of his emotions, from recognition of the skillful building up of the musical form, and from the sensuous beauty of production. The story in opera is, to repeat, chiefly to give a setting and a significance to the music. Sometimes, as in *Tristan und Isolde* and in *Pelléas et Mélisande*, the drama is almost entirely in the feelings of the characters; physically they do nothing, or next to nothing, that is of itself interesting or exciting. But what is evidenced as happening in their souls is the most poignant drama to those who can understand and be moved by the musical expression of the tragedy of inner struggle. This drama of the spirit of man is important; the overt physical action is for the most part to explain what is going on within, what each character feels, and how that feeling manifests a change in his destiny.

For a hundred years or more the importance of song in early opera was so great that audiences accepted the convention that it could be given with little relation to the dramatic story. At the proper time one or more singers would step forward and sing a set piece, as the chorus in *Samson et Delilah* still does, and at its completion step back into the action of the drama. It was conventional to write a libretto so as to give occasion for set pieces such as a serenade, lullaby, dream, or farewell, a jewel song or flower song, a "patter" song, ballad, or prayer. These usually permitted excellent opportunity for vocal display. More recently, however, every effort is used to make all music, instrumental as well as vocal, an integral part of the whole opera composition, rather than a series of detachable formal pieces that can be played or sung almost as well in a concert. Even set pieces are made a natural part of the developing plot; for example, Desdemona's prayer as she prepares for bed. The actors sing "in character," each one in a position that the drama requires.

The convention of opera permits a singer unnatural physical postures for the satisfactory production of tone. This sometimes results in contortions, especially by those who are improperly trained or who have developed unfortunate mannerisms, that are likely to be distracting unless the auditor wills himself to ignore them. Much arm-waving by singers is said to be an effort to free the body from tenseness so that beautiful tone can be more easily produced. Gestures and attitudes are conventionally exaggerated.

In opera we must expect and accept some unnatural situations that make song possible. More than one lover continues to plead his cause long after everyone knows that his lady has yielded to his pleadings, and Gilda is not the only character who revives from death chiefly that another song may be made possible.

A subtle but by no means unimportant opera convention is that the singers are not supposed to hear the interpretations of the characters and situations that are given by the orchestra. When Siegmund tells in *Walküre* of having sought in vain for his father, the trombones play softly the Valhalla theme telling us what Siegmund himself does not know—that his father Wolfe is really Wotan. The instrumental music may contradict the words that are being sung, but it never contradicts the characters or the action. When Mime is trying to deceive or preparing to kill Siegfried he cannot know that the orchestra is depicting his meanness or his deceit. Ortrud does not hear in Act II of *Lohengrin* the orchestral F minor fortissimo warning to Elsa, nor does Venus hear in the flute and oboe the faint sound of the bells that disturbed Tann- häuser in his dream. The orchestra may reveal to the auditors the motive for actions even though they be unknown to the character himself. Declares Lavignac,

The special mission of music, as conceived by Wagner, is to place the spectator in direct communication with the very spirit of the characters, to reveal their most secret thoughts, and to render them transparent, so to speak, to their hearers, who will thus come to know them better than they know themselves.

Other conventions of the opera which one must accept are the usual libretto, the stage settings and costumes, the casting, the acting, the gestures, the ballet, the prompter's box (which arouses curiosity as to what is going on in it), the horrendous cacophony of applause, which if we did not accept the con- vention would go far to destroy the effect of the beautiful music that excites it, and the shouts of "Bravo!" a form of applause peculiar to opera. Few operagoers are more than momentarily disturbed by the fact that the parts of Orpheus, Cherubino, Siebel, Feodor, and Octavian are sung by women.

Chapter Four

HOW TO PREPARE FOR AN
OPERA EXPERIENCE

UNDERSTANDING and accepting the conventions of opera that other auditors generally accept, one is ready to prepare to experience * his first opera. Preparation is necessary if one expects to understand and to learn fully to enjoy what he is to see and hear. [Some preparation is desirable for any art experience, but for such enjoyment as opera offers, extensive preparation is desirable. If one goes to opera expecting it to make its own appeal satisfactorily by what is sung and acted, he is likely often to be mystified, confused, disappointed, and perhaps cynically contemptuous of the music drama and of its conventions.] It is true that he may get some pleasure from the music, but not nearly as much as if he had learned beforehand what it was composed to interpret. The opera has too much to give for one not to make the preparation necessary for the fullest possible enjoyment and appreciation.

The following suggestions for preparation by a beginner may seem too many and too detailed. One may feel that if

* As there is no word in the English language meaning both to see and to hear, the word *experience* is used to characterize what one does at the opera.

47

the opera requires so much it is not worth the trouble. Very well, then; if you feel that way, give up the hope of enjoying the opera as it may be enjoyed, or learn by inevitable disappointment and tediously what you can learn more quickly and more assuredly by following the suggestions of one who has taken the long and wasteful way of achieving something which he would have achieved more economically with such help.

If the suggestions seem to demand more than you care to do in preparation for your first opera experience, follow such of them as appeal to you as most interesting and most promising for immediate profit. You will probably come sooner or later, if you like the opera, to do all, or at least most, of the things suggested. The more enjoyment you get, the more you will want. But, to repeat, don't attempt any opera unless you like music. Learn from what has been presented on the preceding pages what to expect and then:

Familiarize yourself with the story of the opera * and with the libretto. It will not be sufficient merely to read the story, in synopsis or in full, for as you watch the development of the drama you will want to know what is going on at every step. In all probability you cannot understand during the performance all of what the characters are trying to express in song or of what the instrumental music is interpreting unless you know at every point of development the exact status of the story. You will not be able to understand enough of the words, in whatever language they are sung, either to get the complete development of the drama or to know precisely what any character is singing. Therefore, study the libretto until you know the plot somewhat in detail and in order. If you can read it in the language in which the opera is written, you will gain greater appreciation of such poetry and drama as it presents, and perhaps during the performance you can catch enough of the words as they are sung to prompt your

* For a list of books containing stories of operas, see Appendix B, page 243.

memory. Do not be disappointed if the plot and the diction are not all that you would expect in the spoken drama or in a published poem. Other people, probably quite as gifted as you, have been able to tolerate both. Remember the necessities of composition that have already been mentioned and concentrate on the dramatic framework for expressive music.

Try to understand the development of the drama that is presented, drawing on your background of knowledge of the techniques of both story and drama. As in the spoken drama, there are exposition, development, contrast, suspense, climax, and denouement. If the opera is based on such a well-known story as that of Tristan and Isolde or on the philanderings of Don Juan or a novel like *La Dame Aux Camélias* or a poem like *Faust* or a play like *Othello*, you will probably bring to the preparation much knowledge and a set of emotionalized attitudes that the author assumes in a cultured audience. When you find in your reading of the story the most dramatic points, especially the climaxes, minor as well as major, try to feel the emotions that should fill the characters and be conveyed in music. How should you feel if you were in the place of the character on the stage? What sort of expression of your feelings should you be inclined to give? What would be satisfactory musically? One of the functions that all the arts serve is to express for us what we have felt vaguely but are unable to express satisfactorily for ourselves. With such preparation you will be better able to understand what the music is imparting and to appreciate its success.

The rare person who has some skill with pencil or paint brush will learn much by attempting to construct imaginatively for one or more scenes, settings that will not only satisfy the demands of the plot but be beautiful in themselves and aesthetically harmonious with the story and the characters. Remember that they should also in mass and color and lighting give immediately a suggestion of the atmosphere in which the action and the music of the scene are to be developed. Few amateurs will have the creative imagination to anticipate the gorgeous pageantry of the Metropolitan setting for the second scene, for instance, of *Boris Godunov*, or the peaceful beauty of the Elysian scene in *Orfeo ed Euridice*, but the attempt to put together a setting harmonious in an art sense and practical for acting will contribute materially to appreciation of the professional scene designers' achievement.

Many opera settings are in themselves highly pleasing artistic productions. The art of the scene designer is not recognized by the amateur operagoer as it should be; indeed, the artist sometimes is not even noted on the printed program.

Similarly, if you have the interest, challenge yourself to imagine what would be appropriate costumes for the well-characterized actors, each one not only correct for the time and plot of the story and pleasing in itself, but also combining well with the others worn on the stage to give a harmony of the whole color effect. Like the preceding, this activity is not essential in preparation, but it may lead those who are especially interested and gifted to a series of entertaining inventions that are contributory to appreciation of one of the lesser arts in the opera. If the costumes worn on the stage are well designed, we are likely to give them little attention. Only when they are obviously wrong in themselves, unbecoming, or lacking in color harmony with others do they call attention to themselves and distract attention from the opera.

Familiarize yourself with the important music, at least with the set pieces such as the overture and the intermezzi, if any, the arias, and the ensembles. A list of the more important compositions of the best operas can be found in the catalogues of makers of recorded disks for phonographs, and in *Opera News*. If you are musician enough to read the score, that will of course be the best thing for you to do; but most of us have to depend on some friend who will play the music for us, or, what is usually more convenient, play it for ourselves on a phonograph. Play the important numbers over and over again, giving such close and intelligent attention that you will not only remember the themes well enough to recognize and identify them when heard later, but also to understand as best you can what each composition is attempting to make you feel. Knowing the music, you can concentrate during the performance on its interpretation by the singers and the orchestra. If the composer uses leitmotifs, musical phrases always associated with and identifying characters, places, or things, learn them by heart. One of the keen pleasures to be had from listening to familiar music is the anticipation, exact or even vague, of what is coming next, and then enjoying the gratification when the performers correct or satisfy the anticipation. If you know enough of musical theory, you will increase your appreciation by studying the form of each composition, the way it is technically put together. A person who can do this probably needs no stimulation to analysis.

Associate the words with the music. After you have become fairly familiar with the music, hear each piece over again, at the same time reading the words. To do this you will need a score of the opera, which presents the words along with the music, usually in an arrangement for the piano.* A score can be borrowed from many libraries or it can be bought for from two to five dollars. As you listen and read, try to understand the feelings that are being expressed, interpreted, and intensified. This association of words and music will materially help your memory when you hear the opera, and it will stimulate your imagination and the development of appropriate emotions more than either can do alone.

Then study the chief characters so that you will know each one as a distinct and individual personality. Some, but not all, operas are as skillfully effective in characterization as any novel or spoken drama. You should know Wotan, Rhadames, Carmen, Violetta Valery, and Mephistopheles, Turiddu, and Canio so that you not only understand what each one does and how he feels but also how he would act and how he would

---

* An unusually good source is Henry W. Simon's *A Treasury of Grand Opera* (Simon & Schuster), which contains the principal music numbers of seven frequently presented operas.

feel in a somewhat different situation. Without such an under-standing of the more important characters well delineated by both librettist and composer one will miss many of the sub-tleties of the opera. The better you understand the characters, the more thoroughly you will appreciate their dramatic and musical expressions.

Note where a spectacle or a ballet is indicated, and decide for yourself whether it is included to forward the progress of the drama or either wholly or largely as a *divertissement* for decorative pleasure. If it is for the former purpose, appreciate what it is likely to contribute to the dramatic spirit or de-velopment. Imagining how the spectacle or ballet will be staged will add to your pleasure when you see it performed.

Be willing to enjoy what you are to see and to hear. Nathaniel Hawthorne was entirely right when he said that no artist could make him feel anything against his will, or, it may be added, without his active cooperation. There is no more foolish person than one who goes to the opera and chal-lenges the performers to entertain him. You must be in the right mood and that must be one of charitable and even eager receptivity. Remember that in the appreciation of any art at least two people are necessary—the artist and the one who enjoys the product. You must in your way be as intelligent, as alert, and as active as the cooperating artists. Do your share.

No amateur can fully enjoy an opera without preparation. It is true, of course that those who have had some training and experience in music can without special preparation get some enjoyment, though not the fullest, from what is played and sung. But as has been repeatedly emphasized, the opera is more than music, vocal or instrumental; it is a fusion of all the contributing arts to make each one more effective than it could be alone in helping to produce the combined appeal to the emotions. The better preparation you make, the more enjoyment you will get. It is foolish to spend time and money to see and hear what you do not prepare yourself to enjoy.

Chapter Five

HOW TO EXPERIENCE AN OPERA

FOR your first operas get a seat where you can both hear and see well. If you fail to do this, be prepared to sacrifice a part of enjoyment. In some opera houses the cost of a seat is not entirely an index of its value. After you have learned to enjoy opera, and especially after you have heard one often enough partly to supply from your memory or imagination what you cannot see well, you can afford to be economical by taking a poor seat or even by standing. But not at first. Don't let penny-pinching prejudice your attitude and your prospects of learning to share in the pleasures that other cultivated people get from a great art.

During the performance ignore the people around you— both their personalities and their remarks, if they are inconsiderate enough to make any. You must concentrate on the performance, which so far as you are concerned is for you alone. Whatever your efforts, however, you are likely to be influenced, willy-nilly, by the evidences of enjoyment or of boredom of those near you. Share in their enthusiasm and during the intermissions learn from the comments of those who are intelligent about opera, but so far as possible ignore everything else.

Be considerate of others in the audience. Be in your seat in ample time. Take a comfortable position and do not move unnecessarily or wiggle, which you will not be tempted to do if you are understanding and enjoying the opera. It should not be necessary to caution you not to whisper to a companion or to hum a tune that you recognize; people have been murdered for less. If you are sitting in a balcony, do not lean forward, for thus you may blot out for those behind you much of what they came to see.

If you take a libretto with you, do not try to consult it during the performance. In the first place, you will not be able to read by such lights as are in the house, and if you use an electric torch, however small, you will distract and annoy your neighbors. In the second place, any attempt to consult a libretto during a performance will take your attention away from the combined appeal by the artists. If at times you forget parts of the story and do not entirely understand what is being expressed by voice and instruments, redouble your attention in an effort to get what they are trying to convey to you. You will be pleased to find that you will rapidly grow in power to do this. You can well use the libretto during the intermissions to acquaint yourself with exactly what has been going on or to refresh your memory as to what is to come.

Try to appreciate the performance with all of its elements fused. Attempt to gain an interpretation of each unified dramatic situation and to feel unrestrained the emotions that it calls forth. Remember always that the opera is a co-operative appeal by all the arts involved. It is probably impossible constantly and consistently to make the desired fusion. Your attention will wander, from time to time concentrating on one element or another more or less in isolation—partly because this is the way the human mind tends to work, partly because the impresario has not been entirely successful in getting his artists to make a complete fusion of their efforts. At one time the instrumental music will be so outstandingly beautiful that one would be foolish not to give it such attention as appreciation demands; at another time the vocal display, the dramatic situation, some subtle or masterful piece of acting, or even the cleverness of the stage setting may deserve the focus of attention momentarily. But your responsibility is to make as complete a fusion as you can for yourself. When you find that you are concentrating on one part of the opera, bring the other parts back into focus. Certain elements may be less worthy than others, but what is intended and what you should help the impresario to get is a complete impression from the whole complex presentation. The extent to which you are able to do this will largely determine your enjoyment of opera.

Ignore the conductor. Some people cannot break the bad habit, which is derived from a strong impulse to follow with the eye a moving object, of watching him beat time. Although the master of the production, the conductor is merely a performer, like a fiddler, only playing a larger and more complex instrument. It would be distracting from the opera to watch the fiddler's bow move back and forth across the strings; it is distracting and neither pleasurable nor profitable, to watch the conductor waving his baton. He is merely giving signals to the players in order that they may cooperate harmoniously in producing music that will please you. Concentrate on the production, not on the performers. Fortunately in most opera houses the conductor and orchestra are more or less concealed in a pit.

If there is an overture, listen closely to learn how it sets the tone and creates an atmosphere for what is to follow. In the theater, music is sometimes used for this purpose, and always the skilled dramatist writes his first scene or two partly to tune the audience, which is the complex instrument on which he will attempt to play for the next two hours. The opera uses the overture largely for this purpose. Listen to it closely to get the atmosphere of the opera and sometimes a musical summary of what is to follow.

When the curtain is drawn it says "Once upon a time,"

and as when listening to a story we should as quickly as possible put away thought of everything else and submit ourselves wholly to the charm of the performance. Give a swift
consideration to the scenery, the stage setting, and see what
they contribute of atmosphere and of anticipation. If in preparation for your experience you have attempted to imagine
what the setting for a scene should be, compare it with the
one that you see and try to understand and appreciate the differences. Most of this comparison you may well make during
the intermission. As the drama develops see how appropriate
the details, as well as the whole, of the stage setting are. You
may be interested similarly to consider the costumes, but for
the most part they are of much less importance, being chiefly
for the purpose of heightening the illusion of dramatic reality.

As the characters appear identify each one quickly and
surely. See how the personality and performance of the singer
modify the concept of the character that you had formed in
your study of the libretto and of the music, but do not permit
anything in the singer's personality to irritate you and thus to
prevent your enjoyment of the opera as a whole. Remember
that the singer was chosen as the best person available to present through music and action the emotions of the character
that he impersonates. What he lacks you must supply from
your imagination. Watch the development of the character:
at his first appearance he is no more than a dummy in costume.
Everything that he sings or does, everything that the orchestra
plays, many of the things that the other actors sing and do,
clothe him gradually with personality and breathe into him
life and character. Long before the final curtain he should
have become a real, vivid person. The understanding of personality is easy with such simple characters as Mimi or
Santuzza, more difficult with Carmen, and a serious challenge
with Hans Sachs and Kundry.

Enjoy the music for its own sake. Most set pieces in the
opera, arias, ensembles, and choruses, are highly enjoyable
when entirely dissociated from their setting—heard in concert

or on a reproducing machine. Enjoy them as music, but never forget that the setting contributes to the music as the music contributes to the setting. Try sometime reading the balcony scene in Shakespeare's *Romeo and Juliet* out of its context. It has undoubted beauties of its own, but without intimate association with what has preceded and without the physical setting in which the lovers speak, it may sound too sentimental and even insincere. Hear the dialogue, however, as spoken by the ill-starred lovers in romantic costume in a setting of moonlight, with flowers growing in the garden and certainly perfuming the soft Italian air, and how infinitely more beautiful and sincere it is. Similarly the "Fire Music" in *Die Walküre* or "La Reve" in *Manon* or "The Evening Star" in *Tannhäuser* or "Salut demuere" gain immeasurably from their settings, both physical and dramatic. Enjoy the music, then, as music, as you would enjoy it in a concert, but do not at the same time fail to appreciate the augmented beauty that comes from the dramatic setting and situation.

Especially try continuously to blend the orchestral and the vocal music into one unified harmony, as if it were given out by a single complex instrument. Only a connoisseur or the rankest kind of ignoramus would allow himself to concentrate on the *vox humana* or the salicional stop of the organ when it is producing a masterpiece of music. Only one who has not learned what the opera is or who is an irrational admirer of some performer will lose most of the beauty by long focusing his attention on an individual singer, or an instrument, or on the means of producing an effect. The vocal and the instrumental music, though given different emphasis at various periods of the development of opera, are cooperating parts to produce a single effect. You must learn to fuse them for this result.

Of course at times, for reasons already given, an auditor will attend most closely to the voice parts or to the orchestra. If trained or greatly experienced in music, he may get a peculiar pleasure from analyzing the form of a composition or from explaining how an effect is achieved—the tone color from muted French horns or the vocal technique displayed by shifting from chest tone to head tone, for example. But however interesting such matters may be in themselves, they distract from enjoyment of the opera during the performance. No amateur who expects to get from it the pleasure that it is designed to give will permit his attention long to wander from the complex unity of the whole effect.

At least at the beginning of your opera experiences avoid a critical attitude. If you think you detect faults, ignore them at the time of the hearing; later you may try to explain them and to imagine how they could be remedied. A carping attitude inhibits appreciative reception and enjoyment. Concentrate on the good, and in reflection, on the way home or at another time, explain to yourself why it was good. That is what you came to hear and to see. If you don't find it and enjoy it, your evening will have been largely wasted, and your progress in opera appreciation will be impeded if not stopped altogether.

At every intermission attempt a summary, not only of the scene just concluded but also of everything that has gone on up to that time. It is remarkable how this will help you to remember, and the more you remember the more you will be able to increase your enjoyment at a subsequent performance of this or another opera. One test of the success of an opera is the desire that you have to experience it again and the new and increased enjoyment that you will get at the next experience. The habit of summarizing will also increase your ability to understand what you have heard and seen, to appreciate the contribution of each part, and to realize the complex unity of the whole.

Some people without true experience think of the opera as a form of entertainment to be enjoyed without effort. Nothing is farther from the truth. One should not expect to get much from the opera without serious intelligent preparation and without unremitting active attention to all details, which he continuously synthesizes into an increasing unity. One should not go to the opera to relax. The cinema or an easy chair at home may be used for that purpose. When you do your part, by preparing and by actively responding imaginatively and aesthetically, the opera will afford not only diversion but also immediate and later pleasures that spring from the use of your highest faculties.

Chapter Six

WHAT TO DO AFTERWARD

AT the fall of the final curtain on the opera I personally resent the burst of hand clapping and the raucous voices calling "Bravo!" Both are a barbarous but conventional violation of the harmony that has just been heard for three hours. But I resent even more the necessity of moving out into an alien crowd to subway or taxicab that will bear me homeward. If one has had his emotions, the most truly personal element of his self, genuinely aroused, he leaves the land of make-believe with reluctance; he wants privacy for readjusting himself to the world of reality; and he does not want to be hurried. He wishes to reflect on what he has seen and heard, to recall the experience imaginatively as far as possible so that he can understand it better and enjoy it again and yet again. But we have to compromise with necessity.

The pleasure that one gets at an opera performance is only a beginning. If it has been genuine, he will want to hear the same opera again. One test of the greatness of a work of art is that it gives more pleasure every time one experiences it. Knowledge of an opera enlarges one's world; it gives one a wealth of memories; it makes the excerpted music later heard in concert or over the radio richer and more meaningful; it creates contacts with cultured people who have had and enjoyed the same or similar experiences; and it may stimulate a dormant creative ability to expression in an art medium—words, music, dance, line, or color—with which one has some degree of skill.

After hearing an opera one should consolidate and seek to understand his experience by as serious effort as he gave to preparation. The sooner he does this, the more profitable the effort will be.

Alone and in quiet, if you can arrange it, recall the whole experience as completely as you can. Follow the story through in detail from beginning to end, whenever in doubt consulting the libretto and the score, if you can read it. The chances are that such recall, besides fixing the opera in memory, will bring a better understanding of the construction of the plot and to some extent will remove the criticisms that seemed important when the libretto was first read. At the same time recall the stage settings and the costumes of the actors and try to see what they contributed to the effect. How was the personality of each character presented and developed—by verbal or by musical description and exposition, by costume, or by action? What acting and what stage business contributed notably to the effect? Don't hurry this recall; take plenty of time to make it as complete and as real as possible. It will repay you, immediately and in the future.

Recall as much of the music as you can. Especially try to make this recall in connection with the development of the plot and in association with the characters. However dim in your memory the music may be, such an attempt will make some of it clear, and it will also help you not only to recognize and appreciate it when you hear it again but also to learn to retain it better in memory. Only after you have made your most serious effort to recall the music, especially of the set pieces, play it over again and again on a piano or on a reproducing machine. Make your own for permanent retention in memory the numbers that you like best.

After the recall of plot and of music make a criticism—or, rather, an evaluation—of the opera as a whole and then of the several contributing elements. Be entirely honest with yourself: decide what you liked and what you did not like, and force yourself to formulate justifying reasons. "Impressions" are not sufficient. Relatively few people force themselves to this discipline, for it is difficult to do such an unaccustomed thing and it takes time; but those who do so are the ones who grow in competence to have sound judgments and thus later to get greater and more intelligent enjoyment. Being unsure of himself in an unfamiliar field, the amateur is usually interested to know how other people felt and therefore, he thinks, how he *ought* to feel. The surest growth in appreciation and in competent judgment does not come that way. One should begin as he should continue, by being entirely sincere and honest: "I feel thus and so for such and such reasons." Only after he has made such an honest review of his own is he ready to profit from what critics of wider experience or more extended knowledge may have to say.

Then read an interpretation and an evaluation of the opera as given in books written by experts. These books consider opera as a work of art apart from any special performance by certain singers. For a criticism of the performance that you heard, read in newspapers the reviews by several different critics to learn what they think were the outstanding merits and shortcomings. These critics, usually having heard the opera many times before, are sometimes inclined to be captious, partly because their standards are high, and partly, perhaps, to advertise their superior knowledge. And, unfortunately for your purpose, they are more likely to comment on details of the performance—that one singer was in good voice, that another is well fitted for his part or is poorly cast, or that at a certain point dust came from his costume—than on the opera as a work of art. But the best critics who write for the metropolitan newspapers, being themselves well-trained musicians, scorn the flippant wisecracking of the popular critics of the spoken drama and seek seriously to promote both appreciation and the steady improvement of public tastes. You will profit most from reading criticisms if you honestly, regardless of deference to experts, evaluate each one in terms of your own responses to the opera, agreeing when you see good reasons and disagreeing without apology when you can justify your judgment to your own satisfaction. The critic may be right when you don't agree with him; but no one is on the road to sound and substantial growth in appreciation of any art unless he respects his own judgments until he is convinced that they are wrong. You will learn more by focusing your attention on what critics praise, especially when they give reasons, than on the defects that they point out. Certainly you will thus learn to get more pleasure from the opera, in reflection or in future experiences with it.

If you are truly interested in the opera and wish to develop a more intelligent understanding of it along with improved critical standards, read such books as are suggested in the Appendix, page 241. Some passages in several of these suggested books will probably prove too technical, but even such parts will lead to some degree of appreciation of the ingenious invention by composers when solving problems of a technical nature. Most of what these books contain is so simply stated that you will understand it readily. Remember while reading that you are developing your own critical powers as well as gaining information, either factual or the opinions of others.

Added understanding and appreciation will also come from reading in the history of the opera. Probably the best books for the beginner are those by Apthorp, Dickinson, Streatfeild, and Dent, any one of them supplemented by special articles in Grove's *Dictionary of Music and Musicians* or in the more recent *Oxford Companion to Music* or the *International Cyclopedia of Music and Musicians*.

The best thing to do in order to promote one's competence for enjoyment after hearing one opera is to hear others. If you like your first experience, you will like successive ones even better, provided you choose wisely what you hear. Some operas that are greatly loved by those who have had many experiences are ill suited for the beginner. The following list is suggested for the amateur. Though the order is intended to have some significance, any one of the operas may be safely chosen for a first experience.

COMPOSER	OPERA
Verdi	*Aïda*
Bizet	*Carmen*
Verdi	*La Traviata*
Mascagni	*Cavalleria Rusticana* ⎫ *
Leoncavallo	*I Pagliacci* ⎭
Rossini	*Il Barbiere di Siviglia*
Verdi	*Tosca*
Gounod	*Faust*
Verdi	*Otello*
Puccini	*Madama Butterfly*
Wagner	*Die Meistersinger*

Other operas which an amateur may find enjoyable and gratifying are:

COMPOSER	OPERA
Gluck	*Orfeo ed Euridice*
Gounod	*Romeo et Juliet*
Humperdinck	*Hansel und Gretel*
Massenet	*Manon*
Mozart	*Don Giovanni*
Mozart	*Nozze di Figaro*
Puccini	*La Boheme*
Smetana	*Bartered Bride*
Strauss	*Der Rosenkavalier*
Wagner	*Lohengrin*
Wagner	*Tannhäuser*

No two people would suggest the same list of operas for a beginner. However, the operas suggested above for initial ex-

* These operas are usually presented as a double bill.

perience by an amateur are, in my opinion, those which are most likely to make an immediate appeal and to give assured pleasure.

Willis Thomson, who has had much experience in preparing young people for their introduction to opera, says that in selection he would use seven criteria:

1. There must be many arias of pleasing and marked melody.
2. There must be a strong melodic line.
3. There must be a lyric singing.
4. There must be colorful sets and costumes.
5. A ballet or other spectacle is desirable.
6. The orchestration should show great musical craftsmanship.
7. There must be only a few long passages that will not be music to the novice.

Especially the operas suggested in the first list satisfy these criteria reasonably well. In this list comedy may seem to be unduly neglected, and many maintain that it is the easiest approach to opera. Much can be said in favor of such a beginning. Mr. Thomson has successfully used *The Gondoliers* as a preparation for greater opera. He says, ". . . probably the step from Sullivan to Verdi is not nearly so great in appreciation as it is in musicianship." I have neglected the lighter opera partly because there are relatively few examples of it in the usual repertoire, but chiefly because it seems to me just as well to use the higher form of grand opera as an approach to what one will hear most frequently and from which he will ultimately get the most substantial pleasure.

In the first list I have also neglected Wagner, suggesting only *Die Meistersinger*. Although I personally have come to enjoy Wagner's later music dramas more than most others, I hesitate to suggest them for the beginner, partly because they are so different from all other operas and partly because they are much more difficult to understand and appreciate. *The Ring* requires long study, which will amply repay anyone who will give it; but it can, I think, be more profitably experienced after an introduction to opera that is easier and more immediately enjoyable. *Tristan und Isolde*, which contains some of the most beautiful music in the world, is hardly a drama in the ordinary sense of the word, but a musical expression of tragic spiritual struggle; and *Parsifal* is to me the most impressively beautiful of all. But I should advise the beginner to defer them until he is more nearly ready for the experience —I say "more nearly ready," for every hearing will reveal new meaning and new beauty. However, if the amateur who loves music should hear one of these great music dramas early in his experience, the chances are that he will at least be so impressed that he will be drawn to them again and yet again.

Aïda is my suggestion for a first opera: it has everything— a good melodramatic plot, intense dramatic situations, a marvelous interpretation of the drama by music, tuneful and at times magnificent orchestrations, eloquent lyrics, a steady succession of highly effective solos and choruses, spectacular settings, and an impressive grand march. It is probably the best opera for the beginner. The last scene is guaranteed to awaken the most lethargic person and to make him enjoy every second of it. One leaves a performance of this opera with a haunting melody in his ears and with a desire to return for renewed enjoyment.

Instead of attempting at the beginning to experience as many different operas as possible, the amateur would do well to hear a few over and over, after each one making such additional preparation for the next as he feels necessary or desirable. One virtue of a great work of art, as already mentioned, is that each experience not only repeats in undiminished degree former pleasures but also reveals new ones, some previously unsuspected.

CONCLUSION

With preparation, attention, and reflection one who loves music will assuredly come to consider the opera one of the great arts. But there are operas and operas, just as there are novels and novels or paintings and paintings, and even the best ones will vary in their appeal, according not merely to the way they are set and presented but also to the taste and the mood of the auditor. Though constantly seeking to understand, to appreciate, and to enjoy, one must at the same time respect his own judgment when it decides that some element is in varying degrees bad or absurd. One does not have to suspend his judgment or to lose his sense of humor when he goes to an opera; but the wise operagoer will, while recognizing defects, subordinate them to concentration on what is good and hope that they will be less obvious the next experience.

It was a lover of the opera, Sutherland Edwards, who wrote this witty imitation of Panard's song in "Le depart de l'Opera" (1733):

> I've seen Semiramis, the queen;
>   I've seen the Mysteries of Isis;
> A lady full of health I've seen
>   Die in her dressing-gown, of Phthisis.

> I've seen a wretched lover sigh,
>   "*Fra Poco*" he a corpse would be,
> Transfix himself, and then—not die,
>   But cooly sing an air in D.

> I've seen a father lose his child,
>   Nor seek the robbers' flight to stay;
> But in a voice extremely mild,
>   Kneel down upon the stage and pray.

> I've seen Otello stab * his wife;
>   The Count di Luna fight his brother;
> Lucrezia take her own son's life;
>   And John of Leyden cut his mother.

> I've seen a churchyard yield its dead,
>   And lifeless nuns in life rejoice;
> I've seen a statue bow its head,
>   And listened to its trombone voice.

* Of course he does not.

I've seen a herald sound alarms,
   Without evincing any fright;
Have seen an army cry "To arms"
   For half an hour, and never fight.

I've seen a maid despond in A,
   Fly the perfidious one in B,
Come back to see her wedding day,
   And perish in a minor key.

I've seen the realm of bliss eternal,
   (The song accompanied by harps);
I've seen the land of pains infernal,
   With demons shouting in six sharps!

There are other amusing criticisms of opera, most of them written by those who have enjoyed it, which an amateur may find entertaining. One of the most pointed is Weber's satirical outlines of an Italian, a French, and a German type opera, which one can find quoted in Chapter 8 of George R. Marek's *A Front Seat at Opera*. Newman Levy, in his *Opera Guyed*, gives in witty verse exaggerated outlines of several popular operas.

Chapter Seven

OPERA MUSIC BY RADIO
AND PHONOGRAPH

NOWADAYS there is frequent opportunity to hear operatic music over the radio. On Saturday afternoons during the season the Metropolitan Opera Company is on the air, usually casting its best singers in a series of the best operas. Reports evidence that these broadcasts have been heard every week by literally hundreds of thousands, perhaps by millions. Who does not get a thrill from knowing that he is one of a vast audience, peoples of all kinds and of all ages in all parts of the country, who are at the same time enjoying the same thing, the beauty of music that arouses the finest human emotions?

In addition, nearly all radio stations include in their programs from time to time excellent renderings of opera music, occasionally whole operas in a condensed version; and broadcasts of the best symphonic concerts often present, with or without voices, excerpts from the operas. It is from these sources that most people become acquainted with operatic music, both that in the standard repertoire and that which for one reason or another is seldom or never now performed. The frequency of opera music in broadcasting programs is con-

69

vincing evidence of a genuine and widespread interest; probably millions of people who have never seen an opera have developed from these radio broadcasts an ardent desire to do so.

If you are interested to know how opera broadcasts are made, you will enjoy Chapter XXII in Taubman's *Opera Front and Back*, or the account in Part III of Heylbut and Gerber's *Backstage at the Opera*. Without the skill and, one may truly say, the artistry of those who control transmission of the music, we get less beautiful and appealing renderings.

Supplementing the radio, we have marvelously faithful phonograph records not merely of single vocal and instrumental numbers from many of the operas but also of entire works. The cost of recordings of full operas may seem high, but actually when one realizes that they permit an indefinitely large number of playings at any time that is convenient, it actually is most reasonable. Fortunately an increasing number of libraries and schools have a selection of records which may be used by those who take the trouble to ask for them. In all probability it will not be long before there are also many rental libraries of records. Those interested in selecting records will find helpful the catalogues of phonographic companies, and such books as David Hall's *The Record Book*, R. D. Darrell's *The Gramophone Shop Encyclopedia of Recorded Music*, and Brockway and Weinstock's *The Opera*, pages 485–562, Irving Kolodin's *A Guide to Recorded Music*, and B. F. Haggin's *Music on Records*.

But with applause for these broadcasts and recordings and with full appreciation of their high excellence, it must be said that they are not opera. Repeatedly in the preceding pages emphasis has been laid on the fact that opera is a combination of several arts cooperating to present a dramatic story in such ways as to make the strongest appeal to the emotions. Ballet alone may be enjoyable, but it loses much of its appeal when out of its dramatic setting. Whatever its merits, a ballet cannot now be broadcast by radio, though it can be televised.

Pantomime and other acting cannot be indicated by radio or by phonograph records. Use of a libretto may supplement broadcasts. Though music is the dominant element, it alone is not opera. However beautiful and artistically presented, when heard without the setting of stage scenery and costumes, and when lacking the interpretation by skilled actors and the colorful support of scenery, spectacle, and ballet, music of necessity lacks what the ensemble of the several arts can contribute. When opera is televised, as occasionally it is, we shall be able to get more at home than we can now by radio.

These other elements of opera the radio commentator attempts so far as it is possible to give. Before the music begins and during intermissions he narrates the story, he sometimes gives a description (necessarily sketchy) of the scenery and costumes, he occasionally tells something of the high points of the acting, and he recounts anecdotes that aid understanding of the characters and of the actors. Because of limited time, if for no other reason, he offers relatively little, however, of what one would experience at the opera besides the music; he cannot make us see, and what we cannot see we cannot combine into the desired fused impression. The commentators are highly skillful in their art and there are reasons to believe that they are greatly aided by responses from auditors more and more to enrich their comments. What they actually do give is very helpful, especially to the listeners who use active imagination to vivify and to synthesize what they are told with what they already know and with what they hear of the music. But even with the help of the best commentator, an opera heard over the radio cannot equal the verisimilitude of colored motion pictures of operas, which will be increasingly numerous.

What has been said is in no sense meant to deprecate the broadcasting of opera music. We are profoundly grateful for it. It gives exquisite enjoyment that could not otherwise be had by perhaps millions of people; it stimulates the intention

of thousands actually to experience the opera; it is an excellent
means of preparing to experience opera; and probably it gives
most pleasure to those who, having had the actual experience,
can to a large degree supplement what comes over the air by
what they remember having seen on the stage. This combination of what is newly heard with what is remembered can
often arouse in sensitive listeners almost the same emotions
that they felt at the actual visible performance.

In some respects the listener at the radio has certain advantages. He does not have to leave his home, he can be as
comfortable physically as he likes, and he need suffer no
distractions from strangers all around him. At home he can
follow the score, which he can borrow from a library if he
cannot afford to buy one. A new score containing the music
and the words, in the original language and in English, costs
only about five dollars; a used one can be procured for less.
This is far better than a libretto alone, for it gives the words
exactly as sung, with all the repetitions and other adaptations.
If one is able to follow a simple two-staff score of the notes, he
will also find such a book helpful not only in understanding
the music as it is played or sung but also in reviewing it later.
Even an amateur can appreciate the added richness that the
complex orchestra contributes to the simple outline presented
in the popular piano score.

The advantages of listening at home should not diminish
one's sense of responsibility to give attention actively, not
passively, every moment of the time, with his intelligence as
well as with all of his senses fully and steadily alert. Sewing
and solitaire are poor aids to a radio listener to opera music.
What a listener to an opera broadcast gets depends largely on
his powers of concentration and on his imagination. Sitting at
home he is denied appeal to the eye, which not only to an
extent relieves the ear but also subtly stimulates and enriches
hearing; in addition, he does not have a consciousness of others
nearby in rapt attention, a social impetus to concentration
that is far from neglible. For such reasons the listener, appre-

ciating the rare opportunity of hearing at no cost great music presented beautifully by the greatest artists, cannot afford to relax his attention even for the briefest time.

Enjoyment of opera broadcasts can be greatly increased, of course, by much of the preparation already suggested for actually experiencing opera. The fact that it is a broadcast should challenge one even more than an actual performance does to make careful preparation, for the listener to the radio is given much less and in consequence must himself supply much more. Try hearing a broadcast after making such preparation as has been suggested, and you will realize an additional enjoyment that will repay your pains.

The suggestions for the listener while the opera is being presented are equally good for one who wishes to increase his intelligent appreciation and his pleasure by means of broadcasts. If the suggestions seem to be too numerous or to require altogether too much effort, accept one or more of them at a time. If you find that you profit from them and that your understanding and enjoyment have increased, you can add others as they promise to be worth your effort.

Similarly, use as many of the suggestions on "what to do afterward" as appeal to you as likely to be profitable. After listening at home, you do not have the annoyance of getting out of the crowd and of traveling. It is easy, especially if you have a libretto, a book of stories of the opera with pictures and important musical themes, or best of all, a simplified score of the music with words, to review the whole performance in the ways suggested. And it is not difficult to make an early opportunity, after you have reflected on your experience, for discussion with others, either those who, like you, have listened over the radio or those who have actually experienced the opera in person. An exchange of impressions and judgments, each one made definite and justified as thoroughly as possible, will be highly pleasurable and profitable. But concentrate on appreciation of the beauty, not on unimportant criticism of details.

Chapter Eight

SYNOPSIS OF CARMEN:
A FIRST OPERA

It was this drama, swift and undisguised in its music, with its overheated southern temperament, dazzling and vital orchestra, wonderful harmonics, inescapable melodies, that called forth the enthusiastic homage of Nietzsche, who saw in *Carmen* the eternal model of the lyric drama.

Carmen will remain one of the greatest creations of the musical stage, a work whose popularity is not excelled by any other lyric drama, for it is the ideal drama, enjoyed by connoisseur and uninitiated alike.[1]

THE welding of music, drama, and the allied arts into an effective unity finds one of its most perfect realizations in Georges Bizet's *opéra comique, Carmen*. The choice of Prosper Mérimée's novel for lyric treatment was indeed a happy one, for the story abounds in situations and characters that cry for a stage and music to express the intensity and depth of their elemental passion. In rendering the book into libretto form, Bizet was served by two master craftsmen, Henri Meilhac and Ludovic Halévy, whose years of experi-

[1] P. H. Lang, *Music in Western Civilization* (New York: W. W. Norton).

74

ence in the theater qualified them for this important commission. With their knowledge of the stage and of the special requirements of the lyric drama libretto Meilhac and Halévy did not hesitate to alter the Mérimée story to suit their needs. Characters and situations were invented to meet the existing conventions of the *opéra comique* genre. Their work is frankly an adaptation and not an attempt at literal translation.

Here is a fusion of music and drama in almost perfect balance. Few are the moments when the music forgets the play and tends to become music merely for the sake of music. The drama rushes on to its inevitable tragic denouement with a directness and a realism that are classic in their economy. This is concentrated drama of great passion that can find release and expression only in the heightened accents of musical speech. The dynamic force and impetuous nature of the drama do not allow fine nuances of language and subtleties of verbal idiom. Librettists less skillful and stage-wise might have ruined a good story by insisting on its literary values to the detriment of its broader and more sweeping dramatic values.

The fierce tempo of the drama makes itself felt in the throbbing rhythm of the quick march with which the prelude opens.

This bright, gay music heard again at the beginning of the fourth act for the entrance of the toreadors and picadors into the bull ring has a holiday spirit far removed from the stark tragedy with which the opera ends. In this potpourri overture the second theme is the refrain of the well-known Toreador Song, a perfect characterization of the suave, swaggering bull-fighter, Escamillo, who appears in the second act, attracts

Carmen's attention by his bravado, and becomes the third figure in this triangle drama.

After a repetition of the quick march, a tragic note is heard in the following fate motive, which is to haunt the drama to its tragic end:

This motive is so closely associated with Carmen that it soon becomes evident that she is a *femme fatale*, a victim of her own exotic personality and the cause of Don José's ruin. After a short development of this theme, the prelude comes to an abrupt, dissonant, and suspensive close, leading directly into the first scene.

There are two ways of presenting *Carmen*. The traditional way is to make everything romantic: Seville is clean and colorful; the soldiers wear yellow uniforms and have plumes on their caps; the factory girls are clothed in baby blue skirts, over which are striped aprons; and Carmen herself is dressed as a seductive charmer rather than as a cigarette maker. The 1952 production at the Metropolitan Opera House in New York emphasized reality: the soldiers were still in a supposedly Spanish uniform but wore no plumes; the factory girls were in dirty grays and soiled petticoats; the boys who followed and imitated the soldiers were ragamuffins of the streets; and Carmen appeared first in a short-sleeved black blouse and skirt tied at the waist with a dirty rose sash.

The curtain opens on a square in Seville. The glare of the midday sun is reflected by the yellow stucco houses, providing a brilliant setting for this torrid drama. There is a cigarette factory where Carmen is employed. On one side is a guardhouse in front of which Corporal Morales and a group of soldiers are lounging. They idly watch the life of the square and comment on the passers-by. Soon appears Micaela, a shy young girl, who by her timid glances and hesitant manner betrays an interest in the soldiers. Morales approaches her and with a show of gallantry asks whom she is seeking. "I am looking for a corporal," she replies. "Here *I* am," says Morales. Micaela explains that she is looking for Don José. Do they know him? Yes, indeed. He is not a member of their squad, but he will be coming on duty soon when the guard changes. While waiting for him will she not enter the guardhouse and rest? Micaela thanks the soldiers for their kind offer and refuses. "I will return when the relief guard replaces the retiring guard," she replies, employing Morales' own words and musical phrase, a little ironic touch that often escapes interpreters and auditors. Micaela thinks it more prudent to leave and bids the soldiers goodby. They resume their idle pastime of watching the life in the square.

In the distance a bugle call is heard. This is answered by a bugler on the stage, and the company of soldiers falls into formation. The relief guard approaches, led by Lieutenant Zuniga and Corporal Don José. Bizet has assigned the role of Zuniga to a bass, thus adding dignity and age to the characterization of the superior officer. Don José is sung by a tenor, the high male voice which has long been associated with youth and romance. A crowd of street urchins wearing paper hats and armed with toy rifles precedes the soldiers in their best military manner. The boys voice their enthusiasm for army life in a spirited unison chorus.

The music of this march and boys' chorus has a light, comic-opera make-believe character that is quite in keeping with the drama up to this point. It forms a part of the stage setting against which this human tragedy is played, and by the lightness of its gay, inconsequential tunes brings into high relief the dark-hued themes that later speak of death.

Following the change of guards, Zuniga engages Don José in conversation. "Is it in that tall building that the cigarette girls work?" he asks. "It is, indeed, and nowhere will you find girls so free and easy," Don José replies. "But are they pretty?" Zuniga continues. "Sir, I do not know, and do not bother about such things." From this it is evident that Don José is a serious young man who has not abandoned himself to reckless living since coming to Seville from his native Navarre. Zuniga remarks that he knows who is occupying Don José's thoughts. It is Micaela, a charming young girl in a blue skirt and with braided hair. Don José admits it.

At this moment the factory bell rings, announcing a rest period for the cigarette girls. A group of men gather and sing a charming daytime serenade, one of them using a guitar for accompaniment. Soon the girls appear and acknowledge the men's song with a graceful chorus comparing the lover's words to the smoke of their cigarettes, represented by floating notes by the flutes. The smoke, the girls say, rises, turns, and vanishes in the sky.

"But where is La Carmencita?" ask her admirers. Immediately the orchestra announces her entrance with a capricious diminution of the fate motive.

So spirited and gay is the motive in this metamorphosis that one barely recognizes it as the theme of the fate which is to doom Carmen to her death. A comparison of musical examples No. 3 and No. 5 will reveal the interesting fact that they are the same melodic theme. A quickened tempo and slight rhythmic change have completely altered the character and emotional connotation of its later appearance.

With the appearance of Carmen, sometimes gayly costumed in a yellow dotted green skirt trimmed in red, the drama takes on new life. Carmen is a child of nature with an animal magnetism that dominates her associates and her environment. The wild intensity of her eyes and her free, sinuous walk give the spectator an indication of her character and personality before she utters a word. She is one of those unmoral, lawless, fascinating women who take their prey where they find it.

The role of Carmen is one of the most alluring and graceful characterizations in the entire operatic literature. It is not strange that prima donnas have coveted this role and essayed it in public often despite disqualifications of voice and temperament. The part demands an actress of the first order, one who can portray the most violent passion with an intensity of concentration that hypnotizes all who come under her spell. The music calls for a mezzo-soprano or a contralto. Though it has often been sung by sopranos, there are a tone color and emotional association in the quality of the soprano voice that make it seen incongruously inconsistent with the warm, sensuous nature of Carmen. There are few opportunities for sustained dramatic singing, the Card Song in the third act being one of the notable exceptions. More important is the singer's ability to declaim the text in such an intelligent and imaginative manner that the meaning will be suggested by the subtle nuances and color of the voice. Singers of such diverse vocal and histrionic talents as Emma Calvé, Schumann-Heink, Mary Garden, Maria Jeritza, and Rosa Ponselle have been identified with this role. It taxes the imagination of the opera lover of this generation to visualize the heroic Schumann-Heink, respectfully remembered for her noble characterizations of Wagnerian roles, as the wild, wayward Spanish gypsy. Styles and tastes have changed in the theater as they have in all activities of life. Our parents, not yet conditioned by the realism of the moving picture, were perhaps less critical of what they saw on the stage than we are today. It is also possible that being accustomed to a higher standard of vocal art than now prevails, they were more critical of what they heard.

The men crowd about Carmen and demand, "Tell us the day, Carmen, when you'll give us your love." Her enigmatic answer is, "When will I give you my love? I do not know. Perhaps never! Perhaps tomorrow! But not today, that's certain." This short recitative is a model of character delineation, for in these few words Carmen has revealed her tantalizing fickleness and caprice that later drive Don José to his own ruin, and her willfulness which brings her to her own death.

It may be noted here that when Carmen was first performed at the Opéra-Comique, in Paris, March 3, 1875, it was produced in true *opéra-comique* tradition, with spoken dialogue connecting the musical numbers. The recitatives were later composed by Ernest Guiraud, French opera composer and professor of harmony and accompaniment at the Conservatoire. Guiraud's additions to the Bizet score were made with such sympathetic understanding and artistry that it is hard to believe that they were not penned by Bizet himself.

This recitative leads directly into the popular Habanera, in which Carmen sets forth her views of life. Love she compares to a wild bird, "a gypsy child, who has never known law." The persistent rhythmic *ostinato* figure in the accompaniment, characteristic of the popular Spanish dance, habanera, achieves through two verses a definite cumulative effect. Over this simple, almost primitive accompaniment, Carmen sings a melody of seductive beauty and sensual allure.

One who is interested in looking more deeply into the composer's technique will note the chromatic quality of the melody, its portamento (smooth movement up or down the scale), its rhythmic freedom, the characteristic use of triplets, and the change from minor to major mode, all of which contribute to the character of this famous song. Carmen has sung the song for the benefit of Don José, who sits over by the guardhouse busily engaged in making a leather chain for his sword. He has manifested not the least interest in Carmen or her song, but it piques and challenges him nevertheless. With instinctive acumen Carmen directs the final warning of the song to her latest infatuation, "You don't love me, but I love you, and if I love you, then beware!"

The men crowd about Carmen again, declaring their love and begging her for a response. With characteristic boldness she pushes them aside, fixes her eye on Don José, and hesitates a moment before turning toward the factory. Then she retraces her steps and goes straight to Don José, takes a flower from her bosom and throws it in his face. This pantomime is accompanied in the orchestra by a dark and foreboding exposition of the fate motive. With a laugh she runs toward the factory, turns and for a long moment fixes a final hypnotic glance on her victim, then enters, leaving the cigarette girls to mock Don José with a phrase of the Habanera.

The factory bell rings again, calling the girls and men to work. The soldiers enter the guardhouse. Don José picks up the flower Carmen has so tauntingly thrown him and reflects on her. "What a look! What effrontery! But the flower is pretty and the perfume is sweet! And the woman! If there are sorceresses, she is certainly one." This recitative is supported in the orchestra with fragmentary reminiscences of the fate motive and the Habanera.

In the midst of this soliloquy Micaela timidly calls to him. He welcomes her with joy and asks for news of his mother. Micaela has brought him a letter and some money which his mother sent to supplement his pay, and a kiss which after hesitation she chastely imprints on his forehead. Micaela continues with a recital of the mother's message:

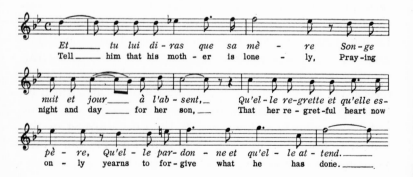

Et____ tu lui di - ras que sa mè - re Son-ge
Tell____ him that his moth - er is lone - ly, Pray-ing

nuit et jour____ à l'ab - sent,_ Qu'el-le re-grette et qu'elle es-
night and day ____ for her son, ___ That her re - gret-ful heart now

pè - re, Qu'el - le par-don - ne et qu'el - le at - tend.____
on - ly yearns to for-give what he has done.____.

Thoughts of his mother and fond memories of his village move Don José to a simple song in which Micaela joins him. Critics and purists have long ranted against Meilhac and Halévy for the creation of this colorless character not found in Mérimée's story. It must be remembered that the Victorian stage, even in France, would not accept a direct dramatization of Mérimée's *Carmen*, with all its stark realism. Micaela represents a personification of homely virtue that serves as an excellent foil against which the cruel, heartless Carmen and her smuggler friends stand out in bold relief. Micaela's goodness is at times irritating, but it is much better to accept her as a convention of the drama than to cavil at her secondary role in the opera. Were she not in the play, we should miss some delightful singing.

The song ended, she modestly leaves Don José alone to read his letter while the orchestra furnishes a commentary, a repetition of the theme (No. 7) with which Micaela conveyed his mother's message. He understands his mother's wishes and will obey them. He loves Micaela and will take her for his wife. As for the flower of that shameless woman. . . .

His thought is interrupted by screams from the cigarette factory. Zuniga comes out of the guardhouse to investigate the cause of the disorder and is surrounded by a group of girls calling for help. They attempt to explain in a frantic chorus the quarrel that has occurred in the cigarette factory between Carmen and La Manuelita. The girls disagree violently in their interpretation of the fight, one faction averring that Carmen started the trouble, the other group maintaining that La Manuelita struck the first blow. The arguing increases until the square becomes a seething mass which is not restored to order until Zuniga commands a squad of soldiers to clear the street. Then Carmen is led from the factory by Don José, followed by two other soldiers.

After hearing Don José's report, Zuniga turns to Carmen and says, "You hear the charge. What is your reply?" Carmen answers with an insolent phrase, refusing to tell him anything.

Tra la la la la la la la, *Cou-pe moi, brû - le -*
                          You may flay me or

moi,   *je ne*   *te*   *di - rai*   *rien* _____
burn   me, but   no - thing   I'll   tell _____

Zuniga orders Don José to tie Carmen's hands and conduct her
to prison. In an aside remark, "What a pity, for she is really
nice," Zuniga betrays his own infatuation with the prisoner.

Carmen and Don José are now alone in the square. She asks
him where he is going to take her. "To prison," he replies;
"there's nothing else I can do." Carmen resorts to feminine
wiles to attain her ends. "I know that in spite of your superior
officers you will do what I wish, because you love me. Yes,
José, the flower I gave you today, the flower of the sorceress,
you may throw it away now. The charm is working." Don
José forbids her to speak to him. The music leads into the
Seguidilla which Carmen with seductive action sings to tan-
talize Don José, the while tapping the rhythm with her feet.

Près des rem - parts de Se - vil - le
Down by the walls of Se - vil la

Chez mon a - mi___ Lil - las Pas - tia___
Stands___ Li - las Pas - tia's gay ta - vern_____

She will go down to Lilas Pastia's tavern by the fortifica-
tions of Seville, and there she will dance and drink. For company she will take with her a lover. Just yesterday she showed
the door to her latest one. Now her heart is free as air. She
has gallants by the dozen, but they are not to her taste. Who
wants her love?

Don José, though shocked by the wantoness of the woman,

is nonetheless affected by her bewitching ways. He musters his moral forces and orders her to be still. Carmen replies, "I'm not speaking to you. I'm singing for myself and I'm thinking. It is not forbidden to think. I'm thinking of an officer who loves me and whom I could love." Her officer is no captain, not even a lieutenant. He's only a corporal, but that's quite enough for a gypsy girl. Don José can stand no more. He agrees to release her if she will keep her promise to love him. Carmen consents, and Don José loosens the cord which binds her hands, but in the later action she holds the rope so that others think she is still bound.

A pianissimo passage in the cellos announces Zuniga's entrance. He hands Don José his orders, with a warning to be on his guard. In a quiet aside to Don José, Carmen explains her plan of escape. On the way to the jail she will give him a push. He is to let himself fall; the rest she will take care of. She then turns to Zuniga and impudently taunts him with the refrain of the Habanera. As Carmen and Don José arrive at the bridge, she shoves him sprawling into the crowd and escapes amid the cheers and laughter of the people.

The entr'acte or curtain music which precedes the second act is based on the song with which Don José later greets Carmen on his release from prison. (See theme No. 12.) The masterful orchestration of this gem of curtain music with its bassoon solo and alternating string and wood-wind choirs is one of the notable achievements of the composer.

The curtain rises on the interior of Lilas Pastia's tavern. It is late at night and a crowd of gypsies, smugglers, and soldiers is at the height of its revelry. In the romantic production soft lights shed a languorous atmosphere over the vivid beauty of the Spanish girls who grace the balconies of this roadside tavern. Gypsy girls, in brilliantly colored shawls, are dancing to the accompaniment of guitars and tambourines. In the new Metropolitan production the girls are gay, but less glamorously costumed, and Carmen wears a faded red shawl, its shabbiness emphasized by slashed fringe, over her orange skirt, which is flared at the hem to permit freedom for her dance. Carmen, traditionally gayly dressed in a red waist and a black skirt on which there are large red flowers and at the bottom of which there is a vivid green border, and intoxicated with the excitement and the throbbing rhythm of the delirious music, sings the Gypsy Song, in the chorus of which she is joined by her two friends, Frasquita and Mercedes.

Les trin - gles des sis - tres tin - taient, _____ A -
The sound of sis - trum bars did greet _____ Their

vec un é-clat mé-tal li - que, Et sur cette é-tran-ge mu-
ears with dry, me-tal-lic ring - ing, To this strange mu-sic soon up-

si - que Les_ zin - ga- rel - las se lé - vaient_____
spring - ing The_ gyp - sy- girls were on their feet _____

Frasquita announces that Lilas Pastia wishes to close the tavern for the night. Zuniga prepares to leave and invites Carmen to join him. His vanity is piqued by her refusal. She must be thinking of the young soldier who was imprisoned on her account. "Well, he is free now," Zuniga tells her, whereupon Carmen expresses her satisfaction and dismisses her many admirers.

In the distance are heard cries, "Viva the Toreador, Viva Escamillo!" A torchlight procession in honor of the winner of the bullfight at Granada is passing. Zuniga invites Escamillo (who is attired in a silver-gray bolero and trousers, a gray silk waistcoat, and pale gray sombrero) and his followers to join the party in a drink and proposes a toast to the bullfighter's old successes and to those of the future. Escamillo thanks the company for their toast with the Toreador Song, in which he gives a dramatic and highly colored account of a bullfight.

Vo - tre toast, je peux— vous le ren - dre, Se -
For a toast. your own— will a - vail— me, Se -

ñors, se - ñors,— car a - vec les sol - dats—
ñors, se - ñors !— For all your men of war —

Everyone present joins in the repetition of the chorus of
the song. This piece, with its driving, insistent rhythm of the
verse, and the suave, unctuous melody of the chorus, is highly
descriptive of the popular hero.

At his entrance Escamillo, buoyant and excited, kisses the
first girl he sees, but Carmen feigns indifference to him. It
soon becomes apparent from her furtive glances that this is
merely a pose to pique the interest of the swaggering bull-
fighter. He falls prey to her feminine fascination at first sight
and when he finishes his song, approaches Carmen and asks her
name. In his next encounter, he says, he will call on her when
confronted with danger. To his question whether or not he
may love her, she parries with a tantalizing reply that it is
permitted to wait and hope.

Zuniga, annoyed that Carmen will not join him, tells her
that he will return. Carmen's direct answer is, "You'll make
a great mistake." The toreador leaves with his men to the
accompaniment of his song, but before going he seizes Carmen
and gives her a passionate kiss.

El Remendado and El Dancairo, leaders of a band of smugglers, are then questioned by Frasquita for news of their activities. They have planned a big project, but to carry it
through successfully they will need the help of the women.
Carmen, Frasquita, and Mercedes crowd about the two men
and listen to their scheme with keen interest. Frasquita and
Mercedes are ready to leave at once. Carmen surprises them
all by announcing that she will not leave. To their coaxing
and pleading she remains obdurate. At last they ask her reason
and receive a greater shock when she tells them that she is in

love. To them that is a great joke, but Carmen insists that this time she is madly in love. El Remendado and El Dancairo ironically remind her that this is not the first time that she has managed to combine love and duty. Carmen insists that this time love takes precedence over duty. The breath-taking virtuosity and the rapid patter and wit of this quintet distinguish it as one of the finest ensembles in operatic literature.

Carmen admits that she is waiting for the soldier who went to jail on her account. El Dancairo suggests that since he has had time to reflect, he may not come. But just then Don José is heard in the distance, singing a soldier's song used previously as the theme of the curtain music of this act.

In a bit of recitative, usually cut in performance, El Remendado and El Dancairo suggest that Carmen invite Don José to join them in their smuggling enterprise. Carmen agrees to try. Before Don José enters, Carmen smooths her hair and makes herself as attractive as possible, but when he comes in she sits as if unaware of his presence. Are these merely woman's wiles, or is her desire for him already waning? Two months he has spent in prison on her account, and if it were necessary he would stay there longer. He adores her and

shows no little jealousy when Carmen tells him that his officers had been there earlier in the evening and that she had
danced for them. She picks up a pair of castanets and soothes
Don José by telling him that now she will dance and sing for
him alone.

Carmen is in the midst of her dance when bugles are heard
in the distance. Don José asks her to stop a moment. Yes, it
is the call to retreat. Carmen resumes her dance with greater
abandon. "It is melancholy to dance without an orchestra,"
she remarks, "so thanks for the music which falls from the
sky." Don José interrupts again. It is the retreat calling him
back to camp for the night. Carmen, stupefied, repeats his
last words, "back to camp for the night?" with a rising inflec-
tion. At last she realizes that he is serious, and the animal fury
of her nature breaks forth in a torrential harangue that knows
no bounds. She throws his helmet and his sword at him and
orders him back to his barracks.

Don José attempts to assure her of his love, but she does not
wish to hear him. Taking from his breast the flower which
she threw him in the first act, Don José shows it to Carmen,
then tells her in the Flower Song

how much this token consoled him during his days in prison. He admits that there were moments when he detested and hated her, and questioned the fate that had brought them together. But always his one desire and hope was to see Carmen again. At the end of the aria Don José throws himself passionately across the lap of Carmen, who is seated in a chair; but the fact that she gives him no caress or comfort indicates that her infatuation is already waning. The introduction to this aria brings again to the listener the familiar fate motive, this time played by the melancholy English horn.

The beloved Flower Song arioso has a climax that has affected listeners ever since it was composed. The boldness of the modulation at the end, where the orchestra comes in against the words "Carmen, je t'aime!" ("Carmen, I love you!"), suggests the delirious passion of the young soldier. This is again brought out by his frenzied responses to Carmen's seductive "Là-bas, la-bas dans la montagne" ("Away to the mountains"). The third act finds the character further developed —a new dramatic accent comes into his voice in the great finale.*

Carmen listens quietly to Don José's protestation of love, but she remains unconvinced. No, he does not love her, else he would be free and independent, with no officers to obey. She paints a bewitching picture of a wandering life beneath the open skies, the whole universe for one's country, and for law one's own will, and above all, that which gypsies prize most, liberty.

José struggles manfully to resist. Finally tearing himself away from her embrace, he refuses to desert his army. "Go then," Carmen shouts at him. "I hate you. Goodby, but goodby forever."

As Don José is about to leave a knocking is heard at the

* Program note.

door. Zuniga has foolishly disregarded Carmen's advice and returned, as he promised he would. Realizing the danger that attends Don José if Zuniga finds him there, Carmen refuses to open the door, whereupon Zuniga forces an entrance. He recognizes Don José, then turns to Carmen and chides her for taking a common soldier when she could have an officer. Zuniga orders Don José to leave, but he refuses. In the quarrel that follows Don José seizes his sword and attacks his superior officer. Carmen calls loudly for help and the gypsies and smugglers enter. El Dancairo and El Remendado seize Zuniga and disarm him, addressing him in terms of mock politeness and formality while keeping him covered with their pistols. For their own safety, they say, they are obliged to detain him for an hour or more. Carmen asks Don José if he will join the band now. What choice has he? The answer is not gallant, Carmen remarks, but what does it matter? He will agree, once he has tasted the joys of gypsy life. The smugglers and gypsies join Carmen in her song and the curtain falls as they are about to set out on their expedition.

The orchestral intermezzo which prefaces the third act can be regarded as a part of the scene in which the act is played. A flute solo, over harp accompaniment, suggests the peacefulness and tranquillity of the mountains in the stillness of night before the storm of passion breaks loose between Carmen and Don José, bringing them into violent conflict.

The smugglers have encamped in a wild mountain pass and are awaiting the arrival of their gypsy colleagues. A horn signal, followed by a stealthy, cautious march, played pianissimo by the orchestra, announces their coming. They join in a unison chorus, urging one another to take the greatest care lest they make a *faux pas*. There follows a sextet in which

Frasquita, Mercedes, Carmen, José, El Remendado, and El Dancairo sing the praises of the smuggling trade, stressing always the dangers that surround them. This number leads directly to a repetition of the march movement in which all join in their admonitions to be careful. In a short recitative El Dancairo suggests that the company rest an hour; meanwhile they will assure themselves that the road is free and that they can move their contraband goods safely.

Carmen (in the Metropolitan production wearing an outdoor costume of brown leather and high boots) observes Don José gazing into the valley below and asks him what he is looking at. He replies, "I was thinking that down there lives a brave old woman who thinks me an honest man. But she is wrong, alas." Don José's reflection is interrupted by the motive (No. 7) which has earlier been associated with thoughts of his mother. "Who is this woman?" Carmen asks in a cruel tone. He replies that it is his mother. "Well, then, go back to her at once," Carmen advises. "Our trade is not for you. And you'll do well to leave as soon as possible."

The suggestion is startling to Don José, who is torn by two devotions. Again the fate motive is heard in the orchestra. "We separate? Carmen, listen, if you repeat that word. . . .," Don José threatens. Carmen counters, "Why then, perhaps you'd kill me. What a look! You don't reply! What does it matter? After all, Destiny is the master." This scene is set in recitative, and an understanding of the words is essential to a complete understanding of it. Those who think of opera only in terms of music will miss here one of the dramatic moments of the piece and a key to much of the action that follows.

Carmen has made it evident that she is bored with Don José and would like to be rid of him. It is this incident which motivates the revenge he silently plots in sullen desperation.

Frasquita and Mercedes amuse themselves by telling their fortunes with cards. A bold young lover, the cards say, is to carry Frasquita off to the mountains. Mercedes' lover is rich and old, but he speaks of marriage, and will establish her in a royal castle. The girls vie with each other in their readings of the cards, reaching a moment of excitement when Mercedes discovers that her lover dies, leaving her a substantial inheritance.

The fate motive accompanies Carmen's action as she takes the cards and proceeds to read her own fortune. "Diamonds! Spades! Death!" she cries as she turns over the first cards. "I, the first, then he. For both of us, death!" In the serious, brooding Card Song Carmen voices her fatalistic philosophy and resignation.

En vain pour é - vi - ter les ré - pon - ses a
In vain, to shun the ans - wer that we dread to

mè - res, En vain tu mè - le - ras _____
hear, _____ To mix the cards we try _____

It is futile, she says, to try to better one's fate by reshuffling the cards. They are sincere and will not lie. "Yes, if you're doomed to die, you may try twenty times, but the pitiless card will repeat 'Death.'" Frasquita and Mercedes resume their duet, each intent upon her own fortune, while Carmen contemplates her fate. For Frasquita, it is love; for Mercedes, wealth; for Carmen, death.

The intensity of the scene is momentarily relieved by El Dancairo's orders and instructions to the gypsies to take to the road. He warns them of three customs officers against whom they must be on their guard. Carmen, Frasquita, and Mercedes, in a sprightly trio in which they are joined by the gypsies, assure El Dancairo that they know how to deal with the guards.

The smugglers have barely left their camp when Micaela appears, usually costumed in white bodice and a blue-gray skirt, in marked contrast to Carmen. Micaela is frightened to be alone in this strange place among these outlaws, but vows to accomplish the mission with which Don José's mother has entrusted her. This recitative is followed by a graceful aria in which she prays for courage and protection.

Though the music of this number is less characteristic than other parts of the score, it holds its appeal to the public by virtue of its pure vocal line. It is skillfully scored. The halting arpeggios give a hesitant effect in keeping with the character, and the predominance of the horn not only is beautiful in itself, but somehow emphasizes the feeling of the woodland loneliness of the scene.

Micaela calls to Don José, whom she recognizes in the distance. She watches him take aim with his rifle and fire on a man. Micaela, in terror, hides behind the rocks. Escamillo enters, having narrowly escaped Don José's shot. He introduces himself to Don José, who welcomes him because of his reputation. Unaware of Don José's identity, Escamillo confides in him his love for Carmen. "She had a lover, a young soldier, who deserted for her. They adored each other, but that is past. Carmen's loves do not last six months." Those who take away a gypsy girl must fight. Escamillo agrees and the two men draw knives. In the encounter Escamillo's knife snaps and Don José is about to strike when Carmen rushes in with the gypsies and prevents the blow.

Escamillo is enraptured that it was she who saved his life. As for Don José, their scores are even, and any time he wishes to resume the contest, Escamillo is at his service. Before leaving, he invites everyone to the bullfight at Seville. "All who love me will come," he repeats as he gazes at Carmen. In bidding farewell he embraces Carmen. Don José makes a desperate effort to attack him, but is held back by El Dancairo and El Remendado. He turns menacingly to Carmen and warns her to be on her guard lest she drive him too far.

The gypsies are about to take to the road when El Remendado discovers Micaela and leads her forth from her hiding place. She has come to ask Don José to return to his mother. Carmen urges him to go. Don José answers, "You tell me to leave so that you can run after your new lover. No, indeed. Even though it cost me my life, I will not go. And the chain which binds us shall hold us until death. No, no, no, I will not leave you!" In his frenzy of passion he seizes Carmen and continues, "Ah, now I have you, you fiend, and I shall force you to submit to the destiny that binds your fate to mine. Even though it cost me my life I will not leave you." The music of this last outburst is the same as that of the first, transposed a half tone higher, a device which adds much to the intensity and excitement of the repetition. These pages are without doubt among the strongest of the musical score and contribute much to the full development of Don José's character.

Micaela makes one last appeal. Don José's mother is dying and would like to pardon him before she dies. He starts to leave, then turning to Carmen says, "Be satisfied. I am going, but we shall meet again." The fate motive makes a prophetic reappearance in the orchestra as Don José and Micaela leave. In the distance Escamillo is heard singing the chorus of the Toreador Song. Carmen tries to run to him, but is intercepted by Don José, who threatens her with a menacing gesture. She then seizes the cards and tries her fortune again. Again they say "Death!" and she tosses them high into the air in tragic resignation as the curtain falls to the strain of the Smugglers' March heard in the orchestra.

The orchestral interlude which precedes Act IV is based on a genuine Andalusian song and dance known as the *polo*. Oboe and flute solos over a guitar accompaniment, simulated by pizzicato strings, are additional examples of Bizet's feeling for tone color and mastery of orchestration.

The curtain opens on a square in Seville. At the back are the walls of the ancient amphitheatre where the bullfights take place. The place is crowded with vendors of fans, oranges, programs, water, cigarettes, and wine, all calling their wares in a lively chorus. Everyone is dressed in holiday attire of the most brilliant colors. A spirit of excitement and enthusiasm prevails as the crowd eagerly awaits the arrival of the toreador, Escamillo, and the beginning of the bullfight.

It has become traditional to introduce a ballet at this point, using music from the L'Arlesienne Suite which Bizet composed for Daudet's play, *L'Arlesienne*. Though it is a pleasant diversion to watch a good *corps de ballet* dance to Bizet's brilliant music, one may resent the retardation of dramatic action at a time when the inevitable tragic end is anxiously awaited. Introduction of ballet in the last act of the opera is a French convention that has established itself through years of usage.

The crowd in the square welcomes the toreadors as they arrive in quadrilles to the accompaniment of the march first heard in the prelude to the opera. Enthusiasm runs wild when the great hero Escamillo enters with Carmen. The people break into a stirring chorus of the Toreador Song. Carmen, aglow with pride and love for Escamillo, is gorgeously dressed for this gala occasion. The white lace mantilla and dress with its red velvet bolero and gold trimmings set off her dusky gypsy beauty. Before entering the arena Escamillo assures Carmen that if she loves him she will soon have occasion to be proud of him. She takes up the same melody, telling him that she has never loved anyone as she loves him. This short duet is interrupted by the entrance of the Alcalde on his way to the amphitheatre. The procession of gayly dressed, excited people bound for the bullfight is gorgeous and stirring. The arrival of the high magistrate is a signal for the beginning of the bullfight, and the crowd rushes into the arena.

The description above is of the way the Act IV begins in the romantic tradition. In the realistic production the setting is quite different. The scene discloses high-arched windows, from which a crowd of fight fans on their way to the arena comment on the procession, which is not visible to the audience. For the remainder of the act the arches are removed to provide for the action, which takes place in a suite of rooms where a party is being prepared to celebrate Escamillo's forthcoming triumph.

At the right is a large, heavily screened window, through which Carmen gazes out to see the bullfight beyond. At the left is the small chamber reserved for the toreador, where he is joined by Carmen for their duet, while at the right, under the window, stands a table behind which she will seek a moment's protection from Don José.[2]

Frasquita approaches Carmen and warns her that Don José is hiding in the crowd. Mercedes joins Frasquita in advising Carmen to be on her guard. Their anxious warning is given over a perfectly unconcerned background of flutes in thirds. Carmen's reply is characteristic. "I am not a woman to be afraid of him. I shall wait and speak with him here. I fear nothing." The two girls after a final warning leave Carmen and enter the amphitheatre. A transitional passage of music reflects the psychological state of Carmen. Fragments of the march are interrupted by a foreboding chromatic descending figure in the bass and finally displaced by a reappearance of the fate motive.

Don José, who has been lurking in the background, seizes this opportunity to speak to Carmen alone. His appearance presents a strange contrast to Carmen's resplendent toilet. He

[2] *Opera News.*

is unshaven, in torn clothing, a man completely demoralized and desperate. Emphasizing his state, he wanders about, dropping first his hat and then his coat to the ground. Evidently he is a broken man. Recognizing him, Carmen begins the conversation. Don José tells her that he does not threaten her; he begs and implores her. He will forget the past if she will go far away and begin a new life with him. Carmen is inflexible. She has never lied. Between them all is over. Don José renews his plea. There is still time to save herself if she will consent. Carmen remains firm. She realizes that her hour has arrived, but whether she lives or dies, she will never yield to him.

"Then you love me no more?" Don José asks. He repeats the question in desperation. He will join the band again, he will do anything she wishes. Her reply is, "Carmen will never yield. Free she was born, and free she will die!" The cheers of the crowd in the arena interrupt as a brass band is heard playing the march (No. 1).

Over the trumpet fanfare there rises the cry of victory for Escamillo. Carmen starts for the arena. Don José bars the way. His jealousy drives her to bold declaration of her love for Escamillo, "I love him, and even in the face of death I repeat that I love him." At this point the drama is accelerated to breath-taking speed. The battle of wills between Carmen and Don José is made the more dramatic and vivid by the background music of brass band and chorus, suggesting the intense excitement of the crowd absorbed in the bullfight and completely unaware of the life and death encounter that is taking place outside the amphitheatre.

As the crowd renews its cheers for Escamillo, Carmen again attempts to enter the arena but is stopped by Don José. Note the dramatic effectiveness of the distance kept between Don José and Carmen; at no time in this wild scene does he touch her. The orchestra punctuates Don José's wild declamation with fortissimo phrases of the fate motive. In the wildest rage he asks if he has lost his soul so that she may laugh at him while in the embraces of his rival. No, it shall not be. Carmen must follow him. "Well, then, strike me down, or let me pass," cries Carmen as she makes another attempt to enter the area.

Within the walls the trumpet fanfare blazes forth and the triumphant cry of the crowd is "Victory!" "For the last time, fiend, will you follow me?" Don José screams. Carmen answers by removing from her finger the ring which Don José had given her and throwing it in his face. At this instant the crowd is heard within the arena singing the Toreador Song. Carmen makes another attempt to enter. Don José anticipates her movement and plunges his dagger into her heart.

The crowd pour out of the arena and surround Don José as he kneels beside Carmen. In deepest agony he cries, "You can arrest me. It is I who killed her. Ah! Carmen! My adored Carmen!" Don José's last words are punctuated by fortissimo statements of the fate motive in the orchestra.

The poignant anguish of these instrumental phrases surpasses in expressiveness the words of Don José. The fate of Carmen and Don José, first suggested in the overture, has been fulfilled.

PART TWO

The Elements of Opera

Chapter Nine

THE LIBRETTO

SOME people get their greatest aesthetic pleasure from having their emotions excited and developed by words in poetry or in elevated prose, others from the drama, and others still from dance, physical form, color, or music, instrumental or vocal. The opera alone of art forms uses all of these elements, fusing them so that together they make a moving appeal to those who are sensitive to beauty.

WORDS AND MUSIC MUTUALLY CONTRIBUTORY

Experts who have advanced far on the road toward the understanding and mastery of music maintain that it expresses emotion better and more completely than words can ever do, but the amateur is far from holding that opinion. He is accustomed to words; he thinks in words, and he is likely to feel the need of words to define his feelings. Listening to a grand opera and not understanding the words, Rufus Choate is said to have exclaimed to his daughter, "Interpret for me the libretto lest I dilate with the wrong emotion." The great majority of people, and this includes most musicians themselves, recognize that words add to music as music adds to words. Mendelssohn to the contrary notwithstanding, most of us like for his "Songs without Words" titles that direct our imaginations to a clearer perception of the ideas and emotions that he intended, and some would like them even better if they were a setting to sentiment expressed in definite diction.

Music can to some extent, though not with any accuracy, suggest the direction in which the emotions are to be worked upon, but, declares J. A. Fuller-Maitland,

... this direction once being given from outside, whether by a "program" read by the listener or by the action and accessories of the stage, the force of feeling can be conveyed with overwhelming power, and the whole gamut of emotion, from the subtlest hint or foreshadowing to the fury of inevitable passion, is at the command of him who knows how to wield the means by which expression is carried to the heart's mind. And in this fact ... lies the completest justification of opera as an artform.[1]

Owing to its greater indefiniteness of utterance, music uses a greater and more conventional definiteness of form than words do. "Music does for the idea what style does for it in the case of the poet—raises it to a higher emotional power, gives it color, odor, incandescence, wings."

In the *Republic* Plato expresses the idea in a sentence which I quote in a meaning slightly different from the original, "What a poor appearance the tales of poets make when stripped of the colors which music puts upon them, and recited in simple prose." And Robert Browning has an apposite passage in *Pauline*.

> For music (which is earnest of a heaven,
> Seeing we know emotions strange by it,
> Not else to be revealed) is like a voice,
> A low voice calling fancy, as a friend,
> To the green woods in the gay summer time.

Ernest Newman has in his writings indicated time after time most clearly that music is in many instances superior to words

---

[1] In *The Well-Tempered Listener*, pages 235–57, Deems Taylor delightfully discusses program music, its possibilities and its limitations, and reports the results of Rigg's experiment, which showed that without verbal help music conveys its meaning very imperfectly, even to those with more than average training.

in the interpretation of the dramatic, in the expression of feeling, and in suggestions too subtle for verbal utterance. When planning *Rigoletto*, Verdi was quick to see that some of the most effective situations in Victor Hugo's play

. . . could be touched in with very much higher lights and deeper shadows by means of music. For example, the father's curse could be made much more sinister by means of the brass of the orchestra; far more dramatic point could be given to the ballad sung by the Duke in the tavern, and again as he is leaving it; while only such an art as music could do complete justice to the double scene inside and outside the hut . . . , for only in music can a number of characters all say different things at the same time with results agreeable to the listeners.[2]

And later Newman speaks of the orchestra as "an extra voice taunting the unhappy Monterone," of the "gruesome suggestiveness impossible to words alone" when the orchestra comments on the Sparafucile theme, and in the last act of what the music contributes in "the accumulation of horrors, the contrast and combination of effects, and the suggestion of atmosphere, particularly during the storm." Everyone who has experienced opera will recall many other instances of the contribution of music to words, such as the dramatic poignancy at the death of Butterfly, and how earlier, during her long vigil, it supplants words altogether.

Music is effective partly because of its sensuous appeal and to those who understand it because of its perfection of form. But a large element in its appeal is dependent on the richness of the hearer's previous experiences and on his imaginative responsiveness to aesthetic appeals for its recall. "All music is what awakes from you when you are reminded by the instruments," says Walt Whitman in "A Song for Occupations." Music is rich as the hearer is rich, not only in his own actual experiences but also in the experiences of the race which he has shared vicariously.

[2] Ernest Newman, *Stories of the Great Operas* (New York, Alfred A. Knopf, Inc.), II, 46.

Great music is a psychical storm, agitating to fathomless depths the mystery of the past within us. Or we might say that it is a prodigious incantation. There are tones that call up all ghosts of youth and joy and tenderness; there are tones that evoke all phantom pains of perished passion; there are tones that revive all dead sensations of majesty and might and glory—all expired exultations, all forgotten magnanimities. Well may the influence of music seem inexplicable to the man who idly dreams that his life began less than a hundred years ago! He who has been initiated into the truth knows that to every ripple of melody, to every billow of harmony, there answers within him, out of the Sea of Death and Birth, some eddying immeasurable of ancient pleasure and pain.[3]

But words are a great help to music, too. Everyone has felt the appeal of "Home, Sweet Home." Although the words are banal, they convey an appealing idea of universally experienced nostalgia. The music would not rank high by technical standards, and it could never alone be aesthetically effective; but it is sufficient to envelop, to reiterate, and to decorate the idea until an emotion suffuses one, when, like Ruth,

> sick for home,
> She stood in tears amid the alien corn.

In *The Ring*, Wagner wove in music a continuous emotional tissue, but it required the framework of poetry to make it definite.

Words are necessary for opera; indeed they are an essential part of it. They furnish for the audience a basis for the music, giving it not only meaning but direction and opportunity for elaborating and developing the emotional significance. For the singers and, to a lesser degree, for the instrumentalists they afford an illusion, as it were, from which they can get the interpretation that they attempt to convey by artistic means. No vocalist and no audience would enjoy or would long tolerate a continued succession of meaningless vocalized syllables, however ravishing the melody or however technically perfect the production.

[3] Paul Elmer More, "Lafcadio Hearn," in *Shelburne Essays* (New York: Putnam's), p. 164.

The superiority of opera can be appreciated when one compares an aria, or even an instrumental passage, presented in its dramatic setting and, on the other hand, dissociated from it in concert. In the latter it may be beautiful in itself; but in the former it also has significance, being suffused by all the meaning and the emotions that the developed situation contains. "One Fine Day" is a beautiful song; but in the opera we hear it as the expression of unshaken faith by the lonely Butterfly, who still believes that the man whom she worships will keep his promise and return to her when the robins nest again. Our knowledge that he has no intention of keeping his word makes the song infinitely touching. Of course if one knows the opera, from memory and imagination he supplies to concert excerpts the setting and the significance that must be entirely absent from listeners who lack his experience and imagination.

LIBRETTO OBSTACLES

Recognizing the mutual contributions of words and music, we must admit that the libretto is usually the greatest obstacle to the amateur who seeks to know something of opera and to enjoy it. For this fact there are several reasons. Not all stories set to music are good, even for opera. Some, such as the confused and unnecessarily complicated plot of *Der Freischütz* and the preposterous story in infelicitous diction of *Un Ballo Maschera*, are bad by any standards whatever, and when judged apart from the music as literature they are weak, silly, or absurd. But, as will be argued presently, no opera libretto should be judged by the criteria that are proper for the text of a spoken drama. By itself a libretto is scarcely more than an articulated dramatic skeleton, a form to be covered with the beautiful flesh of music and animated by the spirit of the singing actors in an appropriate scenic setting. No one would ever read an opera libretto, even the best, for its literary values alone.

As Oscar Thompson has said,

The good libretto is not necessarily a good play. And whether it is good or bad is to be determined, not according to how well it can stand by itself or with the addition of a little music, but by the opportunity it affords a composer to realize in terms of music what is theatrically effective and stimulating when bodied forth in those terms. . . . A good score can be helped or hindered by its libretto and sundry stage considerations. But it is the music that draws a particular listener back for his third, tenth, twentieth, or fiftieth performance of a given opera when the stage action of the work is an utterly old story.

Preparing for his first opera, the amateur is likely to read "a summary of the plot." Such a summary of even the greatest dramatic literature is seldom impressive. Read a brief summary of a great play—of *Lear* or of *The Hunchback*, for instance—or of the plot of some current play and see how little you get that makes you respect the dramatist or his work. The summary of an opera plot is likely to be disappointing, or even to seem extravagant and absurd, especially when prepared, as it often is, by a hack writer who does not appreciate his responsibility or seize his opportunity to present an outline that is intelligent and also attractive. In one summary in the printed libretto of *L'Amore dei Tre Re (The Love of the Three Kings)* one cannot learn until near the end that the old King Archibaldo is blind, a fact that makes the drama possible. One should not condemn an opera plot merely from its summary, even though it be made by a skilled writer. After you know some opera pretty well, read a summary of its plot and you will to some extent realize how little anyone is likely to get from it alone.

The wiser and less hurried amateur will go farther than the summary and read, or try to read, the entire libretto. I say "try to read," for the inexperienced are likely to make the mistake of identifying an opera libretto with the complete text of a spoken play, which it is not, and attempt to read it in the same way. It is, rather, an outline of a story with dramatic possibilities, an outline which one must read with a lively constructive imagination, filling in what is merely suggested, visualizing the complete action, and anticipating the

emotions that will be developed by the music. Even the form
of this outline is modified by the necessities of the composer,
who must have time for the development of his musical numbers; and these numbers must be placed not wholly in terms
of dramatic effectiveness but also in terms of distributing the
arias, ensembles, choruses, and spectacles according to the demands of opera conventions.

No worse mistake can be made by the amateur than to judge
an opera libretto by the standards that he has accepted for the
spoken drama or for the cinema play. The discriminating will
realize that plays to be personally acted on a stage have different standards from those that have been developed for the
drama of the motion picture. Note the many changes made in
every stage play before it is filmed or the changes that would
be necessitated if the process were reversed. Judge an opera
libretto for what it is, an outline of a dramatic development
that will offer opportunities for music to interpret and present,
as words alone are inadequate to do, the emotions that are
suggested in each of the unified succession of situations. In
good opera, words and music supplement each other, or,
rather, they are so inextricably interwoven that neither alone
can produce the effects possible from both together.

The amateur who can read a libretto in the language of its
origin is fortunate; but if he must depend on a translation he
finds an additional obstacle to appreciation. The original
diction was approved by the composer, who fitted his music
to it, or in some instances, the words have been written to conform to music already composed. A translator has a difficult
task in attempting not only to give the original meaning but
also to convey the nuances, the delicate suggestions and shadings that the original poet has expressed. That is exceedingly
difficult, as anyone who has ever attempted translation will
realize; a reading of several translations of the same original
will emphasize the difficulty. But when, in addition, a translator attempts to arrange his words so that they can be sung to
unchangeable music, success is hard to achieve. The wonder
is that translated libretti are not worse than they are.

The translator makes his task doubly hard by attempting to do two different things simultaneously: first, to give a reader who is preparing to enjoy an opera the detailed text so that he can know what is being sung at every moment of dramatic progress; and, second, a very different thing, to present words that can be sung if the opera is presented in English.* The latter is necessary, of course, for such operas as those originally composed in a language that cannot be sung by the members of the opera cast; for example, the Russian *Boris* and the Bohemian *Bartered Bride*, or when any foreign language opera is to be sung in English. That it is possible to do both successfully is illustrated in the Italian and English libretti of Menotti's *Amelia Goes to the Ball*, in Dent's translation of *Le Nozze di Figaro (The Marriage of Figaro)*, and in the Martins' translation of *Die Zauberflöte (The Magic Flute)*.†

* Illustrative of how bad an English version of a libretto can be are the following unsingable quotations from a translation for *La Pique Dame:*

> Our noble host invites you all to come this way;
> He has prepared a pyrotechnical display.

> Yes, nowadays I think society has lost its brilliance.

† In translating Schikaneder and Gieseke's libretto for *The Magic Flute* Thomas Philip Martin and Ruth Kelley Martin set themselves the following difficult requirements:

1. The music should remain untouched.

2. The accent of the declamation should be strictly observed, even in ensembles.

3. All forced methods of making lines fit by means of abbreviations, twisting of phrases, or contractions like e'er, you'll, he'd, etc., should be avoided, except when typical.

4. The number of syllables in a phrase should never be augmented or diminished.

5. The organic breathing points should be accurately preserved, no phrase distorted by an inorganic splitting, nor false connections altering the original phrasing.

6. The original vowel should be maintained to the greatest possible extent at all exposed places where the nature of the vowel is part of the musical effect.

7. To insure clear enunciation and good diction, words which are difficult to pronounce should not be crowded, especially in rapid passages.

8. Throughout the entire opera, the translation should endeavor to follow the original as closely as possible in the conviction that the further a translation digresses from its original, the less it will preserve the unity of words and music.

The translator puts on himself a quite unnecessary task when he attempts to write poetry or even rhymed verse. For one who is preparing to experience an opera, good prose is far more acceptable than bad verse.

For the amateur a libretto is most useful after he has learned the story as told in some such books as Newman's *Stories of the Great Operas*, one of the best, or in other books listed in the Appendix, page —. Having become familiar with the story well told so as to bring out its dramatic features, one preparing for an opera experience can then profitably use the complete libretto so that he may be informed as to what is going on at every stage of progress. He will want to know, for example, that Fafner and Fasolt are quarreling and about what, even though he may not be concerned with every word that they sing.

Detailed diction is not so important in opera anyway as is ordinarily thought. Neither was it in the ancient Greek tragedies, which the earliest opera was intended to imitate. The Greek tragedies were founded on stories the outlines of which everyone knew; they developed their plots in big steps, after each of which the chorus gave interpretation through comment. The audiences no doubt caught words here and there, enough to stimulate their memories and imaginations to follow the story and to get a gradual build-up of feeling. The fact that the actors wore masks is evidence that their enunciation could not have been as important as is sometimes argued, and no one who has stood in one of the ancient amphitheatres and tested its boasted acoustics can believe that any considerable part of the spoken text could have been understood from any but the nearest seats. Moreover, a study of the printed texts very clearly reveals that what Aeschylus and Sophocles and Euripides sought was not verbal subtleties and quotable lines or phrases but, rather, big dramatic situations presented in outline with effects cumulative from the slowly unfolded story and gradually developed characters.

Modern opera is more like the old Greek tragedy than it is

like the modern spoken play. It too proceeds, as a rule, by slow steps, using its series of dramatic situations which should be well known to the audience as settings for emotional expression in music. Whatever the language used, nobody in the audience ever understands all of the words. When familiar with the libretto, one can understand enough, however, to know what is going on at any given moment; and even without complete familiarity one can follow the story pretty well, often well enough to get enjoyment. Even when the words are in the singer's native language they cannot all be understood, especially in such a vast auditorium as the Metropolitan Opera House; and many a foreign-born singer could not be completely understood even if he were speaking the alien tongue that he sings.* They may pronounce correctly, but that is very different from pronouncing effectively. Their over-effort to articulate words may be disastrous to the music.

In most ensembles it can be argued that the composer never intended the detailed words to be heard. In the famous *Rigoletto* quartette the words in one passage run:

GILDA. He is false,   My heart is   broken!   'Twas in
MADDALENA. I am proof, my gentle woo-   er
DUKE. With   a   kind word
RIGOLETTO. . . . Thee   silence,   silence, thy tears will
                                                                not avail

GILDA. vain!   for bliss I   strove, ah, all in
MADDALENA. 'Gainst thy sweet and empty noth-   ings, I know them
DUKE. With   a   word end the pangs
                                                                        of

RIGOLETTO. thee,   not a-   vail thee, no, no

GILDA. vain!
MADDALENA. Well!
DUKE. unrequited love!
RIGOLETTO. no!

---

* It is an interesting phenomenon that not infrequently a singer takes more pains to give out clearly the words of a language that he has learned than of the language that is native to him.

It is absurd to think that any auditor could follow such a collocation of words, each of the four singers saying something entirely different. The words have no sense harmony whatever, though they are dramatically expressive of the contrast of four individual feelings. Verdi was interested in the musical harmony and in the dramatic effect, and in both he was eminently successful.

This in part is what Gilda sings:

> Ah, to speak of love thus lightly!
> Words like these to me were spoken!
> He is false, my heart is broken!
> 'Twas in vain for bliss I strove!
> Ah, ah, all in vain!
> He is faithless, my heart is broken.
> Ah, 'tis in vain! He is false!
> My heart,—my heart is broken!
> Ah, in vain for bliss I strove!
> For he is false, my heart is broken!
> Ah, in vain for bliss I strove!
> Ah, in vain, in vain I strove,
> For he is false, my heart is broken!
> Ah, in vain for bliss I strove!
> For he is false, my heart is broken!
> Ah, in vain for bliss I strove!

Whether in the English translation or in the original Italian, such a repetition of words could not be effective as literature whatever their merit when sung. In other words, weak diction or a poor translation cannot be as bad when sung as one is inclined to think. About all that is necessary is for one to know that the light-hearted Duke is pleading for one more conquest, that Maddalena is still parrying his advances, that the disillusioned Gilda bewails her faithful broken heart, and that Rigoletto is reiterating his determined vengeance. All of this one can know from reading even a poor libretto or from catching phrases as they are sung. More is unnecessary. The same is true of the Egitto chorus in *Aïda*, the "Anvil

Chorus" in *Il Trovatore*, and of innumerable other choruses and ensembles. The chief function of words in most opera songs is to give the general idea that is to be expressed and to direct the emotion that the music is attempting to interpret and to emphasize.

In most passages, then, it is not important that words of an opera libretto be heard in detail. As W. S. Gilbert said, not altogether truthfully, of his own composition of words for the comic opera,

> This particularly rapid, unintelligible patter
> Isn't generally heard,
> And if it is, it doesn't matter.

As a matter of fact, Gilbert and Sullivan solved the problem of combining words and music very simply.

Wherever the stage action and dialogue had to be taken seriously, creating the effect of dramatic realism, they resorted to the spoken word, using an easy, conversational prose, like most other practical playwrights. When buffoonery or absurdity was in order, they combined a fast verbal patter with a minimum of musical accompaniment, making quite sure that all the words would be clearly understood and giving them an extra comic appeal with tricky rhymes, puns, and other humorous touches. But when an honest emotion or a romantic thought called for musical expression, they wrote an actual song, with appealing melody and poetic words. The combination is of course irresistible.[4]

In serious opera, words that the composer felt were important to be understood were in an earlier day given in recitative and often latterly to light orchestration or to none at all.

When the Norns sing at length of the impending doom of the gods or when King Mark and Gurnemanz recount their losses, who cares for their exact words? If we know what they are singing about and sympathetically share in their feelings, we should get little more from understanding every word that they utter. In the first act of the *Barber* everyone knows

[4] Sigmund Spaeth, in *Opera News*.

that the Count in his serenade is singing of the coming dawn and bidding his lovely lady awake; that is what all serenaders have sung since the lute or the guitar was invented. It is not hard to guess the expressed thanks of the musicians when he hands them a generous largess, and one's pleasure is not increased by knowing that they are singing, "A thousand thanks, sir, for these marks of favor, for such honor and courtesy; we are, in truth, indebted to you. . . ." Their sentiments are no better in Italian than in English; but their expression gives an opportunity for a chorus, which is a necessary contrast after the Count's "Ecco ridente in cielo" solo. We can laugh at the expression of self-importance of the Factotum when he tells in his Largo of the many things he is called upon to do, but even if we understood every word we could not later recall half of his activities. To appreciate the amorousness of Don Giovanni we must know the general sense of Leporello's recounting of his amours; we neither remember nor care whether the number of conquests in Spain exceeds or is exceeded by the number in Portugal or France.

Words in an opera libretto may from a literary point of view be utterly prosaic or apparently banal and yet present an effective dramatic situation. The Italian words of Sharpless in *Madame Butterfly:*

> Mi rincresca, ma . . . ignoro
> Non ho studiato l'ornitologia

are no more poetic than the English "I am sorry, but I am ignorant of the study of ornithology." Either is so flatly prosaic that one is likely to ridicule the text. But why focus attention on the prosaic diction, which, by the way, is entirely characteristic of the prosaic American consul? It and he serve as a homely background against which we see the romantic Butterfly pitiful in her unshaken faith that her lover will return as he promised when the robin redbreast nests again. If anything can increase our sympathy for the tragic little figure who seeks a crumb of comfort from the man

who knows as little of the tender and constant heart as he
does of ornithology, this should help to do it. When the
Consul offers Lieutenant Pinkerton "milk punch or whiskey"
—a slur, by the way, on American taste in liquors—the commonplace diction emphasizes the commonplace character.

There are some verbal passages, beautiful as literature or
crucial in the drama, which the auditor at the opera may well
wish to hear or to know in detail. When Orpheus surveys the
beauties of the hard-won Elysium he naturally breaks into
song:

> Piu puro e 'l ciel,
> Piu chiaro il di. . . .

I should like to hear every word of Calzabigi's poem, even in a
translation falling short in literary merit of the original.

> How brilliantly here shines the sun!
> I never saw the sky so pure,
> I never saw the sky so clear.
> With what sweet harmony resounds the grove!
> The warbling of the birds,
> The murmuring of the rivulets,
> And the sweet breath of the air. . . .

But I do not miss a great deal if I am aware that he is singing
of the ethereal beauty and serenity of the abode of the Blessed
Spirits, which by comparison with the horrors through which
he has passed seems to him, and to us, a beautiful fit home for
the lovely lost Euridice. Knowing the sense of the song, I
prefer to concentrate on "the entrancing melody of the oboe,
a ravishing evocation of quivering light and the stirring of soft
airs, and the flowing of quiet streams in some imaginable country of the dreaming mind." * If the libretto were written in
the diction of "Ode on a Grecian Urn," we should be so
attentive to hear all of the perfect words that we might miss
a contributing effect of the music and thus lose opera.

* Who could have written this except the late Lawrence Gilman, whose
eloquent verbal interpretations of music every lover of the opera should
know?

Enzo's "Cielo e mar" in the second act of *La Gioconda*,
the words by that incomparable librettist Boïto, is a poem acceptable even without music. The first stanza runs:

> Cielo e mar!—l' etereo velo
> Splende come un santo altare.
> L' angiol mio verra dal cielo?!
> L' angiol mio verra dal mare?!
> Qui l'attendo, ardente spira
> Oggi il vento dell' amor.
> Quel mortal che vi sospira
> Vi conquide, o sogni d'or!

> Heaven and ocean! yon ethereal veil
> Is radiant as a holy altar.
> My angel, will she come from heaven?
> My angel, will she come o'er ocean?
> Here I await her; I breathe with rapture
> The soft zephyrs filled with love.
> Mortals oft, when fondly sighing,
> Find ye a torment, O golden dreams.

But good as the words are, it is not difficult for one seeing
Enzo on his ship looking out over the moonlit sea to understand the sense that he sings and to share in the sentiment that
he feels as he awaits the arrival of his beloved Laura.

Wagner was proud of his libretti, all of which he himself
wrote. They do contain singable and dramatic diction, just
good enough to serve as a foundation for his music and never
interfering with it by demanding special attention. But often
Wagner's words are metrically monotonous, tedious, and
sometimes in bad taste. The words of the "Liebestod" in
Tristan und Isolde begin

> Mild und leise
> Wie er lächelt,
> Wie das Auge
> hold er öffnet:
> seht ihr, Freunde,
> seht ihr nicht? . . . .

> Mild and softly
> he is smiling;
> how his eyelids sweetly open.
> See, O comrades,
> see you not
> how he beameth
> ever brighter. . . .

While ravished by the incomparable music of the orchestra with a vocal obbligato, as it were, and torn by the ineffable tragedy of the apotheosis of human love, who cares about these words, about any words, especially those in the vile translation? We much prefer to share in the grief of the bereft Isolde, understanding in our hearts something of what her torn spirit feels, rather than to hear the intrusive description of the corpse, which is no longer the noble lover whom she and we have known.

And Brünnhilde's defense of her loyal disobedience, beginning

> Weil für dich in Auge
> das Eine ich heilt.

is moving poetry as an expression of a sentiment, even though we may not appreciate the German words. In English she begins:

> Ay, for *thee*, thee only,
> I did not forget,
> When thrall to another,
> Sad and alone,
> Helpless thou didst turn thee away.

Boïto's words for the lovely duet in *Otello*

> You loved me for the dangers I had passed,
> And I loved you that you did pity them (*Otello*, I, iii)

and for Otello's expression of passionate grief in the last act,

> I kissed thee ere I killed thee. No way but this,
> Killing myself, a kiss, another kiss, and yet a kiss!

are illustrative of passages that the auditor should hear exactly or know in order to get full appreciation of the dramatic scene. Also it is important to hear or to know the exact word when the music gives an unusually close interpretation of their sense; for example, in Wotan's monologue in Act II of *Die Walküre*. In *Traviata* "the abrupt change from the tender, reflective mood of 'Ah, fors e lui' to the abandonment of the 'Sempre libra' will mean little to anyone," as Milton Cross has pointed out, "who does not know that it symbolizes a gesture of repudiation and despair."

Similarly there are "tag lines" which it is important to hear, whether they be sung or spoken. One of the most dramatic of these is in the third act of *Otello*. When the Moor, brought to an agony of jealousy by the diabolic machinations of Iago, lies writhing on the floor, the populace outside with flourishes of trumpets cry

> Victory! Long live Otello!
> Hail to the Lion of Venice!

Iago sneeringly comments,

> See, there is your lion.

And one would miss much if he did not know the words in the long dialogue between Ortrud and Telramund in Act II of *Lohengrin*.

The exact sense is often important in comedy, where coruscating wit or even humor is better conveyed by words than by music. Note that the humor in Beckmesser's song in *Die Meistersinger* is expressed by gross exaggeration so that the audience will be sure to understand its absurdity. We must get this or we miss the point in the scene, but we may fail to understand all of the details of Hans Sachs's lengthy passages without serious loss. We will lose much, too, if we fail to understand the Barber's comments when Rosina is sending a letter to her lover. The exact sense of words is important also in passages that inform the audience of something that has happened offstage, perhaps before the play has begun. It may be needed also to give an explanation that cannot be presented otherwise. *Il Trovatore* is greatly weakened by too much of this necessity. Such information is usually given in recitative, the words of which are unfortunately seldom heard clearly. Often it is tedious and ineffective musically. It is felt to be necessary, however, for dramatic continuity. The most skillfully contrived libretti need little of this, the information being given incidentally or implied by action. If words are inferior or obtrusive, one strains to hear them, thus neglecting the desirable fused effect, and he resents them as a detraction from the music.

Opera in English

From time to time there is a lively campaign for opera in English. In so far as this may promote original compositions in the language with which we are most familiar, it has general sympathy. Artistically there is no reason why more operas should not be composed with English words; but when we have listened to *The King's Henchman*, *The Emperor Jones*, *Shawenis*, or *The Man Without a Country*, the same difficulties that have just been discussed are apparent. True, we recognize more of the words than if they were Italian, German, French, or Russian; but at the best performance the keenest pair of ears fails to understand more than enough merely to sketch the progress of the story. My own experience is that when opera is sung in English, either original or a translation, my effort to hear the words interferes with the most complete enjoyment. After a short while I listen almost exactly as I do to opera in a foreign language: if not familiar beforehand with the plot and its detailed development, I try to get from the words that I can easily catch and from the action of the characters and the scenic sets enough of each dramatic situation so that the music has meaning and significance. Of course I lose something, but hardly as much as if

I should give undue attention to the words. Whenever possible, and it usually is, I become thoroughly familiar before the performance with the plot and with the exact words when they seem especially significant.

In the case of such operas as those by Gilbert and Sullivan, the libretto is of much more and the music of less importance than in the operas by Verdi and Piave, Massenet and Gallet, or Puccini and Giacosa and Illica. Note that we always speak of operas by Gilbert and Sullivan, not by Sullivan and Gilbert, whereas it is an unusual operagoer who can even name the librettists of most of the works that he has heard over and over. When there comes another Gilbert whose libretti sparkle with wit, each quip more important than the plot itself, and set to music which has little emotional value and would seldom be considered important for its own sake, then we may have to revise the position that has been advanced and argue for the major importance of words. But even at a performance of *Pinafore*, *The Pirates of Penzance*, or *The Mikado* the pleasure that one gets is greatly enhanced if he is reasonably familiar with the words beforehand. Then he can more easily enjoy Sullivan's clever music and make the fusion of all the elements just as the unique partnership intended and hoped for.

The case for opera of foreign origin translated into English is not a strong one. Although the Italians, the French, and the Germans usually translate the libretti of foreign operas, we in the United States, as Spaeth has said, do not like to hear everyday phrases sung to a musical accompaniment, for they often sound ludicrous. Even if the words are put into a "poetic" English—"locks" or "tresses" for hair, or "raiment" for clothes—the effect impresses us with its artificiality. Such translations as "Still ween'st thou me weaponless" (*Die Walküre*) and "Ha, my blood, merrily flows it" (*Tristan und Isolde*) we cannot take seriously. Seldom, very seldom, is the translation or adaptation in respectable English. The awkwardness, the straining to make words fit the music, and the frequent violations of common idiom are more likely to offend than is the use of a familiar language to help.

Even if the translation be perfect English, all the arguments previously advanced will hold: the audience cannot hear all or any considerable continuity of the words, especially in the ensembles and choruses; it is not important that they should; and effort to hear them is likely seriously to interfere with the enjoyment of the total effect. It is far better for an auditor to make himself beforehand so familiar with the libretto that he knows precisely what is going on at every moment; then at the performance he can understand the general sense of every song and devote his undivided attention to fusing all the elements—dramatic situation, visual setting, acting, vocal song, and instrumental music—into a series of appreciations of beautifully expressed emotions. The slogan "Opera in English" is more attractive than it is convincing.

Why Words at All?

Why is it necessary to have words at all in opera? The answer to this question has already been at least implied. In the first place, opera being the musical expression of emotions caused by dramatic situations, the drama can be presented best by words. In opera they outline the framework, but more important, they aid in completion of the structure being made by the visual setting, the costumes, and the acting. All of these completing elements are in opera, and in addition there is of course music, both instrumental and vocal.

As said earlier, music needs words to indicate the nature of its expression, to give it the definiteness desired by most hearers and also by most performers. It is entirely possible, of course, for a musician to translate notes into beautiful melody or harmony by voice or instruments without the association of any definite intellectual ideas. That is precisely what we have in "pure music" presented in concert. This gives pleasure from its beauty of sound, from its perfection of

form, and from the techniques used. But song always and
to an extent instrumental music in opera, while retaining form
and demanding good techniques of production, are directed
by verbal ideas and are thereby enriched and made for most
hearers far more appealing to human emotion. One may enjoy
the fire music in *Die Walküre* or Brünnhilde's immolation in
Die Götterdämmerung simply as music, but how much greater
the appeal when we have followed the daughter of Wotan
through the series of events that led to punishment for her high
loyalty and later to her grief and sacrifice for her hero so
basely tricked and slain. The performer of such music gets
from the drama expressed in words a richness of understanding and feeling which indicates how he shall translate the
written notes into expressive music. A not inconsiderable
part of opera music has so little importance as technical composition that we never think of presenting it in concert for
its own sake; but given meaning by drama, it becomes
marvelously moving.

Words give direction, then, to the musician so that he more
clearly understands what emotions he should first feel and
subsequently attempt to produce or intensify in the hearers.
They are even more important in helping the auditor. He can
get a certain aesthetic pleasure from the "Flower Song" in
Faust, from "Caro Nome" in *Rigolletto*, from the "Pilgrims'
Chorus" in *Tannhäuser*, from the prelude to the last act of
Carmen, or from the Forspiel to *Das Rheingold*. But how
much richer and more satisfying that pleasure is when he has
followed Faust from despair in his study through all the
development to the happy but fearful lover in Marguerite's
garden; when he understands that the heart of the simple and
sweet Gilda is all aflutter with love for the unworthy Duke;
when he knows the carnal pleasure, the repentance, and the
regeneration of Tannhäuser; when he realizes that all the color
and excitement of the crowd outside the bull ring are a violent
contrast to the impending tragedy to two characters; or when
familiarity with the story of the *Ring* gives meaning to the

restless and inexorable moving of the river. Even when an excerpt from opera is sung or played in concert, the informed audience bring with them for enrichment and significance memory of the developed situation from which the selection was taken. When the concert tenor sings "Che gelida manina" they recall the Bohemian pair falling in love as they search for the key in the darkness; and when the orchestra plays the intermezzo from *Cavalleria Rusticana* all of the tragic and sordid story comes back in memory to give the music meaning.

In opera there is music, of course, for which words are no more necessary than they are for a signal given on a trumpet, such as that in *Fidelio* to announce the coming of Pizarro. It is highly dramatic, but it needs no words. When José sings offstage "Les Dragons d'Alcala" he merely lets us know that the soldier has completed his confinement in prison and is again approaching the web of the gypsy. The words might mean anything or nothing. Rigoletto sings merely "La-ra, la-ra" when he reveals his anguish and suspicion as he searches the faces of the courtiers to discover if they know the whereabouts of his daughter. Given the setting and the dramatic situation, we are quite content to hear no more than a repeated "Ah. . . ." in many a coloratura aria; we need nothing more to understand the emotion being expressed in song. There is the brilliant cry of the Valkyrie, a mere "Ho-yo-to-ho," and the Rhine-Maidens sing meaningless syllables, "Weia waga . . . wagala weia!" But all of these instances are exceptions and are easily explained and justified. They do not need words because words have already given them meaning and significance.

Words outline the plot of opera so that its development may be understood at any point. Music takes time for development and not infrequently diverts the attention of the audience from the drama; words bring it back and contribute to the dramatic progress. However absorbing the aesthetic pleasure in music, it cannot make the intellect resign its function. All but the auditor who goes to the opera for music alone demand that there be a certain amount of reasonableness in what the singers act on the stage, and this the words supply. The libretto is, then, necessary for opera; it performs very definite services. If we keep in mind just what these services are, we are not likely to be so critical of the words as we are when we apply, as we should not do, the criteria of literary merit to which we are accustomed.

SOME LIBRETTI

The libretto has had its ups and downs in the history of opera; sometimes it has been important, but until Wagner it was chiefly considered merely an excuse for dramatic music. In the eighteenth century, when vocal music, especially coloratura solo singing, was at its height of popularity, many opera producers would order from a hack writer a libretto which he would turn over to a composer of music. Few cared much about the dramatic plot, just so it furnished opportunities for song. As a result many early books of the opera were unbelievably bad, especially when read apart from the music. But why should anybody do that except to prepare for a performance? As audiences in the eighteenth century attended opera chiefly for song, little such preparation was made—indeed, the books were seldom printed—and there was little criticism of the literary style or of the dramatic construction. Beaumarchais is credited with saying that what is too silly to be said may be sung. But the librettists Rinunccini, Quinault, Molière, Zeno, and Metastasio were in their time poets of a high order, and the libretti of Da Ponte represent some of the best in the poetry of operatic drama. It may be noted that almost none of the eighteenth century operas with very poor books survive. Gradually there came a demand for better libretti, so that later operas for the most part have at least respectable dramatic plots.

The earliest opera plots were founded on well-known myths and classic folk tales, those of Dafne, Orpheus and Euridice, Ariadne, Ulysses, Phryne, Psyche, Alcestis, Iphigenia, and Medea being favorites. In them the human feelings are presented in the simplest possible form. A little later the dramatists drew their material from Greek, Roman, and Persian history, using well-known characters but inventing incidents in no way authentic, usually conspiracies and love intrigues. Anachronisms were of course common, not merely in incidents but in costumes, other accessories, and diction. There are a number of instances in the early days of more than one composer's using the same story, and even the same libretto, as a predecessor had done. For example, Gluck used for his *Armide* (1777) Quinault's book, which had formerly been set to music by Lully. It is said that more than thirty composers used a single libretto by Metastasio. As devotion to song grew, plots became increasingly artificial and conventional; singers cared little for the words and audiences cared less, entertaining themselves between arias with conversation, refreshments, and games.

A good deal can be said for the use of plots and characters drawn from mythology or from history. In their broad outlines the stories that were used were in the public mind and had already associated with them a certain atmosphere in which appropriate music could be understood and appreciated. Knowing the main trend of the plots, audiences could more or less take the detailed words for granted and listen to the singing to which they were so devoted. It is much more difficult for librettist and composer to build up an illusion of reality using invented characters set in novel situations than it is when they use familiar characters in mythology or history. Moreover, invented characters, especially of lowly station, cannot easily be elevated to heroic or romantic stature, which opera for a spread of generations required.

In the late nineteenth century, composers began to present characters and emotions of common people and incidents in their lives. *Cavalleria Rusticana* and *Pagliacci* were followed by other operas in *verismo*, like Puccini's *Girl of the Golden West* and Charpentier's *Louise*. An extreme illustration is

Berg's *Wozzeck*. Currently we have such operas as Menotti's *The Consul*, *The Medium*, and *The Saint of Bleecker Street*. But it is more difficult to make common people have deep and wide appeal. Drama, and certainly romance, prefers the highborn and the faraway. It is easier to be moved by Juliet Capulet than by Jane Coons.

In the comic opera the task was different and easier, and so we find in *buffa* and *comique* characters of a kind that was common in the acquaintance of the audiences. But they did not have to be elevated in dignity or heroism, and indeed they were not. It was a violent break with tradition when the Romance movement in the latter half of the eighteenth century brought common people into serious opera. Appreciating the advantages of using characters and stories from mythology, Wagner returned to the custom in ways with which all are familiar.

"The average opera before Wagner," says Newman, "was neither a good play spoiled by music nor good music spoiled by a play, but merely a bad play and formless music adding each to the other's foolishness." To this extreme condemnation some exceptions must of course be made, but appreciation of the opera that we now hear, however absurd some of the situations, characters, and words may seem, will be heightened if one realizes the nature of the plots, characters, and diction of operas in the period of evolution. (Read, for example, the plot of *Lucio Silla* in Jahn's *Life of Mozart*, Volume I, page 8.) If there is a more absurd and more confusing opera book in the world than that for Mozart's *Die Zauberflöte (Magic Flute)* it has not come to my attention, and the one for Weber's *Euryanthe* runs it a close second.

The first succesful librettist was Rinunccini, the famous Italian poet, who died in 1629. But the Italians cared little for verbal texts, and this attitude naturally carried over to the French. Molière and Quinault, who were famous as librettists for more than a century, wrote for Lully, and Voltaire for Rameau. Metastasio (1698–1782) was one of the most prolific of all librettists, preparing books that were used by Handel, Haydn, Scarlatti, Spontini, and others of lesser note. He was especially successful in subordinating his work to that of the musician. It was not until Gluck (who died 1787) that protest arose against the flaccid conventional texts, with their sham personages and dramatic repetition of meaningless words. Gluck maintained that a dramatically skilled poet inspired the composer, and he got an improved book for his *Orfeo ed Euridice* from Calzabigi.

In 1781 Mozart wrote, ". . . in an opera the poem must unquestionably be the obedient daughter of the music." Although not fastidious about his early libretti, which present merely a succession of incidents loosely held together by the dialogue, Mozart had such a sense for the dramatic in individual scenes that audiences do not resent the lack of dramatic continuity. In character drawing he has seldom been surpassed. Bekker says that Mozart discarded "lofty feelings far removed from earthly reality" and substituted for singing ideas "singing personalities." Lorenzo da Ponte, Mozart's favorite librettist, after a checkered career which included selling merchandise, running a bookstore, and promoting opera in New York, finally became a teacher of Italian in Columbia College, New York.

Weber had a fairly good book for *Oberon*, but one of the poorest for his *Euryanthe*. Meyerbeer bullied and dominated his librettists, all of whom were skilled writers, so that he got texts such as he wanted for his music but dramatically inferior to what he might have had. In grand opera as a whole, text and music were far from fused. The importance of the libretto grew with Wagner and with the later operas of Verdi.

Wagner wrote his own texts, partly because his comprehensive genius could be content with nothing less, and partly to exemplify his theories, which he did imperfectly.* Although

---

* A few other composers of opera wrote their own libretti; for instance, Leoncavallo for *Pagliacci*, Tchaikovsky for *Eugen Onegin*, Charpentier for *Louise*, and Prokofiev for *Love for Three Oranges*.

proud of his literary production, Wagner was only a third-rate poet, being insensitive to the aroma of words. In many passages he is excessively long-winded, and partly because of the order of composition of the operas in *The Ring*, repetitious. Whatever one may think of the literary merit of Wagner's libretti, he must recognize that this composer did produce a large number of impressive dramatic situations, big conflicts of elemental forces, and crucial moments in the life of the spirit, and that his diction is singable.

Verdi had a succession of libretti that ranged from the conventional to the best that have been written for opera. He demanded clear narration, tension in action proceeding to a dramatic climax instead of merely words that could be set to music. Piave furnished him good texts for *Ernani*, an adaptation of Victor Hugo's drama, for *La Traviata*, for *Forza del Destino*, and especially for *Rigoletto;* and Ghislanzoni is primarily responsible for the basis of *Aïda*. Perhaps the two best libretti in the history of opera are those for *Otello* and *Falstaff*, both written by the brilliant Arrigo Boïto, himself a composer of one distinguished opera. He also wrote the excellent libretto for Ponchielli's *La Gioconda*. Boïto was marvelously discriminating in his selection from the plays of Shakespeare and equally skilled in re-expressing and arranging the material so that it is suitable for opera. He even made additions (such as Iago's "Credo") at which lovers of the English dramatist do not cavil.[5]

A list of other successful librettists must be headed by Augustin Eugene Scribe, "one of the most admirable of all peoples and times, who stands well-nigh unrivaled in his knowledge of stagecraft and of the requirements of music." He wrote texts for Meyerbeer, Auber, Verdi, and Halévy. Sterbini deserves fame for his adaptation of Beaumarchais' comedy for Rossini's *Barber*. Barbier and Carre wrote the texts for Meyerbeer's *Dinorah*, for Gounod's *Faust*, and for

---

[5] See Francis Toye, *Giuseppe Verdi: His Life and Works* (New York: Alfred A. Knopf, Inc., 1931), 434 ff. *et passim*.

Thomas' *Mignon* and *Hamlet*, while Barbier alone wrote the book for Offenbach's *Les Contes d'Hoffmann*. Meilhac and Halévy made the fine book for *Carmen* from Prosper Merimée's story; Meilhac and Galle did the book for Massenet's *Manon;* and Gallet adapted Anatole France's novel for *Thaïs.* Hoffmannsthal, a highly skilled dramatist, composed the texts in elevated prose for six of Strauss's best-known operas. His *Elektra,* first written to be produced as a spoken drama, is excellently composed. Puccini was served by Giacosa and Illica for *Madama Butterfly* and *Tosca.* And Sem Bennelli made an unusually good adaptation of his spoken tragedy for Montemezzi's *L'Amore dei Tre Re.*

The Making of an Opera Libretto

The composition of an opera begins with the selection of a subject. Usually in modern times a composer will be attracted by the possibilities in some hero of history or fiction, let us say William Tell or Lear, or in some story or drama, like *The Devil and Daniel Webster* or *The Girl of the Golden West.* In the subject he sees drama that can be acted and possibilities of musical expression. If he is to have an opportunity to write a score, he must have a libretto; so he seeks out a poet, preferably one who knows opera and its requirements, and a partnership is begun. Much less commonly than in earlier days is a libretto written on a chosen subject and then submitted to a composer for his approval and use.

A consideration of the subjects and plots of most of the operas that are still presented will reveal that for the most part they contain good dramatic material; that they are fairly simple in structure, usually lacking the subtle complications and surprises that are common and desirable for the spoken drama; that they have few superfluous episodes or incidents, those introduced being justified by their making possible some music which otherwise could not be used; and that they demand a small number of principal characters, each one of a distinct type.

If an opera libretto is disappointing as dramatic literature when read, we should not be too critical of the librettist; he did not write it as dramatic literature to be read. Moreover, in its composition and in the inevitable revision we must remember that he labored under restrictions and requirements that are all but paralyzing. He had to plan his plot with due regard to dramatic development; the difficult quick exposition of the situation and of the characters and their mutual relations; the development that introduces conflict, suspense, and variety; and the denouement, which satisfies the curiosity of the audience without being unduly prolonged. More dramas, sung or spoken, are ruined by a poor first scene or by a tedious final one than by weaknesses in between.

The librettist must see at every step possibilities of action. Though less stage "business" usually is demanded for opera than for a spoken play, still the opera must move forward by action made interesting in this fashion. A good dramatist will invent good "theater," like Tosca's setting candles at the head of the dead Scarpia or like Butterfly's long and lonely vigil. He must provide in a limited number of scenes for a continuity in the plot, though in this respect opera is not overly strict in its requirements, as one will realize by referring to *Manon Lescaut, Mignon,* and *Boheme.* Neither is opera strict in demanding that everything be fully explained or reasonable: Rigoletto could hardly be deceived by the courtiers on their abduction prank; Maddalena does not mend Sparafucile's sack; and we have to imagine, rather than see, the Dutchman and Senta rise heavenward, the gods pass over the rainbow bridge, and the Rhine overflow Siegfried's funeral pyre.

Beyond the ordinary requirements of the drama the opera librettist finds many more. He must provide for the distribution, balance, and combination of singing voices, and also for the desired placing of solos, ensembles, and choruses. Although the rules are not so strict as formerly, it is obvious that important arias or solos should not be in sequence, that recitative or its equivalent must be introduced for emotional relief as well as for information and continuity, and that the plot must provide for getting off and on the stage the singers who will give the necessary numbers.

Moreover, all of the incidents must be suitable for musical expression, incidents to which music can give a heightened beauty and a strengthened effect, and all of the diction must be singable. Some ideas are too intellectual to be expressed by music, some situations or incidents are too horrible. It is doubtful if the suffering and the babbling of the mad Lear, for instance, could be successfully interpreted in music. Notably in Puccini there are a number of passages that defy musical treatment. In them the characters talk rather than sing, while the orchestra plays pretty tunes.

Being something of an artist in words, the librettist will labor long to provide the *mot juste* not only in the lyrics but also to a less extent in the continuum, which will be sung in recitative or the equivalent. But words that read well and that are an exact or felicitous expression of meaning may not sing well, and numerous examples will be pointed out by the composer and by singers whom he consults. The librettist has to remember that the melody is supreme and that it will dislocate rhythm, ignore accents, and drown end rhyme at its own pleasure. It also obscures onomatopoeia and verbal tone color. The long-respected convention that an opera libretto should be written in verse has little to justify it. The innovation of Hoffmannsthal in providing for Strauss libretti written in elevated prose is so entirely sensible that it is likely to be increasingly used by others. The libretto must not be too long. The librettist must constantly remember that music requires time for its unfolding. Words can be repeated, as in "Caro Nome," and the action can stand still while musical and even dramatic development is taking place. Think of meeting all these demands and of telling a good story dramatically at the same time and you will get some idea of the challenge that the librettist faces.

But when he has finished his first draft his troubles really begin. The composer will demand all sorts of changes: he cannot "feel" the music for a certain passage; he must have a lyric for music that he has already written; he thinks one set of words is too long, another too short, and another impossible for the musical expression; or he demands the insertion of a setting for a lullaby or a ballad or a prayer, the music for which he has in mind. Some of his first draft the librettist will have to discard, substituting new composition to satisfy the musical composer and at the same time to carry on the drama, substitutions that may not have the freshness or the effectiveness, from a literary or dramatic point of view, of the originals. In some instances, if the librettist and composer are balked by the challenge, there will be a compromise satisfactory to neither of them. It is a wonder that they are ever on speaking terms when the opera is ready for production. In various biographies and reminiscences, notably those of Gilbert and Sullivan, may be found accounts of disagreements, either humorous or bordering on the tragic, between two partners, each a genius in his own way, who had to work in harmony for the making of an opera.

In light of the demands and of the necessary compromises it is easy to be charitable toward an opera libretto. The writing of one is like custom-tailoring a suit of clothes for a person as yet unborn, continued as he grows in stature and in bulk, and many times altered to satisfy tastes which may be mere whims. It is a wonder that libretti are as good as they are. Judged by the satisfaction of the functions assigned to them and not by standards of excellence for drama to be read or presented on the speaking stage, they are not bad anyway.

Those who are interested in the theory of the libretto and in the laws of its construction can find an illuminating discussion with abundant illustration of details in Istel's book on libretti.[6]

[6] Edgar Istel, *The Art of Writing Opera Librettos*, translated by Thomas Baker (New York: G. Schirmer, Inc., 1922). See especially pp. 109–54.

Chapter Ten

VOCAL MUSIC AND THE OPERA

VOCAL music is the most natural, and probably was the earliest, means for the expression of emotion. It is not difficult to imagine the wailing and ejaculations of early man repeated and continued until they developed into a sort of melodic pattern. Gradually this must have associated with itself words—and then there was song.

The single melody singing by minstrels and troubadours, and no less by men and women for their own satisfaction, kept actively alive through the years the natural desire for solo expression. Music has the power of expressing emotions which lie too deep or which are too subtle for speech. And, moreover, one will express freely in song feelings that he may be reticent to put into spoken words.

In the Middle Ages, though simple song naturally continued, vocal music was developed into the complex art of group contrapuntal singing which, charming as it still is, certainly tended to become the artistic expression of emotion by the satisfaction of elaborate rules of composition. Contrapuntal music is a developed choral art-form, two or more relatively independent melodies sounded together and interwoven into harmony.

It was doubtless appreciation of all this, as well as a desire to resurrect what was thought to be the Greek style of presenting its tragic drama, that led the group of cultured Florentines and their successors at the end of the sixteenth century to invent opera. At first it was merely a presentation in recitative, with a bare instrumental accompaniment, of a dramatic story, with occasional melodic comment by a chorus. But very shortly the recitative was supplemented by song—first, by an arioso, which is a combination of recitative and air, and then by the aria, which quickly developed into an elaborate art-form. This development met hearty popular approval. The musical world found in it not merely a means of satisfying the vague yearning that man had for solo singing, but also a vehicle that could be infinitely elaborated artistically.

The Recitative

The Florentine Camerata proposed that the recitative take its form from the text, giving the natural rhetorical accents of ordinary speech, the natural rise and fall of the ordinary voice, using few musical tones, and adapting itself to the changes in thought and emotion. Its musical value is of necessity slight because of the dominance of meaning expressed in words. It is speech sung at much the same pace as that of ordinary talk, and, being simple, it is much more rapid than the aria, which needs time to develop its musical form and substance. For example, in the third act of *Figaro* the intrigue becomes so rapid and so involved that it can be carried on only by a liberal use of recitative, there being no time for developed music. The recitative was at first accompanied simply by chords struck on the harpsichord and occasionally by sustained notes on the bowed stringed instruments or on the bassoon. This is called *recitativo secco*.

The recitative underwent various modifications in the history of opera, and early it was in constant competition for importance with the aria, which developed a dominating supremacy in Italy during the first three quarters of the eighteenth century. One of the changes in the recitative was that, beginning about 1686, it was given a more important and complex instrumental accompaniment, especially when the singer was represented as being unable to control his emotions. This *recitativo stromentato* gradually developed until the orchestra became, as notably in Wagner, a chorus to comment on what is sung and acted, to paint a background, or to give significance by recalling what had happened earlier in the drama.

In France, Lully made the recitative an essential part in the development of the plot. Because of the emphasis always given by the French to diction, there developed in the opera of that country important and effective accompanied recitative. In Germany and in England the recitative was never as popular as elsewhere, often being replaced by speech, a practice which originated in the ballad opera and the *Singspiel*. It was used there, however, on occasion to give the audience an understanding of the story, an outline of which was seldom printed.

Gluck as a part of his reform banished the *recitativo secco* and made the accompanied recitative a powerful means of dramatic expression, being influenced in his later period by the powerful declamation of the French. Mozart restored the former type, but the reform that Gluck advocated eventually prevailed. Rossini shortened the long and dreary recitative, substituting what afterward was used, a more natural and animated lyric dialogue. He accompanied this type with strings and later with the full orchestra; and he even went so far as to introduce into it trills and roulades, rapidly ascending or descending melody sung to one syllable.

Later composers used recitative as such less and less, making little distinction between it and the aria, until Wagner made it in *Tannhäuser* and *Lohengrin* almost fully clothed song. In his later operas the voice parts may "be said to be in recitative throughout, rising in lyrical movements, but without break, into the most continuous and flowing style and sinking to mere dialogue." *

The purposes of recitative have been, and still to an extent are, to give a part of the plot, usually the least emotional, to afford a rest between the decorative arias, and to furnish contrast. The contrast is especially emphatic when recitative is replaced by speech, as was common in all varieties of opera with exception of what is called "grand." In *Der Freischütz*, for example, when Caspar sings in the eerie scene of Act II while Samiel speaks, the contrast is highly effective.

Leonore and the others (in *Fidelio*) use the spoken dialogue for the business of daily life and express themselves in music when their emotional state reaches a certain degree of passion. Then, at the moment when the emotions are strung up to the highest pitch, the string breaks, Leonore's voice gives way [to speech], and the prima donna is a mere woman once more! [1]

The spoken word is used most effectively in the two most emotional moments of *Traviata*, when Violetta to the orchestral accompaniment of the love theme reads Germont's letter, and again just before her death. There are spoken passages in other operas, too, as in *Carmen*, though they are nowadays usually either set to music or omitted for productions in Italy and the United States. Occasionally recitative or speech is used at points where emotional stress seems too high for expression by mere song. Shakespeare for the same reason on occasion uses prose in the midst of verse, as in *Hamlet*, II, 2, 294 ff.

---

* The evolution of Wagner's music from the old-fashioned recitative to the full-bodied orchestral sweep that characterizes his later operas can be observed by the playing of three records: first, the recitative to the "Evening Star" from *Tannhäuser*, with its accompaniment of sustained chords and harp arpeggios; second, the "Narrative" from *Lohengrin*, where the orchestra aids the declamatory passages of the singer at first through shimmering chords by the violin section and later through use of a sustaining melody of its own; and, third, the "Liebestod" from *Tristan und Isolde*, in which the singer and the orchestra are interdependent in bringing the drama to an awe-inspiring close.

[1] E. J. Dent, *Mozart's Operas*, p. 53.

There are recitatives, many of them verging on decorative song, in practically all modern operas. *Pelléas et Mélisande* is practically all recitative or, rather, song-speech, almost like restrained conversation accompanied by music rich in overtones but lacking in melody and to a large extent in conventional harmony. A good modern example of the *recitativo secco* may be found in *Rigoletto*, Act III, "M'odi! ritorna cassa. . . ." ("Mark me! Betake thee homeward.") It is at first unaccompanied, then is accompanied by sustained chords, and later by the humming with closed lips of a chorus behind the scenes. But, as said before, recitative is far less common in modern than in the earlier opera.

THE ARIA

An air in music is an easily recognized melody, usually simple. An aria is an elaborated air, a set song, almost always with a rich orchestral accompaniment, a kind of "soliloquy or oration that does not submit to interpretation or even to eventual discussion." It is always intended to express emotion, though for nearly two hundred years it was in reality a show-piece by which singers could demonstrate vocal agility and their mastery of the techniques of singing. The singer stepped forward to the footlights and sang; this practice is conventionally continued in *Trovatore*. It usually stops the action of the drama, and one of the conventions of eighteenth century opera was that a singer leave the stage at the conclusion of his aria. Even today the aria is for its own sake enjoyed by audiences, whatever its contribution to the drama, as the highest form of artistry of the voice. It is often heard in concerts.

From near the beginning of opera for two hundred years singers were permitted and expected to introduce into the aria, in the first part and especially at the end, improvised embellishments (*fioriture*) to heighten the effect. Such improvisation required not only vocal agility but also real musical skill in invention, for the additions had to be both pleasing and in harmony with the spirit of the composition. Lully,

Gluck, Haydn, and Mozart curbed this license, which was finally abolished by Rossini. He wrote in 1815, "A good singer should only be the conscientious interpreter of the composer's ideas, endeavoring to express them as effectively as possible and to present them as clearly as they can be presented. . . . In short, the composer and the poet alone have any serious claim to be regarded as creators." To maintain his position and at the same time to satisfy both the vanity of the singers and the expectation of his audiences, Rossini carefully wrote out the embellishments for his arias. His contention was sound in principle and justified because the singers of his day lacked the genius and the thorough training that many of their predecessors had. Some of the passages freely sung in the eighteenth century "are so amazingly difficult," wrote Krehbiel, "that few artists today would care to attack them without a considerable amount of preparatory study."

The aria is said to have been introduced into opera by Cavalli (1602–1676) in a simple, concise, and melodious form. It was developed by Monteverdi and Cesti, the former of whom wrote stanzas which were sung to the same instrumental bass, thus effecting a coherence. His aria for Orpheus, "Ecco purch' a voe retorno" ("For you my spirit yearns") is one of the oldest known arias in the concerted style. The aria in the time of Alessandro Scarlatti became strictly organized into a *da capo* form, in which the second part offers a variation in key and general mood, and the third repeats the words and the music, usually with embellishments, of the first. Without such embellishments, which relieved the tediousness of mere repetition, the old arias when sung today lose much of their effectiveness. There were usually an instrumental introduction and a postlude, the latter partly to give time for the inevitable applause.

In the course of time there developed a number of types of arias and rules for their use that were strictly observed. Some authorities list as many as fifteen types, but usually the number is given as five: the *aria cantabile*, with a quiet slow movement, expressing pathos; the *aria di portamento*, with a symmetrical form and dignified rhythm; the *aria parlante*, giving passionate expression of strong emotion; the *aria d' aglilitate*, affording opportunity for extreme vocal acrobatics; and the *aria di mezzo carattere*, furnishing a chance for deep heart-wringing passion.

According to Rockstro, every scene in the heydey of the fashion closing about 1770 should end with an aria; each important singer should have an aria in every act, no one having two in succession; no two arias of the same type could be consecutive; the most important arias came at the end of the first and the second act. The third act concluded with a chorus, sometimes followed by a dance. "In the second and third acts the hero and the heroine each claimed a grand *scena*—accompanied recitative followed by an *aria d' agilitate*" and they united in at least one grand duet. Such artificiality amazes us today, but it had a popularity that gave it approval and long continuance until Handel and his successors dared to venture into originality. The period of the aria dominance was one in which nothing else in opera mattered much, and in consequence the singers were a vain and tyrannical group. There are records of one artist who would not sing unless an aria began with a certain sonorous word, of another who demanded a costume that provided a long plume for his helmet, and of still another who would be satisfied by nothing less than an entry on horseback.

So low was opera, as we conceive it, esteemed and so popular was song that there developed in the first half of the eighteenth century the *pastiche*. This was a concert of numbers taken from well-liked operas, often by different composers. No wonder the time was ripe for the reforms that Gluck proposed, and equally there can be no wonder, so tardily do people yield to innovations, that the reforms were slowly accepted.

The five or more set forms of the aria gradually faded until by the time of Rossini's successors they were not recognized at all. But two new types are found in later opera, the ballad and the patter song. The ballad, which is a simple lyric or narrative song with lyrical feeling, or its equivalent may be found in the singing lesson in *The Barber of Seville*, in "The King of Thulé" (*Faust*), in Senta's song of the flying Dutchman, in Iago's "Credo" and Desdemona's "O salce, salce" (*Otello*), and in "Susie, little Susie" (*Hänsel und Gretel*).

Largely replacing the artificial aria came the "air," which might be essential to the development of the drama or especially of the character of the singer. The songs of Walther in *Die Meistersinger*, of Tannhäuser in the tournament, of the Duke and of Gilda in *Rigoletto* are examples of the airs that are an integral part of the operas. But songs interpolated to give pleasure to the audience and at the same time to give the singer an opportunity to display beauty of voice or skill in using it are not uncommon. A character sings a serenade, takes a music lesson, renders a ballad, utters a prayer, or is given some other reason for displaying vocal beauty. In *Don Carlo* the Countess of Eboli says,

> Since night is yet far off and not a star is out,
> Would you, my fair companions, beguile us with a song?

Thereupon she sings the Saracen "Song of the Veil." Marguerite's ballad of "The King of Thulé," Mercutio's "Queen Mab" song, and Juliet's showy waltz-arietta are lovely additions to *Faust* and *Romeo and Juliet*, but they could be omitted with little if any loss to the development of drama or of character. The airs that Mozart wrote for Cherubino and for Basilio in Act IV of *The Marriage of Figaro* have no dramatic justification. They merely continue a custom of giving the chief characters showpieces every so often.

The patter song is a rapid singing of a string of words, requiring on the part of the singer agility of tongue, careful diction, and expert breath control, and on the part of the audience alertness of attention. It is usually humorous and is particularly effective in Italian, but the Gilbert and Sullivan operas contain many successful examples. Illustrative of the patter song from other operas are "A bird-catcher am I" in Mozart's *Magic Flute*, and Bartolo's "A un dottor della mia sorte" ("To a man of my importance") and the "Zitti, zitti" ("Softly, softly") from Rossini's *Barber*.

The aria was at the height of its popularity and also of its artificiality all during the eighteenth century. Gluck found the artificial female voice of the castrato dominant in the aria, but not, he thought, expressive of real emotion. He attempted to make the art of the voice present and interpret deep human feeling, as it does successfully in "Che faro senza Euridice" ("I have lost my Euridice"). He reduced the coloratura elaboration to a clear vocal line, which is much more effective dramatically. Mozart, being by nature a better musician and a better dramatist, used the aria when he felt it was effective. His *Figaro, Don Giovanni,* and *Cosi Fan Tutte* are all aria-operas, though in none of them does he closely follow the old rules. Some of his arias approach the sonata form in movement; they are, as the musicians say, of compound binary form, with a statement, a development, and a recapitulation.

With the decline in popularity of the aria a great barrenness fell on opera. The solo singing voice was incapable of further development and apparently the vocal artists near the close of the eighteenth century were less gifted by nature and less thoroughly trained than those who had brought the aria to the top of popularity. The aria yielded, then, somewhat to the developing orchestra and ensemble singing, but it still in one form or another remained in opera. Beethoven, primarily an instrumentalist, was not altogether happy in characterizing personalities and in interpreting feeling by solo song, but the three great arias of Pizarro, Leonore, and Florestan in *Fidelio,* modeled after the French revolutionary operas of Mehul and Cherubini, set the style of the immediately following German opera. It used the heroic vocal types of soprano, tenor, and bass-baritone. Following Beethoven, Weber used solos of every sort, from simple songs to grand arias. By his especial contribution in this field of fusing the aria and the accompanied recitative into the simpler *arioso* he is a link between the old opera and Wagner.

Interrupting the trend toward change were the brilliant Meyerbeer and Rossini. The former wrote arias in the grand style for the grandest of grand opera. Rossini made the singer supreme, and though he composed well for the orchestra he never let it intrude on the province of the voice. Wagner said that Rossini gave the aria a semblance of life, seeing that the lifeblood of opera is melody, "naked, ear-tickling, absolute-melodic melody." So concerned was Rossini with the success of his arias that, as before mentioned, he was the first composer to write out in detail the embellishments that were to be sung. He permitted no improvising and no quotations from the compositions of others. Some commentator has said that almost every resource known to the coloratura singer's art is employed in "Una voce poco fa" ("A little voice I hear") in the second act of the *Barber*, an aria difficult to sing, but a perfect expression of Rosina's character. The "Largo al factotum" ("Make way for the factotum") is the finest possible example of the Italian humorous bass-baritone aria of a period when bass singers were expected to have almost the vocal agility of sopranos. But Rossini ran the embellishments (*fioriture*)—trill, roulade, and so on—into the ground. The time was ripe for a new type of solo singing.

Verdi's contribution was not abandonment of the aria but a great improvement in its musical sincerity and its dramatic effectiveness. Though he wrote sublimely beautiful arias, he made them seem not set showpieces for the display of the singer's art, but vital contributions to the exposition of character and the progress of the plot. The lack of arias in *Otello* and in *Falstaff* is explained by the fact that Verdi did not feel they were necessary to these dramas. When one was justifiable in his operas he inserted it. Note Iago's drinking song and Fenton's song of love. "Ah fors e lui" ("One of whom I dreamed") in the first act of *Traviata* is still one of the favorite showpieces of the coloratura soprana, and Count di Luna's "Il balen del suo sorriso" ("The tempest of the heart") in the second act of *Il Trovatore* was probably the most universally popular operatic melody of the middle of the nineteenth century. Others of Verdi's notable arias are the well-known "Celeste Aïda," which is usually sung too robustly, "O cieli azurio" ("O skies cerulean") from the third act of *Aïda*, Germont's "Di provenza" ("Thy home in Provence") in the second act of *Traviata*, and the brilliant "Tacea la notte placida" ("Peaceful was the night") and "Di quella pira" ("Tremble, ye tyrants") from *Il Trovatore*. Listing these brilliant arias, we must not overlook the simple song forms that he also used, such as the "Ave Maria" in *Otello*.

Although in *Rienzi*, to a less extent in *Der Fliegende Holländer* and in *Lohengrin*, Wagner followed the fashion and introduced formal arias, he resented their artificiality, feeling that music should not be given in separate vocal numbers, that it should be for expression of feeling and not for impressing the audiences. He held that instead of appealing through fancy and technical singing, the characters should speak, act, and sing as common sense dictated that they should in each dramatic situation. Even in his early operas he had no coloratura role, and in his middle period he developed a theory that opera should use what he called *Melos*,* a sort of continuous style of singing, a modified recitative that he could make "melodic or harmonic, fluent or abrupt, as the situation demanded." His conviction that music should change when the meaning changes resulted in what many listeners today, accustomed as they are to conventional structure of music, feel is a lack of form; but attentive listening will reveal that there is always a form which is dictated by meaning rather than by

* "Dramatic accent and declamation, sung or intoned," wrote Lavignac, "stand for Wagner above every other consideration, and it is by this means that he obtains truth of language, absolute cohesion between the poem and the measured recitative which the singers have to give forth on the stage, while the symphonic web is being unwound in the orchestra, two elements of equal importance."

technical rules. He wrote for his voices unending melody, building the structure by means of repetitions and elaboration of themes. He characterizes by phrases, in later operas the leitmotifs, instead of by the elaborate melodies of his predecessors. This is a most effective shorthand, which if not overdone moves the drama forward at a more reasonable pace and indicates a unity of the whole.

Another advance that Wagner made was the discovery that emotion can better be interpreted by emphasizing harmony rather than melody. This means that he uses harmony most effectively in all of his operas, beginning with *The Ring*, and the happy results can be noted by anyone who takes the trouble to compare the richness of his music with that of any other composer. The emphasis on harmony later led to the supremacy, contrary to his recorded theory, of the orchestra over the voice, the former having, of course, infinite possibilities of harmony. Although Wagner called *Tannhäuser* "an opera without song" and doubtless would have similarly characterized his later music-dramas, the statement is not quite true. *Tannhäuser* does contain glorious song, as do all of its successors. *Die Meistersinger* is full of set pieces, notably the "Prize Song," and no one can forget the "Liebestod" in *Tristan und Isolde*. But the "numbers" in the Wagner operas are a piece of the whole dramatic structure; no seams show in the closely woven fabric. No singer in Wagner's dramas ever steps out of character and presents an aria, but where formal song is essential to the dramatic development it is provided, contributing to and not interrupting the development of the plot.

Gounod's arias, though elaborate enough for modern ears, are relatively simple when compared with the old style. The cavatina, a short aria in only one section instead of the usual three ("All hail, thou dwelling pure and lowly" in *Faust*), has a fine continuous lyrical development, and the "Jewel Song" is a perfect expression of the emotions of a girl, still little more than a child, dazzled by the sight of gems and overcome by the thought of all they will mean to her. Thomas in the second act of *Mignon* has a brilliant vocal polonaise, requiring light toccata singing, and so difficult that the composer adds a note: "If the singer finds it impossible to sing the polonaise, a cut must be made to the finale." This indicates its lack of dramatic necessity. Puccini composed a number of beautiful arias of the simplified modern type, illustrative of which are "Vissi d'arte" ("Love and music") in the second act of *Tosca*, and Butterfly's pathetic "Un bel di vedremo" ("Some day he will return").

But as a definite form of high importance in opera the aria has passed. Much of its function has now been taken over by the orchestra and occasionally some of it by the chorus. It must not be forgotten, however, that the aria has secured immortality for all the great operas of the past and that when we hear them we must be not only ready to accept the old convention but also alert to get the pleasure that is afforded by a beautiful human voice when exhibiting its technical skill.

VOCAL ENSEMBLE MUSIC IN OPERA

Ensemble literally means "together," and so it would naturally include the chorus. But usually in opera the term ensemble is used to indicate a group of two or more of the principal characters, while a chorus is composed of supernumeraries who take little part other than in mass singing. The amateur who is accustomed to duets, trios, and quartets in which the members stand together and sing the same words in continued two-, three-, or four-part harmony is sometimes confused by the ensemble in opera, where the singers are often widely separated on the stage and sometimes vocalize in apparent disregard of each other. In a duet in the second scene of the first act of Rossini's *Barber*, for example, Rosina expresses her delight at the prospect of meeting her lover, while Figaro, somewhat apart, comments sarcastically on the artfulness of women. Yet their music combines harmoniously. In the third Act of *Boheme* one pair of lovers effect a reconciliation and another pair have a violent quarrel in one coherent piece of music. In the trio in Act I of *Don Giovanni* the Don and Anna express conflicting emotions, while the hidden Leporello comments sardonically.

It is not unusual for an ensemble to consist mainly of what might be thought of as a number of solo parts, but altogether these may be heard as component elements of a single musical unity. Always the voices in the composition combine in harmony, though that may be different from what is heard in parlor singing or in simple church music. In *Rigoletto* two of the members of the famous quartet are inside a house and two outside, each one singing an expression of his own thought and feeling. In the quartet canon * in the first act of *Fidelio* the four characters are widely separated on the stage and each one sings different words. Marceline sings of her love, Leonore of her fears, Rocco of his pleasure at the prospective marriage of his daughter, and Jaquino of his terror at the thought of losing the girl whom he expected to marry. But in both compositions the combined music is a harmonious unity. Note that a composition for two or more voices necessarily requires more time for musical development than one for a solo voice. *Falstaff* is essentially an ensemble opera.

In one of the intermission programs at the Metropolitan Opera Boris Goldovsky pointed out that there are at least three dramatic situations which demand ensemble treatment. The first, as illustrated by the famous quartet in *Rigoletto*, is a situation in which all of the characters are motivated by one emotion. Though the love felt by each character is different, the music spells out unmistakably the several emotions felt, giving a powerful dramatic impact. The second type, illustrated by the quintet in *Carmen*, speeds the action ahead. The animated broken conversation makes us almost forget

---

* A canon is a musical composition in which the same melody is sung by two or more voices, each usually starting after another has begun and sometimes using a different pitch. "Three Blind Mice" is a canon. In the second act of *Cosi Fan Tutte* the lovers sing a three-part canon.

that we are listening to a highly organized piece of music. And the third type, well illustrated by the sextet in the third act of Mozart's *Marriage of Figaro*, which was the composer's favorite section of the opera, requires the singers to express their mixed reactions to a situation which has been explained by a series of four brief solos, each telling what has happened. "These," said Goldovsky, "are all superb examples of what the marriage of words, music, and theater can do at their best."

Up to the early part of the nineteenth century, and sometimes later, the participants in an ensemble, often deserting the drama, as it were, lined up on the stage and sang as they would in a concert. It is thus that the sextet in Donizetti's *Lucia* is still sung. But in later operas the ensembles are usually essential parts of the developing drama; for example, the highly complex ensemble in Act II of *Die Meisteringer*.

In the earliest operas, which were produced on a lavish scale for the nobility, the chorus was large and important in commenting on what was said in the recitative. It declined in importance and use for two reasons. First, when opera was offered to the public, economy forced a reduction in the size of the chorus and a transference of a major part of its function to an ensemble consisting of the principal characters. Second, when composers learned to write more effectively for solo voices, the commenting of the old chorus to give to the audience understanding of plot and interpretation of the singing could be largely achieved by the solo and ensemble singers. However, the chorus continues to have a peculiar function in contributing robustness to a scene. Rossini and his school developed choral finales on a gigantic scale. The chorus is commonly used between arias and often sings lovely music of its own.

From the time of Rameau, the French used the chorus more than the Italians did, often combining it with the ballet. The two groups not infrequently utilized the same music, the chorus singing while the ballet danced. Consequently the French chorus tended to become less like characters that are a part of the drama and more of a pleasing but unessential adornment.

Before Wagner, says Dent, the chorus came to do little but "stand in a row and bawl music that sounds like the middle part of a brass band." In the time of Bellini and Donizetti the miserably paid chorus was recruited of singers, almost exclusively men and boys, the latter singing the women's parts, who could not read music at sight and who contributed little to the dramatic success of opera.

Monteverdi is credited with the introduction of duets, trios, and quartets into opera, and Cavalli introduced two or three solo voices singing simultaneously in harmony. Lully in France, as might be expected from the love in that country for the spectacular, used mass choruses, and the Italian Scarlatti introduced into his later operas combinations of three or four voices, but they were not dramatically effective. Choruses took little part in the operas of Scarlatti and his immediate successors.

The choral finale, so common in later operas to bring an act to a rousing climax, had to wait many years for its development. When invented it was chiefly a massing of voices into a unified whole, without a personality that changed with the dramatic situation from scene to scene. It was in the comic opera that the concerted finale became definitely characterized and was broken into groups that answered each other in an extended piece of music in a variety of keys and tempi, thus opening up new operatic avenues for lyric expression. Says Dent,

> In serious opera it was not considered good manners for three or more characters to carry on a wrangle in a concerted movement. The complex finale was generally kept for the second act of an opera; it obviously could not be repeated in all three, and generally the third act, after the pages of recitative that at last untied all the tangle of misrepresentation on which the plot was constructed, had become rather long and required a quick conclusion.

Although Gluck has a powerful acting chorus in the second act of his *Orfeo ed Euridice*, the use of the chorus in the ways with which we are most familiar was made popular by Mozart. In *Idomeneo* (1781) he promoted the chorus from the part of being more or less a passive spectator with occasional singing comment. "It joins in the drama," wrote Streatfeild, "and takes an active part in the development of the plot, and the music which it is called upon to sing is often finer and more truly dramatic than that allotted to the solo singers." Mozart's music for the chorus is superior to any previous to it in concerted effectiveness. It is progressive, the situation at the end of a finale being not what it was at the beginning. There are fine participating choruses in his *Abduction from a Seraglio*. In his *La Clemenza di Tito* he built up effective choral finales, the first one being notable in that it ends softly, thus signifying horror at the arson that has just been committed.

Beethoven has a moving chorus of prisoners released from jail for an airing, but it is on the periphery of the action. Weber's choruses participate naturally in the action, but for the most part they furnish atmospheric backgrounds for the principals. Meyerbeer gives us choruses for great mass effects, in spectacle as well as in music. His chorus of nuns risen from the grave (*Robert le Diable*) goes to an extreme in the bizarre that fortunately has no imitators. Rossini developed the expressive power of choral ensembles and placed them not merely at the end of the acts, as had previously been customary, but wherever they seemed called for by drama. The vigor of his ensembles had great influence on Meyerbeer, Verdi, and Wagner.

Verdi's ensembles as a rule bring his chief singers together and not only to an extent characterize them but also indicate their mutual relations. His choral masses often sing in unison melody, as in the powerful "Gloria all' Egitto" of *Aïda*. For the most part his big ensembles are in the middle of an act, rather than at the end. The vocal quartet seems to be his ideal for an ensemble, the one in the fourth act of *Rigoletto* being deservedly one of the most famous in the literature of opera.

Of this Newman says, "As a musical ensemble it falls deliciously on the ear, yet, for all its smoothness and technical skill, the mood of each of the characters that takes part in it is truthfully depicted—the despair of Gilda, the brazen light-heartedness of Maddalena, the amorous passion of the Duke, and the gloom and persistence of purpose of Rigoletto."

Wagner in his operas presents many typical choruses, such as the spinning maidens and the seamen in *Der Fliegende Holländer*, the Pilgrims in *Tannhäuser*, the villagers in *Die Meistersinger*, and the knights in *Parsifal*. They all sing glorious music, none of which could be omitted without ruin to the structure of the drama. He also invented a new species of female ensemble, of which the Rhine-Maidens, the Norns, and the Valkyrie are illustrative. The flower maidens in *Parsifal* are a transition; after them Wagner uses no chorus of the older kind. In *Tristan und Isolde* there is hardly a chorus at all.

It is unnecessary to attempt to characterize the ensembles of the successors to Wagner. None of them have made any notable change in the types of ensemble and chorus, in the music assigned them, or in the functions for which they are used. We may note, however, Bizet's extremely successful choruses in *Carmen* and his innovation of forming an ensemble partly of minor characters. Gounod is perhaps typical of a composer who exemplifies the best of the modern tradition. Note the choruses of the Kermesse and of the soldiers in *Faust*. In his quartet in the third act "the music flows on with logical coherence, yet each of the four characters is clearly differentiated from the others, not only in the solo passages but in the ensembles." The trio in the fourth act is also an admirable example of the best of modern ensemble writing.

Uses of the Chorus

In the early opera the chorus provided a framework for the drama, introducing and concluding it. Much later it provided atmosphere, as in Weber and as in the opening act of *Parsifal*. It often gives tone color in broad masses, which adds greatly to emotional values. Certainly it contributes sound values that enrich the opera enormously. Subtract even the most formal and the least dramatically functional choruses from any opera and you will appreciate the tonal contributions that they make. Solo singing and even the smaller ensembles need the mass effects that the chorus gives for the construction of impressive and moving opera. There is something in emotional man's nature that responds to mass singing as it does not to the single voice; and in the chorus there is endless opportunity for the contrast of the female and the male voices.

The chorus also provides a contrast to the solo and a plateau of relief after dramatic intensity of pathos, suffering, joy, or exultation by an individual. Still, today like the Greek chorus of old, it comments on what has happened and it gives the proper interpretation of what has been sung and acted and also of the characters on the stage and their development. In *Don Carlo* when Philip exiles the Countess of Aremberg for not attending the Queen as she talks with her lover, the chorus exclaims "The Queen's self he insults!" It can be an active participant in the development of the plot, as in *Falstaff*, and in the second act of *Orfeo ed Euridice*. And it can afford in a stirring finale a consummation unsurpassed by other means at the disposal of certain types of opera, for example, the joyous finale in *The Barber* and the imposing ensemble at the end of Rossini's *William Tell*.

Voices in Opera

Song determines the nature and the fundamental concepts of the music of early opera. Inasmuch as in the early days the voice was the only instrument that was already perfected by nature and improved by techniques developed during the contrapuntal period, there is no wonder that it early became and long continued to be the most powerful factor in opera. It was not until after Rossini that it deteriorated in importance, and then perhaps because vocal instruction was less excellent than it had been, instruments had been improved and more interest and skill were shown in composing for them, since they could handle dramatic elements with greater effectiveness. Mozart and Verdi have shown that the most intensely dramatic music is often the most vocal and that the voice is likely to make the broadest human appeal.

Italy was the home of brilliant singing, and so long as the Italian influence was dominant the voice was supreme. The Italian language is most easily sung, and naturally in it was developed the virtuosity of the voice. For a long time the soprano voice was considered a lovely instrument, like a flute, but not for the expression of deep human feeling. The French, lacking the natural voices of the Italians and having a less singable language, stressed rhetorical accents, diction in recitative, gesture, dance, spectacle, and dramatic action. The German language is so different that when it is used it requires a different kind of music, as Mozart discovered and as anyone may discover for himself by comparing the operas of Rossini, Verdi, and Donizetti with those of Beethoven, Weber, and Wagner. Wagner recognized this so thoroughly that he created a new theory of operatic song.

Until the nineteenth century *bel canto* (the art of beautiful song), in which beauty of tone made the principal effect, was supreme. It was supported by the adornments of coloratura—decoration of voice melody by substituting runs, cadenzas, trills or shakes, and ornamental bravura for long notes. Berlioz characterized extreme *bel canto* singers as "performers on the larynx." So popular was coloratura that the opera had to furnish abundant opportunity for display singing: the principal character went mad, was a somnambulist, had a dream, soliloquized over fate, broke out into rapture over success (usually in love), or expressed at length overwhelming sorrow. Some operas, like Bellini's *Norma*, still hold the stage because they give the coloratura singer wonderful opportunities for vocal display. When at its best, remarked Kobbe, coloratura singing ravishes the senses; when not at its best, it merely tickles the ear and offends common sense.

Situations in opera frequently offer legitimate occasion for brilliant vocal display. Illustrative are "The Queen of the Night" in Mozart's *Die Zauberflöte*, "Una voce poca fa" in Rossini's *Barber*, "Ah! no giunga" in Bellini's *Sonnambula*, the mad scene in *Lucia*, "Caro nome" in Verdi's *Rigoletto*, and the "Jewel Song" in Gounod's *Faust*. "The coloratura of Violetta's 'Ah, fors e lui' in *Traviata*," remarks Toye, "is truly expressive of the demi-mondaine, just as the coloratura in her preceding duet suggests the frivolity and indecision of her mind."

It was not the general custom at the time when opera began for women to appear on the public stage. During Shakespeare's lifetime the parts of his female characters were all played by men or boys.* This will in part explain the popularity in opera up until about 1800 of the *castrato* soprano and alto, males emasculated in childhood so that their voices never naturally deepened. The operation depersonalized and instrumentalized, as it were, the vocal organism. The *castrato* voice had the brilliance and soft timbre of a woman's with the strength of a man's. It is said to have had a wide tonal range and unlimited capacities for expressing shades of tone and also virtuosity. It is difficult for us to imagine Hercules singing florid soprano arias, but it was the accepted mode.

The emperor Nero, an artificial sentimental soprano, trilled a brilliant Venetian barcarolle, with delicate rhythmic notes and daring coloratura, while he observed Rome burning. It was not even thought incongruous when mighty Julius Caesar, wearing a huge baroque wig, a wooden sword, and a stage toga, sang a sweet love song, or when Cleopatra expressed her undying love by means of a graceful minuet.[2]

Gluck's music for Orpheus was, of course, written for a *castrato*, and it is reported that when in the Paris revision he

* "In one act of *The History of Sir Francis Drake* (1659), Drake is shown a beautiful woman who has been captured by savages and tied to a tree; but as there was some fear of trouble with the authorities, the bride was represented only by a painted canvas. No woman took part in this opera, although *The Siege of Rhodes* (1656) had seen the first appearances of any woman on the public stage in England."—J. M. Dent, *Opera*, p. 146.

[2] Paul Nettl, "Laughing at Opera," *Opera News*, February, 1948.

substituted a tenor, there was a distinct loss in effectiveness. The last appearance of a *castrato* singer in opera was in Rossini's *Aureliano* in 1814. The use of *castrati* in place of women naturally made the characters unreal and impersonal, and this in large part explains why there was so little love interest in the opera before the nineteenth century.

Women had on occasion sung in opera from the early years of the seventeenth century, especially in Naples, but the female voice dominated only between the disappearance of the *castrato* and the end of lyric opera. Gluck gave to the female voice but little, if any, real feeling. Mozart and Verdi made it an equal partner with the male. We are accustomed to the soprano not infrequently as the leading voice, but usually it is paired in importance with a tenor, a baritone, or a bass.

To be successful a singer must not only have a beautiful natural voice but also be able to produce with the minimum appearance of effort a pure, even tone at the proper pitch, molding and shading one musical phrase after another, no matter at what length, and always maintaining a pleasing flow of line. In opera, the singer must also make his voice interpret the drama of the situation in which he is put.

In opera, roles usually require appropriate types of voices. Verdi was the first composer who assigned roles to those voice qualities and ranges which seemed exactly to suit the characters. He would not release *Trovatore* until he found singers whose voices in his opinion exactly suited the music that he had written.

Coloratura sopranos have a field all their own, and it is only occasionally that a lyric or a dramatic singer can invade this field successfully. Operas like *Lakmé*, *The Daughter of the Regiment*, and *La Sonnambula* are now seldom heard, in part because of the difficulty of finding singers for the chief soprano roles. These operas are brought back to the stage only when a Pons appears on the operatic horizon to thrill audiences with roulades, trills, and other vocal gymnastics that made opera dear to the opera audiences in the days of Jenny Lind. One must not expect too much in the way of volume in a coloratura's voice; it seldom possesses that quality in a marked degree. Only very occasionally has a singer gifted in coloratura stepped into dramatic roles with success. Lilli Lehmann, the great Wagnerian soprano, began her career as a coloratura, but she was an exception. A famous coloratura and great artist, Nellie Melba, once attempted Brünnhilde in *Siegfried*, but with such disastrous results that she never tried it again.

The separation between lyric and dramatic soprano roles is not so distinct. It is not unusual for the same singer to undertake such roles as Marguerite in *Faust* and Sieglinde in *Die Walküre*. But ordinarily only a lyric soprano sings Mimi and a dramatic soprano Tosca.

The introduction into opera of alto and contralto voices was roughly similar to that of the soprano, but neither is usually given parts of the highest importance. Probably the greatest showpiece in operatic literature for a mezzo-soprano is "Ah, mon fils" in Meyerbeer's *Le Prophete*, and "Mon coeur s'ouvre a ta voix" ("My heart at thy sweet voice") from Saint-Saëns' *Samson et Dalila* is an ever-popular number for contraltos. Contralto or mezzo-soprano roles in opera demand a voice of range and power, at the same time retaining the tone color that naturally belongs to the lower voice. Maddalena could be only a contralto. Usually contraltos are trained to ignore head tones and to throw their voices forward except in the lower notes, which they sing as chest tones. As a result of such training, operatic contraltos usually have a brilliance in their upper tones that is often lacking in other voices. Much of the music written for contraltos or mezzo-sopranos is dramatic. It takes an excellent singer and a capable actress to portray Amneris, Brangäne, Azucena, or Ortrud.

The tenor voice is the one we are likely to think of first as representing the hero in opera, but it was not given an important dramatic role until that of Admetus in Gluck's

Alceste. Mozart used the tenor to represent youth and to sing lyric passages, but he was not inclined to make it heroic. Many later composers have felt that the tenor is radiant but representative of a frail personality, to be used chiefly as a duet voice or as a shuttlecock between opposing forces. There are not a great many heroic characters among the lyric tenors of opera. *Tenori robusti* are required for Florestan, Lohengrin, Tannhäuser, Walther von Stolzing, Tristan, Parsifal, Siegmund, Siegfried, Rhadames, Manrico, and Faust, all of whom live and have real manly strength.

The darker male voices did not come into their own until relatively late. For a considerable time the bass was given importance only in comic opera, filling there a role that it marvelously exemplifies as late as Osmin in Mozart's *Entführung aus dem Serail.* In Handel's time, basses were cast almost entirely as villains, old men, and foils. The first baritone in tragic opera was Orestes in Gluck's *Iphigenia en Aulide* (1772); Marschner a generation later elevated it to real dignity. Rossini favored the baritone and Verdi often made it the central voice. Famous characters with the deeper voices are Don Giovanni, Hans Sachs, the Dutchman, Wotan, Hunding, Hagen, Rigoletto, Amonastro, Falstaff, Germont, Scarpia, Escamillo, Archibaldo, Dodon, and Boris. This list gives evidence that in the later opera there has been no prejudice against the bass or the baritone, in fact, that they are recognized as best for men of vigor and strength of character. At the close of the second act of *Tristan und Isolde* the repeated questioning of the bass King Mark, old, heartbroken, and not knowing the reason for his betrayal, is one of the most touching things in musical-dramatic literature.

Voices are not beautiful or fitting merely because of their register; each one has its own peculiar tone color, which may make it fitting or impossible for a certain role. Every producer of opera is faced by the difficulty of selecting for a cast voices that blend well or that afford the desired contrasts. Ideally, singers should be selected, even for such minor characters as

Mercedes and Frasquita in *Carmen*, so that their voices clearly differentiate them when they sing together. Aïda and Amneris should possess voices the tone colors of which are not merely appropriate to the characters but also furnish distinct contrasts. In the "Solenne in quest' ora" ("Swear in this hour"), one of the loveliest duets in opera, the voices of Caruso and Scotti blended perfectly; but there was so little contrast between them that it was at times impossible merely by the ear to tell which was singing. The voices of Flagstad and Thorborg were so similar in color that they did not furnish as much contrast as is desirable when they sang the parts of Isolde and Brangäne. And in the dialogue of Don Giovanni and Leporello one wished that Pinza were a baritone when he was on the stage with Baccaloni. A voice is also influenced in its effectiveness by the personality and the pulchritude of the singers, and even by the costume worn and the acting that accompanies the singing.

When listening to an opera be careful not to let any of these factors weigh too heavily; enjoy a voice for what it is and for the way that it is used in song, especially for dramatic effect. Finally, learn to note the characteristics of the music that is written especially for the voice; how different it is— though composers like Beethoven may attempt to conceal the fact—from that written for instrumental production. No composer of opera can be entirely successful unless he writes always with the voice of a prospective singer in his ear. The voice is the most marvelous of all musical instruments; it can thrill as no other one can, and its imperfections of quality and production can ruin the most beautiful passage assigned to it. The operagoer must enjoy vocal music and should learn to appreciate at least something of its techniques, but he also should always try to fuse its contributions with those of the other elements that make up the music drama. Unless he fuses them into a single impression, he might as well enjoy them separately, in concert, on the speaking stage, in the cinema, or in art galleries.

Chapter Eleven

THE ORCHESTRA

In modern music the orchestra is the most impressive instrument. Although it is composed of many individual instruments grouped in four choirs, it should really be considered and listened to as a single complex producer of music. It is comparable to the pipe organ, but far superior in its resources and in its effectiveness. A generation ago an orchestra in the United States was a rarity, practically always an organization of paid professional musicians in one of our largest cities, while today, as a result of music education, it is common even in relatively small communities. Secondary schools and even elementary schools have their orchestras; the professional organizations regularly draw large audiences and are heard by multitudes over the radio; and the sales of phonograph records of orchestral compositions is evidence of the developed appreciation throughout the country.

An orchestra is not merely a number of instruments that play together. It is a number of instruments so carefully selected that in combination they produce solid and satisfying effects. Balance of tone is necessary. By the use separately of harmonious groups of instruments, peculiar tonal effects are produced, which in series give contrasts; and by mixing the

159

tints, as it were, using in sequence one instrument, say the violin, with flute, oboe, harp, or horns, and by changing the dynamics from soft to loud, or the reverse, and by other such devices infinite variety is possible. Solidity, balance of tone, contrast, and variety are the principal requirements of a good orchestra.

Like other complex instruments, the orchestra seldom uses all of its possibilities at the same time. It may play *tutti*—that is, all of its instruments together—but far more commonly some are silent for periods. In a famous symphony composition one instrument plays only three notes. The violins may announce a theme which is repeated, first by the wood winds and then by the horns, before it is developed by all or by any pleasing combination of the instruments. Variety is also effected by the use of mutes, which soften and muffle the tones, by playing stringed instruments pizzicato—that is, by plucking the strings instead of setting them in vibration by the bow—and by numerous other devices that any attentive listener will soon recognize.

The Conductor *

It is the function of the conductor, the performer on this majestic and complex instrument, to decide what effects of the music are desired and then so to direct the performers on the several instruments that they all together produce these effects for an audience. He indicates the tempo (the rate of playing), the accelerandos, the degree of *piano* or of *forte* (that is, of softness or of loudness), the crescendos and the diminuendos, the exact time when each performer joins the choir and when he ceases to play. In short, he gets from all the parts of the orchestra a performance that results in a unity producing the effects desired.

The conductor of the opera orchestra is potent in the production of good musical drama. Upon him depend not

---

* An excellent exposition of "The Art of Conducting" is given by Leonard Bernstein in his *The Joy of Music*.

merely a satisfying instrumental performance but also the integration of all the instruments of the orchestra into unity, the balance, the pacing, the coordination of the orchestra and singers. However, he himself is held in restraint and directed, as it were, by the composer's instructions—either oral or written on the score—by tradition, and by restrictions laid upon him by the stage manager.

In early opera there was no conductor in the modern sense. For a century and a half the orchestra was led at the first performances chiefly by the player of the harpsichord, who usually was the composer, thus insuring such interpretation of the music as he had in mind. Lully (1632–1687) is said to have been the earliest conductor to attempt to secure from his instruments a true organic unity. The harpsichordist was assisted, especially in setting the beat and in keeping the instrumentalists together, by the concertmaster, the leader of the first violin section, who could indicate the tempo by raising and lowering the neck of his instrument or at times by waving his bow.

The modern conductor ordinarily uses a baton in his right hand for beating time, indicating with his left hand the effects that he desires. This simple procedure evolved slowly. Lully and his successors indicated the tempo by striking a large stick on the floor. Even as late as 1768 Rousseau speaks in his *Dictionnaire de Musique* of the "insufferable noise made by the conductor's baton, which covers or drowns the whole effect of the symphony." The concertmasters, especially in Italy, formerly beat time audibly with their bows, rapping either on the violins or on the music desks. Spontini (d. 1851) used a long baton, grasping it at the center and moving it much as a drum major would today. The modern use of the small baton and of the left hand did not become common until well along into the nineteenth century.

With the refinement of dynamic effects and especially with the emphasizing of instrumental colors, the separation of the conductor from the cembalo (harpsichord) became inevitable. A personality was needed whose task it would be to specialize in controlling the balance of the dynamics and colors, in defining the more and more complicated rhythms, and in being generally responsible for correct execution in accordance with the composer's instructions.[1]

For such reasons Haydn presided at the harpsichord while Salomon assisted with his violin in conducting. The harpsichord was eliminated from the orchestra by Gluck and Mozart, and the piano, its successor in some instances, was finally discarded by Rossini.

The first opera conductor in the modern sense was Weber who, using a roll of paper instead of the later popular baton, led the performance as a whole and assumed responsibility for the success of the entire opera. Wagner was one of the greatest conductors, as well as composers. He assumed direction of the whole opera—stage management, acting, costumes, properties, and music. To satisfy his demands he finally had built for his music-drama the unique *Festspielhaus* at Bayreuth. Conductors nowadays usually have responsibility only for direction of the music and for coordinating it with the singing and acting.

COMPOSITION OF THE ORCHESTRA

The modern orchestra is composed of four choirs—strings, wood winds, brasses, and percussion instruments—of which the first is the basic element. For the information of those who have as yet given no attention to the composition of the orchestra the instruments are listed in the following groups. The numbers are approximately those used in a full symphonic orchestra, but for the opera usually fewer are found, eighty or ninety altogether.

STRINGS	WOOD WINDS
16–18 First violins	2–3 Flutes
14–16 Second violins	1–2 Piccolos
10–14 Violas	2–3 Oboes

[1] Paul Bekker, *The Story of the Orchestra* (New York: W. W. Norton, 1936), pp. 138–39).

8–12 Violoncellos
8–10 Double basses

1 English horn
2–3 Clarinets
1 Bass clarinet
2–3 Bassoons
1 Contra bassoon

BRASSES

4 (occasionally more)
  French horns
2–4 Trumpets
3 Trombones
2 Tenor tubas, alternating
  with the horns
1–2 Bass tubas
1 Contrabass tuba (occasionally)

PERCUSSION
INSTRUMENTS

2–4 Kettle drums
1 Bass drum
1 Snare drum
1 Chinese drum
Cymbals
Castanets
Triangle
Tambourine

In addition to the more commonly used instruments there are harps, celesta, xylophone, glockenspiel, and tam-tam or Chinese gong, instruments which are occasionally used for special effects. They do not easily classify under any of the four usual choirs.

Each conductor arranges the instruments before him according to a plan which he thinks will give the best effects.

The amateur will do well to learn not merely what the several instruments are but also to recognize their voices, whether sounded normally or muted, and to know the general effects that each one, alone or in combination, produces. Such knowledge adds greatly to one's understanding and appreciation of orchestral music.

DEVELOPMENT OF THE ORCHESTRA

Before the invention of opera there was no such thing as an orchestra. It is true that there were in use a variety of instruments—such as viols, rebecs, theorbos, lutes, lyres, trumpets, and trombones—which were the ancestors of the instruments that are used today; but they were crude and in many respects inferior. Moreover they were never used in combination to produce a complex but unified musical effect. In the sixteenth century there was no interest in instrumental music, no ensemble playing for its own sake. The human voice was supreme. The contrapuntal music, to the making of which the genius of composers and of performers alike was devoted, used combinations of the human voice much as we now use instruments, to produce highly technical effects, as in motets and madrigals, some of which have been sung in recent revivals.

But the invention of opera, which at first was designed to reproduce what was thought to be the ancient Greek form of tragedy, a succession of songs connected by justifying explanation in recitative, required instrumental accompaniment. Peri, the composer of *Euridice* (1600), the first opera that had a public performance, doubtless gathered up such instruments as were available—a harpsichord, a large lyre or guitar, a lute, and a few viols (the ancestor of the violin)—and had them play chord accompaniments to the recitatives.

Seven years later when that great genius Claudio Monteverdi produced his *Orfeo* he had an orchestra (doubtless similarly limited by the instruments and players at his disposal) composed of two harpsichords, one small portable organ, two organs with wooden pipes, ten viols, two French treble violins, three bass viols, two bass lutes, one double-strung harp, one small flute, one trumpet, two cornetti (an old instrument with cup-shaped mouthpiece and finger holes), and four trombones. Although these instruments were all somewhat different from those that we know today, it is easy for the veriest amateur to realize that in combination they would be too heavily loaded with brass and that the sound produced would, to our ears, be far from harmonious.

However, they were a beginning of an orchestra. Monteverdi was much too good a musician to use them all together often or at length. Although he had not learned that the string choir is the best possible foundation, he used his instruments in well-defined groups: a harpsichord with two viols or two flutes, cornetti with trombones and organ, and so on. And he used one group, which he doubtless thought best to express the atmosphere or feeling desired, throughout a whole movement or scene. Lacking solidity, balance, frequent contrast, and variety, a performance such as at this early opera would seem to us monotonous and musically uninteresting; but such was the beginning of the orchestra in opera.

In the first Italian operas the players of the orchestra were hidden behind the scenes; later they were in a gallery over the stage, unless the plot required their presence as a part of the action. Before the end of the seventeenth century, however, the orchestra was given the place that it now occupies, between the stage and the audience, though not sunk from view until the innovation was made by Wagner.

In the early days the instruments for the most part merely accompanied the singers, and such music as they played was essentially vocal music. Naturally composers had not yet learned to write for instruments. Gradually they perceived the wisdom of doing this, but the learning took several score of years. They learned, too, that a combination of stringed instruments is the most effective basis for an orchestra. After much experimenting they agreed that a four-part string choir—first and second violins, violas, violoncellos, and double basses—such as we use today, was the best possible combination.

There have been three major periods in the development of the orchestra. The first, a period of exploration and invention, lasted from 1600 until approximately 1750, though no sharp change must be understood to have occurred then. In this period the string choir became dominant, though the cellos, and often the violas, played in unison but one or two octaves higher with the double basses; bassoons, seldom heard alone, strengthened the basses; the oboe and the flute were the principal wood-wind instruments; the brasses had hardly become a self-contained group at all; there was little differentiation in part writing; and the harpsichord, which supplied most of the harmony, was always present. In this period, which ran up to Gluck, interest was primarily in the melody and in simple harmony accompaniment, and very little in the several instruments themselves. The orchestra was small, the instruments were far from perfect and badly tuned; no marks indicating the way in which the music should be played were found in the score, and indeed considerable liberty was allowed the players in the matter of improvising within the general scheme of the melody. The chief principles for the use of instruments were doubling one with others, augmentation to effect simple harmony, and simple contrasts of strings with other instruments, especially the wood winds.

The second period may be said to have begun with Gluck (1714–1787), who had vigorous notions as to desired reforms in the opera. He also had novel and, to us, entirely sound notions as to the desired reform of the orchestra. In the first place, he eliminated the harpsichord from the orchestra, where it had never belonged except as an accompaniment of a small body of strings, as the color of its music is different from that of the other instruments and does not combine well with them. Without the harpsichord Gluck felt the necessity of writing full harmony for the strings, the wood winds, and to a less degree for the brasses. In consequence we find in his music a substantial solidity for the strings, with no gap between the violins and the brasses. Gluck sounded from four to six notes in chords for the strings, while Handel had been content with two or three. He also used the wood winds to supply harmony, emphasized the clarinet, and employed a pair of oboes. His orchestral music was no longer vocal music played by instruments but was composed *for* the orchestra. He continued the practice of maintaining essentially the same color throughout a scene. By the third quarter of the eighteenth century the orchestra was well on its way to having a language of its own. Haydn should be credited with laying out the modern score as we know it.

Mozart (1756–1791) belongs to this second period when

the orchestra was growing up and becoming of greater importance than it had been in opera. Although Mozart's themes are melodic, being derived from the vocal songs, he composed many passages in which the musical development was carried on entirely by the orchestra, which he conceived to be far more important than it had ever been before. It was no longer a mere accompaniment. Mozart had the genius to select his instruments as dramatic personalities; hence he had no fixed composition of his orchestra, either for a whole opera or for any major part of it. He constantly used combinations of instruments which he considered most suitable to express and to develop the music needed to convey the desired dramatic effect. He used an opera orchestra, says Bekker, that had "ready wit, epigrammatic brevity, the power instantaneously to characterize a personality or a situation, a dramatic event, or a special mood."

According to Láng, the average orchestra in Germany and England toward the close of the eighteenth century consisted of about 12 violins, 2–3 violas, 2–3 cellos, 2–3 double basses, with an indeterminate number of flutes, oboes, bassoons, horns, trumpets, and kettle drums. For one of his operas Mozart used 14 first violins, 14 second violins, 6 violas, 2 cellos, 6 double basses, 2 flutes, 2 oboes, 2 bassoons, 2 horns, 2 trumpets, and 2 harps.

About 1800 the ideal, largely influenced by Haydn, was for the orchestra to present one fundamental musical motive and to develop it symphonically in all imaginable ways. The orchestra was on its way to overpower the singing voice.

The third period of the development of the opera orchestra includes Beethoven, Weber, Meyerbeer, Rossini, Wagner, Verdi, and others of less note. Of Beethoven (1770–1827), the master of the symphonic orchestra, which he used with great effectiveness in his single opera *Fidelio*, it is unnecessary to write; his contributions are too well known. What Haydn did for the oboe, Mozart for the flute, and Weber for the clarinet, Beethoven did for the horn, trumpet, bassoon, and drum—

popularized them as melodic instruments. He demonstrated the true relationships of all of the instruments, the special character and possibilities of which he thoroughly understood. His phrases are distinctly unvocal, though the music that he wrote for singing is sometimes effective. He demonstrated a unified orchestra, which his successors were to use in their operas.

Weber (1786–1826) simplified the artistic style bequeathed by Mozart and introduced a brilliance in his passage work for strings and more varied color than is usual in Beethoven. Instead of always seeking for effects from the whole orchestra, Weber analyzed the tones and developed the single instrumental voice to new importance, bringing into prominence the neglected viola, oboe, clarinet, and horns. He was peculiarly successful in using uncommon combinations, such as violin and viola with clarinets and trombones, thus producing novel and effective tone colors. His compositions for the orchestra not only are symphonically treated but are designed for dramatic effects, which they successfully achieve. Weber paid great attention to the orchestra and usually gave it prominence in the expression of dramatic climaxes.

Meyerbeer (1791–1864), the German turned Frenchman, was, as W. J. Henderson said, "a veritable trickster with instruments, and could produce a theatrical effect with a penny-ballad idea." If you are fortunate enough to hear one of Meyerbeer's seldom given operas, listen carefully to the orchestra, which is likely to impress you as being highly effective in interpreting the scene for which it was written. Theatrical? Yes; but very good theater for those who love to be stirred by music.

Rossini (1792–1868) was another composer who used all the tricks of the trade to make his orchestra theatrically, and often dramatically, effective. He had sheer brilliance unsurpassed in his time, and his music was colorful and piquant. But to modern ears the orchestra in even his only surviving opera, *The Barber of Seville*, is showy and noisy, but perhaps not too much so for the comic plot. In his other operas Rossini used loud *tutti*, ostentatious passages for the strings, heavy brass, and a frequent crescendo built up by the addition of more and more instruments to an ear-splitting conclusion, to say nothing of shrieks of piccolo, clanging of gongs, and rumble of tympani. There was no monotony in Rossini's orchestral music, which he used mainly to reinforce the vocal effects. He introduced a new style of composing for the horn, treating it with brilliance as a solo instrument. Unfortunately his contemporaries and immediate successors were more influenced by his eccentricities than by the sounder manifestations of his real genius. Richard Strauss used the orchestra much as Rossini did.

On the whole the Germans in this period kept the main choirs of the opera orchestra distinct in their composition, and made contrasts between them important in the structure of the music, which has more solidity and dignity than that of other nationalities. The French were notable for brilliance, clearance, fitness, delicacy, and economy of color, though Berlioz, in his semi-dramatic compositions, had considerable influence in his use of extravagant means to achieve startling effects. He also popularized "inner movement" of music in each choir instead of massive movement by chords from the whole. The Gallic use of wood winds is in general unsurpassed. The Italian orchestra remained essentially one of dominant strings used to accompany the singing voice; but it was not infrequently used for charming and even brilliant overtures and for delightful, often sentimental, intermezzi.

Of the orchestration by the two opera giants of the period, Verdi (1813–1901) and Wagner (1813–1883), only a master of music can speak at all adequately. In all of his operas Verdi strove for dramatic effects to which music was a contribution, not an end in itself. His successful immediate predecessors in Italy also had a keen sense of the dramatic, but they used the orchestra often for musical showiness, giving it clear color, brilliance, and variety more for its own sake than for its heightening of the dramatic effect. Verdi kept alive the good with which audiences were familiar, but he also discovered and steadily revealed new resources of the orchestra. In his conception it was not for brilliance as a complex musical instrument, on the one hand, or, on the other, for mere accompaniment. He developed an orchestra that was balanced and full in tone and also full of tuneful voluptuousness. Although its harmony was satisfying, at least to the amateur ear, rhythm was its most impressive characteristic. More notable still, it echoed and reinforced the dramatic action on the stage and in subtle ways helped as no orchestra had done before to make each singer a real person with an individuality of his own. Instead of striving for independent effects, it fused with the singing, with the characters, and with the action to produce a connected series of dramatic effects.[2] In the operas of his later years Verdi used an abbreviated orchestration, hinting at the full chord by its most characteristic color. He "sought refinement of effect, lightening of the mechanical apparatus, increased flexibility and intensifying of subtle details." Great in his mastery of the orchestra, Verdi was a genius in his use of it to achieve drama.

Wagner had very positive ideas about the theory of everything involved in the opera, including, of course, the orchestra, which he understood as no composer had before his time. His writings on the functions of the orchestra are pondered even today by every serious student of the opera. As is natural, he steadily developed his theory, that of his later years manifesting distinct differences not only from that of his predecessors and contemporaries but also from that of his early manhood. When he violated his theory, as he not infrequently did, it was to get new and successful effects. Understanding as he did the possibilities not only of the orchestra as a whole but also of the several choirs and of individual instruments, he

---

[2] For details of Verdi's subtle uses of the orchestra the interested reader may consult Francis Toye, *Giuseppe Verdi: His Life and Works* (New York: Alfred Knopf, 1931), pp. 404–6, 419 ff., 436–40.

composed music peculiarly for it, music that cannot be produced with anything like similar effectiveness through any other medium. He organized his orchestra about the principle of harmonic display, using a large number of notes in his chords, which produce the full and sonorous volume that ravishes all music lovers today. In his orchestral music there is an impression of maturity and of manly vigor as well as of great sensuous beauty. The opulence of harmony in the wood winds, the daring strong melody in the brasses, the vigor at times of the tympani, and the shattering effects of what had previously been known as cacophony everyone has noted, but the causes of subtleties within the several choirs are often discovered only by the most careful and studious listening.

Wagner was not long in realizing that however thrilling the timbre of the human voice may be, and useful as it is for making clear the course of the action and the sentiments of the characters, the orchestra is the most powerful and resourceful of all the instruments at the disposal of the operatic composer. . . . In the *Rheingold* the orchestral texture . . . frequently . . . merely punctuates or supports the vocal declamation by means of a detached chord or two, much in the way that it used to sustain the older recitative. As the *Ring* proceeds, pages of this kind become rarer . . . the orchestral part of the *Götterdämmerung* would flow on with hardly a break if the vocal part were omitted; so also would large sections of *Tristan und Isolde* or *Meistersinger*.[3]

In consequence, orchestral excerpts from Wagner's operas are often used in concerts, but, it must be noted, most effectively when the audience know and recall the dramatic setting from which they are taken and which they effectively interpret and emphasize. Although not accompanying words or action, the not infrequent long orchestral interludes are vitally a part of what precedes or what follows them in the music drama.

Wagner's emphasis on the orchestra, which in contradiction to his theory came to dominate the singing voice, first comes

---

[3] Ernest Newman, *Wagner as Man and Artist* (New York, Alfred A. Knopf, Inc., 1937), pp. 290–91.

into evidence in *Lohengrin*. For this opera he required besides a large complement of strings, three flutes, two oboes, one English horn, two clarinets, one bass clarinet, three bassoons, four horns, three trumpets, three trombones, one bass tuba, tympani, and cymbals—a large orchestra for the time. Such magnitude he maintained throughout the *Ring*, and he invented, or caused to be invented, the "Wagner tubas," tenor tubas, for especial effects that he needed. He never hesitated to use novel combinations of instruments when he wished to produce novel music to interpret and to reinforce his dramatic ideas.

Lavignac declared,

Wagnerian melody is not subjected to the laws of regular composition, nor forced to move within the limits of one tonality, nor yet to end in a perfect cadence. Wagner's melody is free and infinite in the sense of not being finished, that is to say, never ending and always linking itself to another melody, thus admitting of all possible modulations.[4]

Because of his overpowering success Wagner may be justly charged with stopping, at least temporarily, development of operatic orchestration. Recognizing that they were unable to surpass him and timorous of emulating a style that was distinctively his, successors either to a large extent reverted to the earlier mode or else ventured on experimental novelties, few of which have gained general approval by popular audiences or have been continued in later compositions. Wagner's successors in opera, with the exception of Strauss, have on the whole more or less abandoned the consideration of the orchestra as a unified ensemble and have employed single instruments or groups of instruments for what may be called solo effects. Some of the efforts, more notable in symphonic compositions, to destroy the old harmony have crept into the orchestra of the opera, as in Berg's *Wozzeck*, but so far they have found no sure footing there.

[4] Source unknown.

Puccini (1858–1924) the opera composer after Verdi and Wagner who earned most popular success, was not notable for his treatment of the orchestra. He was primarily interested in melody and therefore used his orchestra not as an equal partner with the singing voice but as a subordinated supporter. His orchestra, either as a whole or in separate parts, plays the melody with the human voice, making it more effective and increasing the sensuous emotion conveyed. Harmony and instrumental effects are to Puccini important only as they contribute to this end.

Debussy's use of the operatic orchestra in his single opera *Pelléas et Mélisande* is in two respects more or less unique. In the first place, the instrumental music is throughout adapted to the interpretation of a vocal drama, the existing form of which absolutely determines the structure of what the orchestra plays. The music can have no elaborate structure of its own, which in other compositions usually causes the librettist to sacrifice the form in which the verbal expression of thought would be most effectively cast. Moreover, it is a drama of the spirit, of the inner emotions of the characters, and not of overt physical action. Thus the orchestra is necessarily subordinated and limited in what it tries to do. In the second place, Debussy uses a newly developed theory of music in which conventional harmony finds but little place. This theory is too technical to be gone into in a book written for amateurs.

Of Debussy's music in *Pelléas et Mélisande* Carse says that it "speaks with a hushed voice in delicately varied and subtly blended tone colors, and often with intentionally blurred outlines," and that "it murmurs dreamily to itself, speaks or suggests in veiled tones, swells up for a moment and again subsides or dwindles down almost to disappearance." Debussy's opera is unique. The amateur who thrills to the conventional opera is likely to be disappointed in this one. But if he attempts the experience he should strive to appreciate how, with complete subordination of itself, the orchestra endeavors almost solely to present an interpretation of the moods and feelings that Maeterlinck has conveyed by means of his verbal text.

Richard Straus (1864–1949) was the last of composers who contributed notably to the development of the opera orchestra. He had a remarkable knowledge of all the instruments and of their possibilities. Moreover, as in his composition of operas as a whole, he never hesitated to experiment. So far did he go in this direction that one is led to suspect that he did not develop, as other great geniuses did, a theory of composition to which he was wholeheartedly devoted. With him the orchestra was far from an independent instrument for the colorful presentation of imagination or feeling. More and more he called on it to express psychic phenomena, for which many think it unsuited. In consequence, while popular audiences may marvel at its "curious and surprising feats," they may not be charmed by the beauty of its music or moved by its heightening of dramatic effects. To this statement there are of course exceptions. But one is less likely to be carried away by the beauty of the music than to be distracted by the size of some of his orchestras, by voices of novel instruments, the unusual combinations of old ones, the forcing of compass beyond that which we normally think of as beautiful, the muting of the brass instruments, the tongue-tremolo of the wood winds, and the score of other tricks that Strauss used in the orchestra. One amateur at least thinks that his orchestra was at its best when it used the conventions to which the opera ear is most accustomed.

Instruments of the Orchestra

Although, as stated earlier, there was at the time of the invention of opera a variety of musical instruments, they were not used in ensemble for the purpose of producing music in the sense that we now use the term. They were reported to have been used to give rhythm for dances, marches, and spectacles, and to create a mood for a scene, and of course single instruments had long been used by minstrels and troubadours for simple accompaniment. It is interesting to learn of the early instruments—lute, lyre, viol, cornetto, and the like; but this is not the place to explain or to discuss them. Suffice it to say that although not one of these existent before 1600 is in use today, they were the ancestors of the instruments of the modern orchestra. Although we find records of flutes, oboes, harps, trombones, trumpets, and drums, for the most part the names represent very different instruments.

For the first operas there were orchestras of a considerable number of instruments, but this number was sharply reduced when opera was publicly presented for profit. The early orchestras were composed of such instruments as were available and not unsuited to accompaniment, or of those for which there were available players. It is difficult for us, accustomed as we are to standard orchestras and to skilled performers, to realize how limited were the resources in the early years of the orchestra. Even in 1800 there was only one double bass in the orchestra of the Paris opera, and that was used only on the fashionable Friday evenings lest it wear out. As late as the middle of the nineteenth century Berlioz records the difficulties that he had, when he was a visiting conductor in German cities, to find instruments and performers required by the scores that he used. It is reported that in France before 1725 there was scarcely a performer on the violin who could read music at sight. There was no definite orchestra as we now conceive it for the opera before the beginning of the eighteenth century. It was more or less standardized by Bach, Handel, and Haydn, but continued to be modified for many years to come.

The violin, the chief of the strings, which are now the basic choir of all orchestras, attained its present form about the same time as the opera and soon became popular because it so perfectly can accompany the human voice, especially the soprano. It developed from the old viol, a similar instrument of slightly different shape with fixed frets, somewhat like the mandolin's, but the violin has a far better tone and is much more flexible. However, its possibilities were learned slowly. Even in the time of Lully (d. 1687) shifting of the left hand on the neck to produce notes above B was unknown. Monteverdi is said to have invented the *pizzicato*, or method of plucking instead of bowing the strings, and the tremolo; but it was not until the time of Gluck (d. 1787) that the sordino, or mute, was used to produce a muffled but sweet variant of sound. Various other methods of playing—with a jumping bow (*spiccato*), playing a number of detached notes with one stroke (double stopping, that is, playing of chords of two notes), trills and shakes, harmonics, and the like—came later. Monteverdi discovered the effectiveness of a vocal solo accompanied softly by strings, but this did not become popular in his time.

The string choir—violin, viola, violoncello, and double bass —by the beginning of the eighteenth century had become the basis of orchestral music, but only after considerable experimentation with three and five members of the family. Weber was the first opera composer to divide the music for first violins into two parts. Later the parts were written differently for as many as eight or ten first violins, though it is hardly possible for even a trained ear to note such fine divisions.

The harpsichord, a predecessor of the modern piano, in which the strings were mechanically plucked by quills instead of struck by hammers, early became the standard chief producer of harmony in the orchestra. Different in tone production from the piano, which to our ears does not belong in the orchestra, it was finally discarded in the time of Gluck and Mozart, composers having learned to produce harmony by means of other instruments of the orchestra. Someone has truly said that what color adds to an engraving the orchestra adds to the music of the harpsichord. For some time later, however, it was still used to give out chords during "unaccompanied" recitative. The harpsichord was succeeded for a brief time by the occasional use of the newly invented pianoforte, which Rossini must be credited for finally discarding. With the disappearance of the harpsichord the inner harmony by the string choir developed rapidly, and later it was supplemented by harmony from the other choirs.

Music for the harpsichord was improvised by the player from what is called the *basso-continuo* or "figured bass." Over the bass part, written for the cellos and double basses, were placed figures which indicated in a general way the character of the accompaniment; that is, of the harmony. The figures left considerable freedom to the performer, however, so that it was necessary for him to be a musician well trained in the fundamental principles of harmony and even something of a composer himself. This practice seems almost incredible today to a generation accustomed to appreciate the importance of exact varied instrumental harmony in the music of the orchestra, but an approximation to it may be heard in the improvisations by members of contemporary "swing" bands. Because figured bass was a kind of shorthand method of writing music, it permitted composers to be much more productive than later, when they imposed on themselves the task of writing down every note that was to be played. *Basso-continuo* was used until the time of Mozart. Because of the monotony it produced, it had to be discarded before orchestral color was possible.

As late as Haydn (d. 1809), whose orchestra consisted of fewer than twenty players, after the harpsichord had been discarded, the strings came to dominate in the full orchestra, the first violins usually playing the chief melody or fragments of melody. A principal reason for this dominance is that the other instruments for variously presenting and for producing glowing colors did not exist or were so made that it was difficult for players to get the effects that later were common.

Flutes, oboes, bassoons, and clarinets, the last of which had been used since the middle of the century, were crude instruments, each a with row of holes that were stopped by the fingers to produce different notes. But if the holes were placed so that they could be reached by the fingers of the player, the sound produced by some stops was badly out of tune. Instrument makers compromised, as they later did for the sharps and flats on the pianoforte, but so much more that neither players nor auditors were satisfied with the results. Certainly the performers could not produce delicate shadings or even respectable music. It was not until 1832 that Theobald Boehm invented for the flute a system of mechanically covering the holes by keys operated by levers, a system that was shortly afterward adopted for the other wood winds. This permits each instrument in this choir to play more easily with accuracy and with expression the complete chromatic scale, and it also extends the compass of possible notes. Without this system we should not have the beautiful varieties of tone color that later composers used so freely. Without it we should have missed the touching *cor Anglaise* solo in the third act of *Tristan und Isolde*, the flute obbligato in *Lakmé*, the lightning music in *Rigoletto*, and many other memorable and loved passages by the wood winds.

A horn in Haydn's time could play an incomplete scale in only one key. When the key of the music changed, the performer had to stop playing altogether or else pause and replace a piece of detachable metal tubing in his instrument with one of a different length, an awkward and time-consuming task. In Mozart's *Don Giovanni* this change was required 35 times. A composer had to allow time, of course, for these replacements, perhaps at a point when the horn would have been peculiarly effective. No wonder it was not more used. Another possibility was the use of two horns in different keys. The trumpet was similarly handicapped. In one of Haydn's symphonies the first trumpet is given exactly three notes to play, one of them at intervals no less than 93 times. The other two notes are sounded only three times and once respectively.

In the early years of the nineteenth century geniuses invented valves, which permit each of the brass instruments to play easily the full chromatic scale within its range. Such valved instruments were used in Halévy's *La Juive* in 1835. So conservative are musicians, however, that it was many years before the improved instruments were generally adopted. Even as late as Wagner we find in the same orchestra, though entirely without necessity, both the old-fashioned and the valved horns. With the improved instruments almost unlimited possibilities in the way of richer harmony and of deeper tone colors were opened up for the venturesome composer. The orchestral music of *The Ring* would be pale indeed, if not impossible, without the mechanically keyed wood winds and the valved brasses.

Before 1810 the harp too had been a difficult and limited instrument. In that year Erard invented a mechanism by which a single pressure of the foot of the performer would raise or lower all of the strings by one or two half tones. That means that almost instantaneously the harpist can change from one key to any other. Thus the harp was made available at any point for producing the music of which it is capable.

These accounts are sufficient to indicate a similar improvement in almost all of the instruments of the orchestra. The violin family alone remains almost unchanged in the near perfection to which the members were brought by the Italians of the early eighteenth century. With improved instruments we have, naturally, improved compositions for the orchestra and also performance of old music such as its composers neither heard nor dreamed of. Fortunate is this generation in a set of instruments capable in the hands of an abundance of skilled performers under the direction of conductors who have refined tastes and perfected techniques of rendering the best music in the best manner that civilization has ever known.

But man is never satisfied. Already the electric organ has practically replaced the old instrument with its myriad of wooden and metal pipes, and there are reports of progress on an electrical instrument that will give with greater refinement and more facile accuracy all of the effects of the present largest orchestra. But until it is perfected we have enough to enjoy, enough to satisfy the most exacting demands of the most fastidious amateur.

THE ORCHESTRA IN OPERA

The orchestra is of course one of the chief performers in the production of opera. It began with opera and was developed chiefly because of the demands made upon it by the growing music drama. At first wholly subservient to the voices, it became a jealous partner and at times demanded, as in the later operas of Gluck, equality of importance. This was possible at a time when the development of human voice production had reached its apogee and the orchestra was growing in power by leaps and bounds. In Wagner it may be fairly said to have become the dominant partner.

Most persons need no training to get sensuous pleasure from an orchestra, and many go to opera chiefly to enjoy the instrumental music. Orchestral selections from opera, as everybody knows, are frequently played in concerts and over the radio, and then, unless the hearer is familiar with their setting in opera, they are just like any other music.

But there is more to the enjoyment of music than just listening to beautiful sounds skillfully produced and combined for rhythm, melody, harmony, and tone color. Like other arts, music has its own peculiar techniques. To get added pleasure one has to learn musical form—the announcement and development of a theme, the contrast with one or more other themes, the development, and the reconciliation to produce a complete unity, and the like. Unless one understands what a fugue is he will fail to appreciate the marvelous dexterity that Verdi manifests in the concluding passage of *Falstaff*. Knowing the technical forms, one gets added pleasure from noting and appreciating production of happy results. Although the techniques of musical form run into realms that are infinitely complex, an amateur can learn by a little study and by much intelligent listening, especially if he has a good musical memory, enough to give not only heightened pleasure

ves precede his "Phoebus does not remain
n *Electra*, Clytemnestra is introduced "with dr
onic clusters . . . which suggest her constant eff
p against the load of physical corruption and men
hat weigh on her by day and by night." And in th
of *Cosi Fan Tutte*, Don Alfonso enters to an orchestr
animent that imitates his panting for breath. As th
e Angelotti in *Tosca* enters the church, he is introduced
hurried and nervous syncopated phrase, and then his
ed flight from prison is marvelously represented by the
mental music.

any composers since Weber have given in the orchestra
haracterizing musical phrase, usually a melodic phrase of
eral notes, called a leitmotif. Wagner was, of course, the
ef exponent of this practice; and we hear motifs occasion-
y in many of the operas of later composers.* Such motifs
e frequent in Strauss's *Electra*—motifs representing Aga-
memnon, his children, especially Orestes, degradation, undying hate, and Electra's ecstasy. The dialogue between
Clytemnestra and Electra is an elaborate network of thematic
references.

Motifs are also used to recall what has happened or to
foretell what will happen later. The marvelous Prelude to
Act III of *Siegfried* makes us understand the fatefulness of the
events that we have been seeing. It recalls the Valkyries,
the Norns, and the Rhine-Maidens, and then foretells the fall
of the gods. The fate motif in the Prelude to *Carmen*, a motif
that is repeated time and time again as the drama develops,
anticipates the final tragedy. Motifs are used to recall a
character or an incident. By the music of the horns we know
that Siegfried is approaching the Hall of the Gibichungs, and
the "Perfect Love" motif brings up vividly his association with
Brünnhilde. The orchestral accompaniment to the conun-
drums of Mime and Wotan introduces nearly all of the motifs

* The motifs that Wagner employed in *The Ring* are recorded on Victor
Red Seal records 11215–11216.

but also a stimulus to continued effort better to understand
what can give unending pleasure.

A function of the orchestra that is seldom noticed by the
amateur is to prepare the audience for sympathetic response.
Coming to the theater in many different moods, they need as
much as the instruments of the orchestra to be tuned for
harmonious response. Inasmuch as an appreciative audience is
just as truly essential for the success of opera as the orchestra
or the singers, the composer, especially by the overture,
attempts to put each one into the proper mood for enjoyment,
to prepare him for tragedy, comedy, or romance. Moreover,
it keeps the audience in the mood of the drama, changing the
listeners from one mood to another as the plot develops. Of
course the orchestra does not do this alone; it is aided by
scenery, costumes, stage business, and the singing actors.

The orchestra creates atmosphere and influences the mood
of the audience chiefly by its tempi, dynamics, and tone color.
The next time you attend opera note how skillfully the
overture suggests what you will see and feel when the curtain
goes up. The earliest composers of opera maintained one
atmosphere and mood throughout a scene; later ones, having
more and better instruments and greater power over them,
frequently demand and get changes, subtle or striking in
contrast, as the drama develops. These changes are usually
emphasized, and sometimes entirely caused, by the orchestral
music. The changes of mood in *Carmen* and in *Rigoletto*, for
instance, are not merely from scene to scene but also often in
a single scene. The orchestra aids the ear as well as the eye
and the intelligence to appreciate what the composer intended.

The orchestra supplements and also interprets the scenery.
For evidence, contrast the instrumental music in the latter
part of the first act of *Aïda* with that when the banks of the
Nile are shown; the gay music that colors Flora Bervoix'
terrace or the square outside the Cafe Momus with the sombre
painting of the mood in Violetta's bedroom and the cold
tragedy of the Barriere d'Enfer. In the first scene of the last

act of *Parsifal* the background is a gentle spring landscape with flowering meadows. When Gurnemanz helps Kundry to a grassy knoll, crying that "winter's fled and spring has come," the cellos mount in a long and restless cantilena that stirs the blood of every listener. Then follows the "Good Friday Spell." There is nothing elsewhere in music comparable with its ecstasy and joy, its superhuman beauty reflecting the spring that has brought back beauty and hope to the world. And in *Orfeo ed Euridice* the magical beauty and serenity of the landscape are caught up into the music of both voice ("Che pure ciel") and orchestra, led by the entrancing melody of the oboe that introduces it—that ravishing equivocation of quivering light, the stirring of soft airs, and the flowing of quiet streams in some imaginable country of the dreaming mind. Compare the music that the orchestra plays when the damned spirits repel Orpheus from the mouth of hell.

As orchestral music interprets the scene in which the drama develops, it also supplements and emphasizes the action of the characters. It supplies crashes and thuds and soft accompaniments at appropriate moments. Moreover, it gives "program effects," imitating by sound what is going on—storytelling or picture-making or other appeals to the senses. At the beginning of *Otello* we hear in music the subsiding storm; in *Rigoletto* the piccolos represent lightning and the heavy instruments give the subsequent thunder; in *Siegfried* we hear music that perfectly suggests the upsoaring fire about Brünnhilde and we also hear the song of a bird; in other operas we hear rushing winds, feel the night, or are made by the music to see sunshine or gloom. The Prelude to *Walküre* represents the storm raging outside Hunding's dwelling, its organpoint suggesting the heavy rain periodically, as the orchestra tells us in the frequent swells, blown by the wind. "The music," says Bekker, "throws our nerves into a state of abnormal excitement, in which our imagination can easily compete with the illusion which the scenery has suggested."

"This," writes Ernest Newman, "is one of the baffling mys-

teries of music how the [...] be made to suggest suc[...] visible world . . ." Wag[...] program music in Berlioz[...] except when it complied w[...] thoroughly justified by the s[...] the scope of musical expression[...] Act II of *Der Fliegender Ho*[...] orchestra imitate the whir of th[...] orchestra portrays the raging of th[...] *Tannhäuser* after Elizabeth ascends t[...] effects in which Wagner excels, in[...] heard are blended into one impression,[...] means of a deep trombone color, that [...] like a dark mantle falling over the cle[...] hitherto prevailed in association with the h[...]

Illustrative of the cleverness of Verdi in[...] music are the following quotations from *T*[...] orchestral details in *Falstaff*:

The two trills on bass and wood wind, the grunts on cl[...] and pizzicato double bass after each of the Fairies' que[...] practical advantages of honor. . . . [And in Act III] t[...] expanding effect of wine is illustrated by a trill progress[...] up by the whole orchestra, including trombones, trumpets,[...] drum tremolo—an astounding piece of virtuosity.

The orchestra often introduces the singing actor, c[...] terizing him both as he appears and as the drama develop[...] prepares for him before he comes on the stage, it clothes h[...] with an appropriate atmosphere, it comments on him contin[...] ally while he sings and acts, and, in short, it reveals the[...] innermost meaning of his character. Gianni Schicchi is made[...] by the music to be just what he is, a scheming and clever[...] rascal. After the curtain rises in *L'Amore dei Tre Re* a quiet[...] theme in the orchestra represents the romantic nature of[...] Fiora. A mighty C-major chord of horns, trombones, and[...] bassoons introduces the High Priest in *Alcestis*, and gigantic[...]

from the two preceding music dramas. When we hear in *Götterdämmerung* snatches of the Fire Music, a whole scene of the preceding opera rushes back to mind, and we read into the situation much more than we see at the time. Like the chorus in the old Greek drama, leitmotifs interpret, reveal, recall, foretell, elucidate, and convey a depth and poignancy of meaning or association that words alone are powerless to convey.

Such subtle musical interpretations may not be consciously noticed by a listener, but they have their effects nevertheless. One of the pleasures of repeatedly hearing an opera is the growing awareness of the skill of the composer to make us understand and feel as he intended us to do.

Of course the most commonly understood function of the orchestra in opera is to accompany the singing. As has been told, in early opera the singing was the most important element, and the accompanying instrumental music was subordinated. Later the orchestral music became more and more important until at times it was dominant, as in *L'Amore dei Tre Re.* Gluck in his eighteenth century reform wrote that he strove "to restrict music to its true office of serving poetry by means of expression and by following the situations of the story, without interrupting the action or stifling it with useless superfluity of ornaments."

All composers of operas that we are likely to hear today attempted to make the instrumental and the vocal music equal partners. But not infrequently one or the other dominates. Regardless of the intention of the composer, the enthusiastic conductor sometimes drowns the voice by the volume of the orchestra. But great conductors make the instruments support, emphasize, and interpret what is sung. It is a miracle that they can produce a great volume of orchestral sound and at the same time permit the voice to soar out in clearness and beauty.

The orchestra does more than accompany the singing. It interprets what the characters are, what they do, and even what they think. It represents the smallness of Mime's mind as well as of his body. It makes Manrico always chivalrous and the Count di Luna violent almost to the point of insanity, and Azucena vitally human and consistent. It tells in sound Beckmesser's temptation, hesitancy, fear, and theft from Sachs's room of the manuscript of Walther's song. Little punctuating chromatic runs in the orchestra indicate the craftiness of Iago in his conversation with Roderigo, and again in the drinking song the instruments portray Iago's sinister nature by the descending runs in the higher voice. The wonderful rush of the violins at the moment when Otello throws Desdemona to the ground and the passage in the double basses that announces his coming to his wife's room for the final tragedy are perfect orchestral interpretations of the action and of what is in the Moor's mind.

What is in the mind of the characters? The well-known Meditation in *Thais* reveals her struggle to make up her mind to abandon her life in profligate Alexandria and to go to austere salvation with Athanael. The soft, undulating figure in strings prepares for Siegfried's dreamy pondering in the Waldleben. The staccato forge theme of Mime is heard as the dwarf enters his mind, but this is broken off by "Ich mag' ihn nicht mehr seh'n!" ("I don't wish to see him again!") The theme of the Volsung race is heard as Siegfried wonders how his mother looked, and the rich and tender motif of filial love precedes his cry "Ach, möcht! ich Sohn meine mutter sehen!" ("O that I could see my mother!")

And, finally, the orchestra maintains a mood while time passes. Butterfly, Suzuki, and Trouble stand long watching for the return of Pinkerton with no word sung or spoken. The orchestra emphasizes the hopeless waiting and resumes the mood when the curtain rises on the last act. It fills in the time while the Meistersingers take their seats for the contest of song. The Intermezzo in *Cavalleria Rusticana* maintains the mood while Alfio is maturing his plan for killing Turiddu and the contrasting holy service is going on in the church. In the last Act of *Romeo and Juliet* there is a long orchestral interlude harmonious with the death-like sleep of Juliet. And the orchestra fills the time while Tosca wets her napkin, washes her fingers, arranges her disheveled hair, finds the safe-conduct paper, lights the candles and sets them by the dead Scarpia, and places the crucifix on his breast. And at the beginning of the last act of *Tosca* there is a long passage for the orchestra while actors come on the stage and leave it without singing. The pastoral sheep bells and the shepherd's distant song are in sharp contrast to the tragedy soon to follow.

TONE COLOR

One does not read very far into the literature of the orchestra without coming across frequent mention of "tone color." It is a figurative phrase drawn from the field of painting, as are the musical terms "chromatic" and "coloratura," and like many other figurative expressions it does not convey an exact meaning. Unfortunately it is used to suggest several different ideas, only one of which is pertinent to our consideration of the music of the orchestra in opera. A careful search in the literature of music fails to reveal a clear and complete exposition of the special meaning of tone color with which we are concerned, though probably at least one exists somewhere. So here is an attempt by a layman to explain to amateurs what professional musicians apparently mean by the term.

Some people have a peculiar gift for associating a color with a musical note, chord, or key, but several studies have shown that no two agree in all the details of such association. Rimsky-Korsakov and Scriabin made lists, each different, showing the colors that the several keys suggested to them; and Beethoven once said that he never composed in a certain key because to him it was dark brown. Two famous musicians indicated in their scores colors that might be displayed during performance—Scriabin for his *Promethee* and Schönberg for his *Die Glückliche Hand*—and several inventors have devised instruments for producing a series of harmonious colors, combined after the manner of music in a symphony. But all this is apart from the meaning of tone color in the orchestra of an opera.

The basis of the meaning is that no two instruments, including the human voice, sound alike when they produce the same note. No one has difficulty in distinguishing an A, for instance, produced by a violin, a flute, a horn, or a drum. Sung by a soprano or a bass, or even by two sopranos, it sounds different. The reason for this, physicists tell us, is the presence of various overtones accompanying the fundamental. A fundamental tone, given most purely by a tuning fork, is produced by a certain number of pure vibrations. Usually these set in motion other vibrations, the most important being an octave higher, that are called overtones or harmonics. The following experiment will show the presence of overtones: hold down the key of A on the piano, not striking it so as to produce a tone, and then strike sharply and release the A an octave below; the higher note will sound, giving one set of the overtones. By adding certain overtones to a fundamental, physicists can build up an imitation of the sound of any instrument. This is the principle basic to the electric organ and to the theremin. The characteristic sound of any instrument is called its tone color. The French *timbre* is used with much the same meaning.

Music undoubtedly began with rhythm, to which it later added melody, much later harmony, and, later still, form. Harmony was developed for combinations of instruments after the beginning of opera.* By the middle of the nineteenth century, musicians felt that they were reaching the limits of the resources of rhythm, melody, and harmony, and so they turned for new effects to the varied use of tone color. Some

---

* And I know not if, save in this, such gift be allowed to man,
   That out of three sounds he frame, not a fourth sound, but a star.
Consider it well: each tone in our scale in itself is naught:
   It is everywhere in the world—loud, soft, and all is said;
Give it to me to use!! I mix it with two in my thought:
   And there! Ye have heard and seen: consider and bow the head!
                                        —ROBERT BROWNING, *Abt Vogler*

of the effects are purely aesthetic and others are connotative; that is, arousing from the experience or imagination of auditors emotions associated with or responding to the peculiar tone colors or combinations of tone colors used.

Composers early learned what combinations of instruments are pleasing. The violin goes especially well with all the other members of its family, with the wood winds, and with the human voice; in fact it combines probably better than any other instrument. But an audacious experiment by Antheil to write a sonata for piano, violin, and bass drum was doomed to failure because our ears do not like the combination of the peculiar tone colors produced. Stravinsky's *Octette*, a far better piece of music, for a similar reason failed to prove acceptable. It calls for a flute, a clarinet, two bassoons, two trumpets, and two trombones. The harpsichord, in early days the foundation of the orchestra, was ejected because its tone color did not harmonize satisfactorily with the instruments that were retained and developed. The combination of the four choirs, with their component instruments, that make up the modern orchestra has already been explained. All together they produce a total palette that is most satisfying.

Multiplying the same instrument also changes the tone color: ten violins, five flutes, four trumpets, or three oboes, played even in unison, give a different effect from one. And there are variations possible on a single instrument by muting or dulling its tone. The violin can be not only muted but also plucked (*pizzicato*), played with a jumping bow (*saltando*), with the wood part of the bow (*con legno*), close up to the bridge or farther than usual from it, given a tremolo, or manipulated so that the strings produce eerie harmonics. The note played by stopping—that is, by pressing the finger on a lower string—will give a slightly different color from the same note played on a higher string open. Other instruments of the orchestra are capable, though to less degree, of similarly having their color changed.

For a long time the instruments of the orchestra were

combined by doubling; for instance, the flute would play a melody with the violins, the violas, the cellos, the bassoons, and the double basses playing the same notes, though one or more octaves apart. This produced color, but no tints. Before the beginning of the nineteenth century, composers discovered that beautiful and otherwise effective shades of color could be produced by giving to the several instruments different parts that combine into a marvelous complex harmony. They broke up the violin family so that there were first and second violins, and eventually three or more parts for the first violins alone. Wagner goes so far in the Prelude to *Lohengrin* as to write as many as sixteen parts for the first violins. By such experimentation composers learned how much mixture of tone color can be appreciated by the human ear.

Recent experiments have introduced into the orchestra for peculiar effects novel instruments, such as the gong and celesta, and into nonoperatic orchestras even such things as whistles, toy horns, typewriters, and airplane propellers. These all give "color," but some colors are not liked well enough for us to demand their repetition.

Some music is capable of satisfactory production by many instruments or combinations of instruments; the "Pilgrims' Chorus," Percy Grainger contends, is beautiful on the piano, the organ, or the orchestra; certainly "The Evening Star" is as lovely on the cello as when sung, but we draw the line at its performance on the piccolo or ukulele. Much music, however, especially that composed since Beethoven and, more especially, since Wagner, seems to demand the color that certain instruments or combinations of instruments can give. The obbligato to "the Bell Song" in *Lakmé* can be satisfyingly produced only by the flute; Siegfried's funeral music could not be. Considerable appreciation of what color in music means can be gained from comparing the same composition played by an orchestra and then by a piano. The rich painting by the former usually becomes by the latter an etching, or at best a tinted print.

Tone color, then, is obtained by the use of different instruments or combinations of instruments, and by varying the ways in which they are played. Since Weber it has been the constant concern of composers for the opera orchestra to assign to music such instruments as will give a series of colors not only harmonious and pleasing in themselves, but also contributing, often in subtle ways, to the emotional response by the auditors. Everyone appreciates the color in the dark music produced by massive octaves that accompanies the giants in *Rheingold* and that in the bright orchestration for Loge. Modern music is rhythm, melody, harmony, form, and tone color—the last steadily assuming a greater importance, with the impressionists in music, such as Debussy, often becoming the chief concern.

To increase his appreciation of tone color an amateur should learn the voice of each of the instruments in the orchestra, and be able to recognize it however much it may be modified by muting or by other devices such as have been mentioned. He should also develop some understanding of its character—strong or weak, sympathetic or brusque, light or dark. Then he will be in a position to listen for its effects, not only when it plays alone or is dominant—like the English horn in the last act of *Tristan und Isolde*—but also in combination with other instruments—like the harp in the Fire Music of *Die Walküre*. Every attempt to analyze peculiar color effects by the orchestra will repay the amateur many fold and will increase his ability to get appreciation and pleasure from intelligent understanding.

SOME BOOKS ABOUT THE ORCHESTRA

PAUL BEKKER, *The Story of the Orchestra.* W. W. Norton and Company.

ARTHUR ELSON, *Orchestral Instruments and Their Use.* L. C. Page and Company. Revised edition.

*GERALD R. HAYES, *Musical Instruments and Their Music, 1500–1750.* Oxford University Press, 5 volumes.

* Comprehensive and technical.

W. J. HENDERSON, *Orchestra and Orchestral Music.* Charles Scribner's Sons.

A. E. JOHNSTONE and E. J. STRINGHAM, *Instruments of the Modern Synphony Orchestra and Band.* Carl Fischer.

DANIEL GREGORY MASON, *Orchestral Instruments and What They Do.* H. W. Gray Company.

*EBENEZER PROUT, *The Orchestra*, Vol. I, "Technique of the Instruments"; Vol. II, "Orchestral Combinations." Augener and Company.

HOWARD D. SMITH, *Instruments of the Orchestra.* R.C.A. Manufacturing Company.

LEOPOLD STOKOWSKI, *Music for All of Us:* Chapter 20, "Voices-Instruments"; Chapter 26, "The Orchestra-Orchestration." Simon and Schuster.

Chapter Twelve

OVERTURE AND INTERMEZZO

WHATEVER the intent and whatever the skill of the creator, no poem, painting, or piece of music has any significance until it is appreciated by someone. In a sense, then, at least two persons are necessary for the creation of art. This is peculiarly true of the opera, the elements of which must be fused by those who see and hear them into a single impression to which each one in its own way contributes. The composer and his associates bring together the materials and indicate how they should be combined; but the actual combining or, preferably, the actual fusion of them must be done by those who actively see and hear what is offered in the performance. "I defy any artist to move and elevate me," wrote Nathaniel Hawthorne, "without my own consent and assistance."

Just as an orchestra is a complex instrument that a conductor plays to produce unified harmony, so an audience is also a complex instrument to be played on by an opera. But it is not only more complex than an orchestra; it is eternally variable, needing to be got into tune before harmonious response is possible. Hardly any two people in an audience have the same knowledge of music, of the story in the libretto, or of the other component parts of the opera to be performed;

and hardly any two at the rising of the curtain are in the same mood for actively participating in the experience prepared for all.

There are a number of devices for tuning an audience at an opera, and one of the most important is the overture.

Purposes of the Overture

The overture to opera is not always the same in form, intent, or effectiveness. In its long historical evolution it has had many purposes, some of which have been emphasized at one period or by one composer, while others have been emphasized at different times by composers with other ideas and theories. The ten chief purposes for which the overture has been used will now be presented and briefly discussed.

To get the audience into their seats, quiet, expectant, and receptive. In the earliest days the first part of this purpose was sometimes achieved merely by a fanfare of instruments, but usually it was attempted by a brief instrumental introduction called a *sinfonia* or a *toccata*. Monteverdi introduced his *Orfeo* in 1607 by a nine-bar toccata repeated three times. Often the introduction was an instrumental arrangement of a popular madrigal. Though such introductions may have been pleasing in themselves and effective for the purpose stated, they were of course dramatically unnecessary and probably at times intrusive and disturbing to the mood of the opera to be presented. In modern opera the overture may achieve this purpose, though the audience is usually seated and attentive before the overture begins.

To entertain as music. Although at the time when opera began there was no such thing as composition for an ensemble of instruments, the overture furnished the challenge that composers needed. Consequently it was not long before there were definite music forms written for the orchestra, and finally, after one or more centuries of experimentation, there was general agreement with Wagner that the overture should form a music artwork complete in itself. The Italians early

invented one form, and the French, under the leadership of
Lully, another, which was used by nearly all composers until
Gluck and Mozart. Purcell and Haydn developed and digni-
fied this French form.

When the overture was merely to give entertainment, it did
not need to show any relationship to the music of the opera
that was to follow, though of course it probably was not of
such a different style as to give offense by contrast. Many
early composers used for an opera an overture composed for
another one, as Rossini did when he introduced his *William
Tell* with a previously used miniature symphony which,
though it has no connection with the opera, does harmonize
agreeably with its general mood. The overture for the first
presentation of *The Barber of Seville* had been used in two
earlier operas. So long as such overtures were entertaining
music, no one in the early days criticized the lack of relationship between them and the opera that followed. In later
opera, the overture, while continuing to be entertaining music,
gradually assumed a closer relationship to the music drama.

To create an atmosphere. Obviously if an overture can
create the atmosphere in which the ensuing opera is to be
developed, so much less is to be done after the curtain goes
up. Asserting that the overture "should prepare the listener
for the action about to be presented and constitute, as it were,
an argument," Gluck prefaced his *Iphigenie en Tauride* with
an overture that depicts a distant storm which gradually approaches and finally merges with the actual storm in which
the first act begins. The overture to Mozart's *Figaro* is also
peculiarly successful in creating an atmosphere for the opera,
as are the overtures to *Carmen, Der Freischütz, Otello, Die
Walküre, Tristan und Isolde,* and many others.

To develop the desired mood in the audience. This purpose is, of course, closely akin to the one preceding; an
atmosphere does much to produce a climate of mood. Gluck
was probably the first composer to use an overture to prepare
the audience for the ensuing action. Wagner contended that

an overture should be simply an ideal prologue, and he well exemplifies his theory in *Lohengrin,* the operas of *The Ring,* and *Parsifal.* Almost every auditor will first thrill to the sunshine and movement in the overture to *Carmen* and then find himself sobered and made apprehensive by the concluding fate motive. The overture to *Rigoletto* puts everyone into the mood of tragedy, a mood that is never dispelled by the gaiety of the court or the cruel fun of the courtiers.

To present themes, or musical ideas, from the opera. This purpose was first sought, though only by a single quotation, by Mozart in *Don Giovanni.* If there is to be in the overture music attractive in itself and harmonious with what is to follow, it is perfectly natural that in the course of time composers should introduce and briefly develop in the overture themes from the opera. Spontini used this method, and Weber developed it into effectiveness. The overture to *Die Meistersinger,* one of the most elaborate of all overtures, passes in review most of the main themes of the opera. Wagner in his famous essay on the overture advocated this purpose, and exemplified it well in *Tannhäuser* and *Tristan und Isolde.*

Quotation of themes is popular with audiences, but in the hands of lesser composers it easily degenerates into a mere potpourri, themes loosely strung together but seldom dramatically effective, however intrinsically entertaining they may be. The overture to Thomas' *Mignon* is of this kind. Much more dramatic is the series of quotations in *Der Fliegende Holländer.*

To anticipate what is to follow in the opera. This purpose carries on the preceding one beyond mere quotation. Seeking it, the composer attempts not only to indicate the atmosphere of the drama but also to tell in a general way what will be developed there. The short and simple prelude to *La Traviata* has such a programmatic significance. The rhythmic figure in the Prelude to *L'Amore dei Tre Re* suggests the vigorous horsemanship of Manfredo. The prelude to Act II of *Tristan und Isolde* "opens portentously with the theme of day. This is followed by the motive of impatience and a new passionate love theme, a short climactic run, and another which seems to grow out of this and which is to have its final flowering in the great 'Liebestod.' "

To give an argument to the ensuing drama, to summarize it. Wagner advocates this purpose and he seeks it consistently in *Tannhäuser*, all of which, some critics have said, occurs in the overture. "Though the overture must not attempt to reproduce, stage by stage all the episodes of the story," Wagner wrote, "it can suggest in its own way the dramatic content of the two main principles of the contest between two symbolic musical ideas: only the working out of these musical ideas must follow from the nature of the themes themselves." Some think that such an epitome makes the overture a concert piece and not properly a prelude to a drama from which it has already taken the edge. But few are likely to enjoy *Tannhäuser* less because they have already enjoyed the condensed summary in the overture.

The fine overture to *Der Fliegende Holländer* also gives in summary the entire story: the stormy sea, portrayed as no other composer has ever succeeded in doing; the gloomy Dutchman, the curse upon him and his longing for redemption; the tranquil motive of Senta, who will bring about the redemption; for a moment of relief, the gay song of the Norwegian sailors, soon overwhelmed in the storm; and finally the crashing of the curse motive displaced by the theme of Senta, glorified and radiant, as it will be heard at the end of the opera, when across the glow of the sunset the figures of Senta and the redeemed Dutchman are seen rising from the sea heavenward. Note that Wagner does not in this overture attempt to introduce into a potpourri all of the elements of the drama, but emphasizes instead the central dramatic purpose of the opera.

Perhaps the most notable exemplification of this purpose is in Beethoven's "Leonore No. 3," one of the several overtures that he composed for his opera *Fidelio*. Wagner says that it really sets the drama before us more completely and more effectively than the ensuing broken action does, but perhaps few amateurs will agree with him. Ernest Newman contends that it anticipates too fully the completed drama: if it is *not* understood by the hearer, because of his lack of knowledge of the opera, it conveys only a fragment of the real message to him; if it *is* wholly understood, it weakens his subsequent enjoyment of the drama itself. This belief leads Newman to suggest that this overture might well be played at the end of the opera, as a musical summary for those who have just had the dramatic experience. Those who know the opera certainly find in the summarizing overture a most satisfying pleasure. When heard in concert it brings back and interprets the whole drama.

Partly because another overture composed for *Fidelio* is too good to omit and partly because "Leonore No. 3" is too colossal as a prelude to the light comedy with which the opera opens, the "Fidelio Overture," which Beethoven composed for the 1814 performance of the opera, in current performances nearly always is used as an introduction, "Leonore No. 3" being inserted between the first and second acts or after the first scene of the second act. This gives a double summary and still further emphasizes the drama. This is especially true in respect to Pizarro's trumpet call, one of the most thrilling musical phrases in all opera.

To be an instrumental beginning of a train of thought and of feeling. The thunderstorm music in the overture to *Die Walküre* begins a train of thought and of feeling which is taken up by the combined libretto and music and carried forward in the first act. The same is true of the beginning of *Götterdämmerung* and of *Das Rheingold*. In the latter the prelude consists of a persistent sounding for 136 bars of the tonality of E-flat. It is meant to suggest the Rhine; and the idea is first of all of a sort of ground swell, then of heavy waves, and then of lighter and still lighter waves. From it we pass to the Rhine-Maidens and Alberich with never a jar to the progress of thought or feeling. The prelude to *Rosen-kavalier* represents more realistically than the subsequent action on the stage the amorous adventure of Octavian and the Marschallin.

To work out one great emotional motive. Instead of epitomizing the whole drama or even its principal conflicts, this purpose is confined to the presentation and development of one broad or basal theme. It is achieved marvelously in *Tristan und Isolde* and in *Lohengrin*. The prelude to the former "gives us the spiritual essence of the drama in highly concentrated form. . . . It is a slow, inexorable working out of one sad mood in all its sweet and bitter implications." Those especially interested in the effectiveness of the overture to *Lohengrin* should read the interpretations given by Wagner and by Liszt.[1]

To be a significant part of the music drama. This purpose is well achieved in many operas when the overture sets the proper atmosphere or leads directly into the action. It is especially notable in those subordinate overtures which introduce some acts subsequent to the first. Note for illustration the beginning of Acts III and IV of *Carmen*, of Act III of *Lohengrin*, and of Act III of *Götterdämmerung*. Wagner turned his *Vorspiel*, as he called some of his overtures, into an integral part of his music drama.

HISTORICAL DEVELOPMENT

As already stated, the earliest form of the overture was an instrumental rendering of a popular madrigal, which was of course in the conventional contrapuntal style, or it was a similarly unrelated short composition for the orchestra. In Italy, Scarlatti developed a regular ternary form, consisting of a slow movement preceded and followed by a quick one, the last sometimes being a minuet. From this eventually developed the symphony and the sonata.

In France, a little earlier, Lully invented a slightly different

[1] Ernest Newman, *Stories of Great Operas*, Vol. I, p. 69.

ternary form, the quick movement, often fugal in style, being in the middle. This form became the more popular and was generally imitated by composers of opera up to and including Handel, who gave it expansion and development. In other hands it became highly formalized and was of course still dissociated from the meaning of the opera that it introduced.

In 1763 Algarotti, who had great influence on Gluck, wrote that the overture "always consists of two *allegro* movements and one *grave*, makes as much noise as it can, is of the same invariable pattern, and is always conducted in the same manner," regardless of the content of the opera. As one of his reforms, Gluck attempted to improve the overture. He discarded the French form and developed some of his overtures into a single movement, usually in the sonata form, but without repetition of the exposition. In his later operas he used the overture to prepare the auditors for the plot of the drama, and several times he ran into the beginning of the play without pause from the appropriate prelude.

Mozart profited from this part of Gluck's innovations and still further improved the overture. His early overtures were entirely separate from the operas, though broadly suggestive of what was to follow. But in *Don Giovanni*, for the first time in opera he introduced into the overture a theme, that of the statue, which was to be used later in the play; and also in the overture he presented in transfigured musical language the contest between the arrogance of Don Giovanni and the anger of the higher power. It effectively prepares for the drama. In the overture to *Die Zauberflöte* Mozart combined the sonata form and the fugue style.

Beethoven being a great composer for instruments could not fail to make the several overtures which he composed for his single opera effective, self-contained tone pieces. The "Leonore No. 3" is in sonata form, with regular exposition, development, and recapitulation. He composed similar brilliant overtures for dramas written by others.

Weber may be said to have developed the opera overture

that was the model of the nineteenth century, for more than anyone else he influenced the great master, Wagner. Carrying on from Mozart's beginning in *Don Giovanni*, Weber constructed his overtures of the melodies in the music of the operas. They are masterpieces of organic design, that to *Der Freischütz* being a perfect symphonic poem. Wagner commended Weber for making his overtures dramatic "without losing and wasting himself in painful depiction of insignificant accessories of the plot." More than any of his predecessors Weber enriched the overture with a lavishness of tone color and he never hesitated to be programmatic; that is, to make music that directly represented and even imitated the sounds of nature and of people in the drama. In both these matters Wagner followed the example. The brilliant programmatic overture—a little symphonic poem, with andante, allegro, repetitions, and developments—to Rossini's *William Tell* is well known.

In the opinion of many, Wagner was one of the greatest masters that opera has known of the overture and of the more dramatic but less musically independent *Vorspiel*, or prelude. Always effective, he wrote no two of his musical introductions alike. The overture to his early *Der Fliegende Holländer* was conventional in that it brought into review the themes later to be developed and used dramatically, but early as it was it is one of the finest overtures in the world. The overture to *Tannhäuser*, like the overtures of Wagner's predecessor and model, Weber, employs the main themes of the opera to summarize the dramatic action; but Wagner raises this form of overture to a height of which Weber probably never dreamed. Howard Murphy has pointed out that "the Tristan Prelude is developed from five important motifs used in the music drama: Tristan, Isolde, The Glance, Love-potion, Longing for Death. After a tremendous climax resulting from a continuation of the first two motifs the first returns alone, and the Prelude closes with Morold's ominous motif in the bass as the curtain rises."

The overtures in *The Ring* are all powerful in dramatic effect, as well as beautiful music. The prelude to *Siegfried* opens to us the machinations of Mime's mind. That to *Die Meistersinger* passes in review most of the themes of the opera, and before the third act Wagner describes in marvelous music Hans Sachs's attempt to reach spiritual happiness through renunciation. The prelude to *Parsifal* is one of the most moving pieces of music ever written, perfectly creating an atmosphere for the succeeding drama. Wagner's influence was toward making the preludial music an integral part of the drama, besides creating in the audience the mood desired and giving an acquaintance with the theme materials that are later used in the structure of the music drama.

Verdi never considered the overture as one of the important elements of the opera in which he was deeply interested. In *La Traviata* he has a short and simple prelude, suggesting the beginning and the end of the play; the *Rigoletto* overture begins with the grim curse that is to work its inexorable tragedy from its utterance to the final shriek by the river side; *Il Trovatore* has barely more than a roll of drums to start it on its way; but *Aïda* in its brief but brilliant orchestral introduction indicates what Verdi could have done if he had been interested. For him the overture was to get the drama on its way quickly and with a proper tonal introduction.

With later composers of opera the overture was not advanced in importance. Leoncavallo introduced in *I Pagliacci* the novelty of substituting for the overture a prologue sung before the curtain. In Gounod's *Faust* the overture is not essential; in fact, it seems to have been written as an afterthought, but it is thoroughly characteristic of the music of the opera. Puccini nowhere considers the overture essential: a brief introduction, a few striking chords, and he is on his way. *Butterfly* seems to invite an elaborate overture, but there is only a short semi-fugal working out of a single theme, and the story begins to unfold.

The tendency seems to be to shorten the overture and to

give it less independence and less importance. The old epitomizing is a practice of the past. And yet most of the operas that we shall hear, most of those that we love, have overtures, and for the sake of the fullest enjoyment we should understand them for what they are as musical compositions and also for what they contribute to the drama.

THE INTERMEZZO

In the early opera the practice developed of having between the acts of the serious or tragic play interludes, called *intermezzi*, somewhat like the *satirae* in the old Roman drama. These were to entertain the auditors who were not too keenly interested in opera, to give relief from such tension as may have been created, to afford rest to the singers, and to occupy the time while the costumes and scenes were changed. Out of such interludes developed the "comic" opera, not always amusing, which after a while became strong and popular enough to be given independently.

For similar purposes there were at times introduced into opera musical numbers, independent and not related to the developing plot. Usually at first they were simple madrigals, or on occasion excerpts, either vocal or instrumental, from other operas. For the same purposes ballets, and even wrestling matches, in the early days were introduced between acts of the opera.

Eventually, however, the physical contests were discarded, the ballet more frequently was incorporated into the opera, the comic element developed into an entity of its own, and orchestral intermezzi were introduced for the several purposes mentioned above. These were especially popular in Germany, where instrumental music was most loved for its own sake. For this reason Beethoven wrote such incidental music for Schiller's *Egmont*, Schubert for *Rosamunde*, and Mendelssohn for *A Midsummer Night's Dream*, which though not operas will serve for illustration. Much of such music, when used, was consonant with the spirit of the opera into which it was interpolated, but was not essential or functional to the drama. Such intermezzi are no longer used in opera.

Examples of intermezzi in modern opera are that which occurs after the Senta and Eric duet in *Der Fliegende Holländer*, the popular dainty gavotte between the first two acts of *Mignon*, "The Witch's Ride" in *Hänsel und Gretel* and the music before Act III of *Manon Lescaut*, which suggests Manon's regrets in prison. With these may be included the postlude to Act II of *Butterfly*, which maintains the Japanese atmosphere and emphasizes the long vigil.

The rare functional intermezzo is best illustrated by that in *Cavalleria Rusticana*, where it is used to indicate in that single-act opera a lapse of time.

Suppose there were no intermezzo, the curtain falling between the two scenes; the break would be intolerable. The drama is so exciting we want to go straight on; yet a certain amount of time must elapse while the people are supposed to be in church. We cannot really wait all that time . . . and if there were a long silence and no fall of the curtain, the audience would resume their talk . . . and lose their interest.[2]

So we have the musical intermezzo, in entire harmony with the play, which almost everybody knows as an independent composition. There is a briefer dramatic-symphonic inter-mezzo in *Fidelio*, when Florestan falls asleep.

If we conceive an intermezzo as a musical passage interposed in an opera and having some connection with its general theme, it is found not infrequently to indicate the passing of time (Prelude to Act III of *Butterfly*), to give actors opportunity to do something essential (as when Cio Cio San gets into her night dress in Act I or when Faust is being metamorphosed into a young man), to reflect what is going on in the mind of the singer, as the "Waldleben" music in *Siegfried*, the "Medita-tion" in *Thaïs*, or when Butterfly in the last act is making up her mind to sacrifice herself. There are in opera many instru-mental interludes that accompany action without singing.

---

[2] Edward J. Dent, *Alessandro Scarlatti: His Life and Works*, p. 44.

One example is in Act I, Scene 2 of *Alcestis*, when the queen and her attendants bring offerings to the temple. The musical interlude in *Louise* represents the Street Cries in Paris and tends to emphasize the city as the central interest of the drama. A true intermezzo has a complete musical form of its own.

Chapter Thirteen

STAGE SETTINGS AND COSTUMES

When the curtain goes up on an opera, usually after a prelude has begun to determine the mood of the drama, the stage setting forwards understanding of the atmosphere of what will be sung and acted. It helps to put the audience into a proper emotional mood and to make them receptive of what is to follow, thus economizing both text and music. It indicates the mood, the place, the period, the season. It suggests the romance or tragedy or comedy that is to take the audience out of the commonplace into the far away and long ago.

It should not be overlooked that orchestral music itself plays no small part in aiding the eye to appreciate the visual setting of the stage. Verdi's music decorates the stage, suggesting to the designer of sets and costumes what is colorful and appropriate. And Wagner is a superb scene painter. His music

. . . has a capacity for bathing each scene, each character in a light and atmosphere of its own. Music like that at the awakening of Brünnhilde would go with nothing but a mountain height in blinding sunlight. Hunding is not physically darker to the eye than he is to the ear in that marvelous tuba motif that accompanies his first entry in *Valkyrie*.[1]

[1] Ernest Newman, *Wagner as Man and Artist* (New York, Alfred A. Knopf, Inc., 1937).

Though a stage setting should be aesthetically pleasing and harmonious with the musical drama, it should not unduly call attention to itself, for it is merely a background. Habitual operagoers may properly applaud a setting that is novel in its beauty or in its significance. But if it continues to draw attention away from the opera itself, it is out of proportion and thereby bad. The amateur may be tempted to peer through opera glasses at the half-darkened stage in *Die Walküre* and other operas in a fruitless effort to see clearly what was intentionally dimmed. The result is inevitably distraction from the music of the orchestra or from the singing artists.

And yet scenery is an important part of opera. *Orfeo ed Euridice* opens with watchers grieving at the gloomy tomb. *Coq d'Or* shows a scene of fantasy. After an introductory scene, *Parsifal* presents a place of worship with the solemn procession of knights marching to holy communion. The boudoir of the Marschallin lit by the streaming sun of the morning sets the mood for *Der Rosenkavalier*. Faust is in his mediaeval study with his books and apparatus, depressed in his reflection on his loss of faith, which is emphasized by the joyous song of students passing by. Gorelik thus planned the set for Faust's study:

. . . a niche in a bare, massive wall. Beyond, dimly visible, a narrow Gothic window. A desk, an armchair; only those properties which are indispensable. The Demon appears. We hear only his voice; but the walls of the study turn crimson, as if blood were seeping through them, the silhouette of Faust becomes a deep purple. These impassioned colors seem to reveal to us a soul torn with loneliness and fearful torment . . . .[2]

Carmen, *Rigoletto*, and *Traviata* begin with scenes of brilliance, but the music hints at tragedy to come. The gnarled scenery in the second act of *The Dybbuk* emphasizes the poverty of the beggars. Scenery assists, clarifies, and stresses what is to be played and sung.

[2] *New Theatres for Old*, p. 177. © 1940, by Mordecai Gorelik. Reprinted by permission of the author and Samuel French, Inc.

The music of opera without scenery would be to the inexperienced little more than an orchestral or a vocal concert. Scenery and costumes help create in singers a mood to interpret the music, and they aid the audience to enter into the spirit of the drama. It is easy to recall what "dressing up" did for us as children when we played make-believe, and certainly behavior at a masked ball or a carnival would be less restrained were it not for the setting and the fancy dress. Some recent spoken drama has been presented without scenery and with the actors in conventional dress, but it is next to impossible to imagine *Butterfly, Aïda, Der Rosenkavalier,* or *The Ring,* without scenery and costumes.

Scenery should of course be appropriate to the spirit of the opera. But scenery there must be. Even the stock scenery of the small town theater is better than none. The flats of painted canvas, the parallel rows of serrated foliage, the artificial stones, and the conventional backdrop fool no one in the audience, but they are accepted as conventions against which the performance is given.

Although scenery should be unobtrusive, the amateur should give it enough attention, preferably in reflection during the intermissions or after the performance, to appreciate the art that has produced the appropriate background for the drama. The more he knows of pictorial composition, the easier appreciation will be. Through experience in the theater he has already become accustomed to the proscenium arch and other stage conventions. He has no difficulty in accepting a room with no front side and perspective by light, color, and lines as representing distance. A set is important for what it seems to be, not for what it is. The Gibichung's dwelling need not be strong, but it must suggest strength; Florestan's dungeon may be of black velvet, but it should give an impression of damp stone. General impressions are more important than details. The amateur does not need to know the technical devices of the stage, however ingenious and interesting they may be—the tormentor, the teasers, the baby spots, and the like. He should just accept scenery as an artistic setting for the drama.

Although producers usually attempt to have scenery that is historically accurate and some critics complain if a nineteenth century chair is used in a sixteenth century story, the only thing really important is that both setting and accessories are consistent with the atmosphere and contributory to it. Who cares if a military uniform is used for a soldier in a regiment disbanded before the uniform was designed, so long as it does not seem unsuited to the character of the man and his action? Only a pedant cavils at the waltzes in *Der Rosenkavalier* because the dance had not been invented at the time of the action. The Scotch kilts in *Lucia* are said to be "correct," but actually they seem somewhat incongruous and ridiculous on stout actors of mature years singing Italian. Historical or archaeological accuracy should concern the operagoer less than an effective contribution to the atmosphere of the music drama. An incongruity is more important than an anachronism.

The designer of modern scenery is an artist in his own right, a combination of painter, sculptor, and architect, but the art of stage settings is not merely one of making pictures: it is the art of relating pictures to living actors. After becoming familiar with the story and the music of an opera, the designer plans sets with definite centers of interest, which are emphasized by the placement of masses, by converging lines, by contrasts of color, and by the use of lights. Long straight lines, horizontal or vertical, give certain effects; lines that are short, irregular, broken, or curved give others. The designer seeks pleasing rhythm in both line and color, and a balance so that the design has unity. He uses proportions to heroize or to dwarf the characters. In current practice he keeps the sets as simple as possible, with no furniture or other accessories that are unnecessary either for the picture or for use. He introduces no detail that attracts attention to itself, unless it has a special importance in the developing story. When it does have such importance, attention is usually drawn to it by lights only at the time when it is used.

The modern designer paints with lights as well as with pigments. It is difficult for us to realize the handicap under which the theater operated before the invention of electric lights. In the first two centuries of opera, productions were illuminated by candles or by oil lamps. The first gas lights were used in London in 1803. Then gas, or a gas flame playing on lime, before which were interposed translucent colors, was common. In 1846 crude arc lights were introduced in Paris. Edison's invention of the incandescent bulb in 1875 made possible a revolution in stage lighting. But for a long time its possibilities were not realized. There was plenty of illumination, it is true; but it was usually glare. Footlights of white, red, and blue, each color used singly or in combination, gave varied effects, but they made the actors seem only two dimensional. Gradually improvements were made possible by the invention of dimming devices, by spotting the light on certain parts of the stage, by combinations that do away with disturbing shadows, and by the use of light reflected and diffused from a plastic dome or from silk hangings. The first act of *Orfeo ed Euridice* as formerly given at the Metropolitan Opera House affords an example of effective lighting. As Orpheus stands on the steps of the tomb of Euridice, he and the tomb above are illuminated by a circle of dim light that comes from directly above. Later the light gradually spreads to show the recumbent mourners, who sing as a chorus.

It was not, however, until the Swiss designer Alphonse Appia presented and illustrated his theories of the spiritual quality of light that it was effectively used to give emotional effects to the setting. Believing in unity and simplicity, Appia effected them by varied lights that not only give mood and atmosphere but also emphasize dramatic values. He used light to affect and to effect emotions. Instead of the old flat lighting, which made chiaroscuro difficult if not impossible, he used broken lights that cast shadows and produced the three-dimensional effects that give emphasis to the bodies of the performers, for he held that scenery should emphasize, not dwarf, the actors.

Light with its infinite capacities for varying nuances was valuable to Appia for its power of suggestion, which has become for us the distinguishing mark of everything artistic. He points out how in *Das Rheingold* one can give the impression of water through the sensation of depth by keeping the stage dim, filling the scene with "a vague obscurity" where contours are not defined. For *Die Walküre* the open air will be felt only if the summit of the mountain detaches itself clearly against misty distances. The flames of the *Feuerzauber* are not to be continued an instant beyond the time allotted to them in the score. Their intensity will be emphasized by contrasting them with "a limpid night sky vaguely pierced by stars." The light in Alberich's cavern, which is illuminated by his forge, is to have an entirely different quality: "The general feeling given will be one of oppression and a lack of light. The proportions of the setting will contribute to this sense of oppressive weight. Reflections of spurts of flame will intermittently illuminate now this detail of the setting now that one; and the setting itself, in blocking the source of light, will cast shadows that produce an ensemble chaotic in effect, of which, it goes without saying, the personages in the scene will be a part." The "Waldleben" in *Siegfried* is to be accompanied by a wavering play of fluttering sunlight and leaf shadows. The forest is to be made by the barest indication of a few tree-trunks and branches. Siegfried will seem to be in a forest because he is tinged in the vaguely green suffusion of light filtered through leaves and bespattered with an occasional sun-spot. The audience will then see a wood even though it does not see all the trees.[3]

Appia further argued that

. . . diffused light produces a blank visibility, in which we recognize objects without emotion. But the light that is blocked by an object and casts shadows has a sculpturesque quality that by the vehemence of its definition, by the balance of light and shade, can carve an

[3] Lee Simonson: *The Stage Is Set* (New York: Harcourt, Brace Co., 1932), pp. 360–61.

object before our eyes. It is capable of arousing us emotionally because it can so emphasize and accent forms as to give them new force and meaning.[4]

The following paragraphs quoted by Simonson serve as an excellent illustration.

Act II: As Isolde enters she sees only two things: the burning torch set as a signal for Tristan and enveloping darkness. She does not see the castle park, the luminous distance of the night. For her it is only horrible emptiness that separates her from Tristan. Only the torch remains irrefutably just what it is: a signal separating her from the man she loves. Finally she extinguishes it. Time stands still. Time, space, the echoes of the natural world, the threatening torch—everything is wiped out. Nothing exists, for Tristan is in her arms.

How is this to be scenically realized so that the spectator, without resorting to logical reasoning, without conscious mental effort, identifies himself unreservedly with the inner meaning of these events?

At the rise of the curtain a large torch, stage centre. The stage is bright enough so that one can recognize the actors clearly but not bright enough to dim the torch's flare. The forms that bound the stage are barely visible. A few barely perceptible lines indicate trees.

By degrees the eye grows accustomed to the scene. Gradually it becomes aware of the more or less distinct mass of a building adjoining the terrace. During the entire first scene Isolde and Brangäne remain on this terrace, and between them and the foreground one senses a declivity, but one cannot determine its precise character. When Isolde extinguishes the torch the setting is shrouded in a half-light in which the eye loses itself.

Isolde is submerged in this whispering darkness as she rushes to Tristan. During the first ecstasy of their meeting they remain on the terrace. At its climax they approach the audience. By almost imperceptible degrees they leave the terrace and by a barely visible flight of steps reach a sort of platform near the foreground. Then, as their desire appeases itself somewhat and only one idea unites them, as we grow more and more aware of the Death of Time, they finally reach the extreme foreground, where—we notice it for the first time —a bench awaits them. The tone of the whole secret, shadowy space surrounding them grows even more uniform; the forms of the terrace and the castle are submerged, and even the different levels of the stage floor are hardly perceptible.

[4] Simonson, *op. cit.*

Whether because of the contrast of deepened darkness induced by extinguishing the torch, or perhaps because our eye has followed the path that Tristan and Isolde have just trod—however that may be, in any case we feel how softly they are cradled by every object about them. During Brangäne's song the light grows still dimmer; the bodily forms of the people themselves no longer have a distinct outline. Then . . . suddenly a pale glimmer of light strikes the right side of stage rear: King Mark and his men-at-arms break in. Slowly the cold colourless light of day increases. The eye begins to recognize the main outlines of the stage setting and its color begins to register in all its harshness. Then as Tristan with the greatest effort at self-mastery realizes that he is after all among the living, he challenges Melot to a duel.

In the setting, cold in colour, hard as bone, only one spot is shaded from the dawning day and remains soft and shadowy, the bench at the foot of the terrace.[5]

On the modern stage most marvelous of all perhaps are the color effects. Lights can be used not only to give any hue and brightness desired, but also to change entirely the appearance of color in setting and in costumes. Modern dyes make possible many effects that before this century no stage could have had. The beauty of the modern stage is far beyond what our ancestors could have dreamed. Further advances are possible by the use of moving picture projections along with material scenery and properties. Some day we may actually see the gods marching across the rainbow bridge to Valhalla, a convincing destruction of the hall of the Gibichungs, and Senta actually rising heavenward from the sea with her sailor lover. In a Paris performance of *Don Giovanni*, a color projection has been used to give an illusion of real trees and sky, with an imposing effect of a huge stone archway in the banquet hall. When the Commandant seized Don Giovanni by the hand and drew him to his doom, the stone walls apparently burst into flame as the two disappeared; then in the wink of an eye the banquet hall reappeared as before. This is certainly an improvement over the conventional trap door from which unconvincing pink steam rolls upward.

5 *Ibid.*

It is better, too, than the colored transparency of Marguerite often shown in the first act of *Faust* and that of Marguerite shown with angels in the last act. Only a colored moving picture could at all adequately present Wagner's conception for Act I of *Tännhauser*, for which he prescribed:

The mist in the background dissolves, showing a cloud-picture of the Rape of Europa by the white bull, escorted by Tritons and Nereids. During the second song of the Sirens, Leda is seen in the soft light of the moon reclining on the bank of a woodland lake, with the swan laying his head on her bosom. As the picture gradually fades away, the mist itself completely disappears.

And of course in Act III of *Walküre* a projection is required to show Grimgerde and Rossweise each carrying a slain warrior at her saddlebow and flying through a glowering thundercloud which ascends from the depths and vanishes behind a fir tree. In *Opera News* (December 10, 1956) Ian Strasfogel tells of experiments with lights before and behind a curtain of plastic.

An illustration of the effective use of restrained light is given by Moderwell in his setting for the first scene of *Faust*.

Imagine a small dark room. In it are only two light spots—one the window in the upper left hand corner of the picture, the other the face of an old man, toward the lower right hand corner. . . . The large, square, drab light spot contrasts with the small tortured face. The livid intensity of the small spot balances with the blankness of the large one . . . This is essentially a pure design in mass. A single straight candlestick on the table contrasts with Faust's bent figure, and this adds a touch of pure design in line.[6]

Since Appia a number of adventurous and clever designers have revolutionized settings for the theater. They have passed from attempts at accurate representation to symbolism. Today the best designers tend to stark simplicity that suggests the mood of the opera, leaving to the audience responsibility for imagining much that was previously presented in reality. Although even in the best opera houses much of the old types

[6] H. Moderwell, *The Theater of Today* (New York: Dodd Mead, 1923).

of stage settings is still used, all of the new sets manifest the tendency toward simplicity and symbolism.

In the 1952 production of *The Ring* and of *Tristan und Isolde* at Bayreuth Wieland Wagner got away from all conventional mountings and accessories. In the *Ring* nobody wore winged helmets and the Rhine was treated not as an actual river but as a symbolic fluid. In *Tristan* the stage designer removed every traditional detail that might detract from the central theme. He swept from the stage every "prop" that could be spared, including the sailors in Act I, who are merely heard as an off-stage chorus. In Act II there is no castle or wood, and even the necessary bench is not immediately visible. After Tristan's arrival nothing can be clearly seen except the two lovers seated motionless far upstage, hazily visible in soft green light. Act III shows nothing but an indefinite wall and Tristan's couch.

For a number of reasons the designer of stage settings is handicapped. He must first of all satisfy the demands of the libretto, and he has always to keep in mind the limitations of cost. He must devise scenery that is easily handled, that can be quickly set up and taken down, that can be stored, and, if the company is to travel, that can be transported with minimum danger of damage. His sets should enable every person in the house to see what happens on any part of the stage. Spectators have many points of view—near, distant, below the level of the stage, far above, from the center, and to one side. The designer draws "sight lines" from every extreme position in the house and attempts to make the essential scenery and action visible to everyone.

Space on the stage of even the largest opera houses is limited, and though the clever use of lights can extend a shallow stage, the designer is hard put to it when he is called upon to represent lofty groined arches or the passage of the gods to Valhalla. One of Gordon Craig's designs called for towers as high as an eight-story building. If represented in scale it would of course have made the actors giants. But there are many ingenious devices that the designer uses to give the effect of great size even though his space is limited. Moreover, stage settings must be practical. There must be doors that open and close, windows through which light enters or through which a vista can be seen, a wall from which Tosca can cast herself; screens for various purposes, as in *Butterfly* and *Rosenkavalier;* tables, as in *Manon* and *La Juive;* chairs, thrones, balconies, statues, and what not that the acting drama demands. Set pieces and other accessories, some commonplace and others highly unusual, also serve to create or to intensify the mood of the opera. The ship of the Flying Dutchman is unlike the ship in *La Gioconda;* Alberich's underground workshop is different from Mime's forge; Sparafucile's sordid dwelling contrasts sharply with the Duke's drawing room; the temple scene in *Aïda* is bathed in mysterious African moonlight, while the triumphal march is drenched with brilliant sunshine.

Then we have ravens, dragons, toads, swans, goats, horses, storms, flames—an endless list of accessories that help create the proper atmosphere of the drama that is being acted and sung. Unfortunately, the difficulties of presenting these accessories, especially the living ones, are so great that the results are sometimes ludicrous rather than effective. In consequence, the stage manager does not introduce Fricka's goats, and the raven is left to imagination. It is far better to imagine the ride of the Valkyries or Grane than to be offended by a poor, incongruous actuality. A person without sympathetic imagination had just about as well stay at home anyway.

Juliet and Marguerite have balconies or windows from which they sing; *Cavalleria* has a church which the villagers enter and from which their song can be heard. Mimi and Violetta and Sieglinde and Brünnhilde each has a different bed on which to lie. The swan in *Lohengrin* must bring the hero and carry him away; the swan in *Parsifal* is shown after being killed. The statue in *Don Giovanni* must look like a statue and yet move and speak. The spinning wheels in *Der*

Fliegende Holländer and in *Martha* must whir; in *Hänsel und Gretel* the oven must receive the old witch; the theater must burn in *Mignon;* and Cavaradossi in *Tosca* must be painting a real picture before the altar. All these accessories either help create or intensify the atmosphere in which the music is interpreting emotions.

Ingenious machinery, along with amazing display of pageantry, was used in opera of the eighteenth century, especially in Venice. It was to some extent revived by Weber for *Der Freischütz* and by the showman Meyerbeer. Wagner made difficult and at times impossible demands of the stage. For the *Götterdämmerung* funeral procession and for the transformation scenes in *Parsifal* he required a painted horizontal curtain, which moved across the stage to evidence progression of the marchers.* Klingsor's spear had to sail across the stage and remain suspended over Parsifal's head and the castle had to collapse; Kundry was to materialize out of the ground; the gods were to march to Valhalla across a rainbow bridge; and the Rhine was to overflow Gunther's palace after *Brünnhilde* had ridden Grane into the blazing pyre. As we know, the impossibles are only suggested, sometimes crudely, on the modern stage, leaving the imagination to create what the composer intended. After Wagner the limitations of stage representation have been recognized and respected.

The mechanics of some of the accessories of opera are marvelously ingenious, but most operagoers prefer to accept them as miraculous actualities and not puzzle about the way that they work. If they are effective, they are good. Those who are interested, however, will find in Taubman's *Opera Front and Back* an explanation of some of the devices in common use, notably for the collapse of Gunther's house, the

---

* Wagner's directions read: "Gradually, while Parsifal and Gurnemanz appear to walk, the scene changes imperceptibly from L to R. The forest disappears; a door opens in rocky cliffs and conceals the two; they are then seen again in sloping passages which they appear to ascend. . . . At last they arrive at a mighty hall, which loses itself overhead in a high vaulted dome, down from which alone the light streams in."

illumined flowers in Marguerite's garden, the statue in *Don Giovanni*, the bird in *Die Götterdämmerung*, Tell's arrow and Parsifal's spear, and the steam curtain in *Die Walküre* and *Siegfried*. Here is Taubman's explanation of the illumined chalice in *Parsifal*.

One of the most startling and stirring moments in the whole calendar of opera occurs in *Parsifal* when Amfortas picks up the chalice that is the Holy Grail and holds it aloft to his disciples of Montsalvat. The grail lights slowly and becomes blood red. The stage is darkened, and the crimson of the Grail dominates the scene with awe-inspiring impressiveness. Here again the Amfortas is not relied upon to turn the light on and off. Hidden under the altar-like structure upon which the Grail is set is a stage hand. There is an opening in the structure, and as the moment comes for the revelation of the Grail, the stage hand turns a little knob at the bottom of the chalice. The Grail is connected to a dimming device, and it irradiates slowly. It is possible to operate the Grail in this way because it begins to light up just as Amfortas touches it and it need not be dimmed and extinguished until he sets it down again.[7]

To achieve success the designer must learn from the director just where the moving performers will be when they sing and act both individually or in ensemble. If success is to follow, the designer must also use colors and lights that will harmonize with the costumes to be worn. All this means that the designer of stage settings, cooperating with the management, the director, and the costumer has a difficult job, one seldom appreciated by the audience.

The chief faults to be found with the usual stage settings, in the opinion of Macgowan, are want of simplicity and of reposeful masses, overloading with superfluous and distracting objects, and architecture that is full of the mannerisms of the designer without helpful contributions to the drama. "Unobtrusive suggestion," he maintains, "is what is needed, not bewildering effects."

The new stagecraft of the theater, which is exemplified far

[7] Howard Taubman, *Opera Front and Back* (New York: Scribner's, 1938).

too little in the operas that we ordinarily see, is said to have three basic principles: simplification, of effect always, of means usually; suggestion, as when a single Saracenic arch gives the background for *Don Juan,* or a single candlestick indicates the Baroque period for *La Tosca;* and synthesis, "a complex and rhythmic fusion of setting, lights, actors, and play."

Some Early Stage Sets

The early opera, produced for men of wealth, in part grew out of splendid spectacles with elaborate and complicated stage settings and scenery. Although, chiefly for economy when opera passed to the public, the magnificence was soon replaced by simplicity, spectacles continued well into the eighteenth century. Ivanovich, quoted by Torrefranca, gives the following description, which though not typical of all opera of the early time indicates what some performances exhibited.

In this theatre are produced, during the Carnival, musical works with marvellous changes of scene, majestic pageants, the finest machinery and miraculous flights, while one may generally view the splendors of the Heavens, Deities, Seas, Kingdoms, Palaces, Groves, Forests, and other beauteous and delightful displays. The Music is always exquisite, selection being made from the best voices of the City, and bringing others from Rome, Germany, and other places, especially women, who with their beauty of face, the richness of their costumes, the charm of their singing, and the action proper to the personages whom they represent cause amazement and admiration. The effects are similar in the theatres of S. Salvatore and S. Cassiano.

So today theatrical performances with music have been introduced as a solace for the spirit, and as a most artistic recreation wherein are displayed Machines of great ingenuity, suggested by the Drama, forming a grand attraction amid the Pomp of the Scenes, and costumes, which gratify in full the universal curiosity. Thus there have been seen, on the stage, real Elephants, live Camels, Chariots drawn majestically by Wild Beasts and by Horses, Horses likewise in the Air, Horses which dance, the most superb Machines, displayed in the air, on the ground, on the sea with extravagant contrivances, and with admirable inventions to bring down from the Air Royal

Halls, with all the Personages, and Musicians, as illuminated by night-time, and to make them reascend in most astounding fashion, and a thousand other things, which being printed in the Dramas, it is superfluous to describe them with particularity, all persons being able to inform themselves fully by reading the same, which will serve as a pleasing and at the same time profitable diversion for Geni virtuosi or, as we should say today, the intellectuals.

Late in the eighteenth century Rousseau puts into the mouth of St. Preux, the hero of his *Nouvelle Heloise,* a sad description of the setting of opera in France.

Imagine an enclosure fifteen feet broad, and long in proportion; this enclosure is the theater. On its two sides are placed at intervals screens, on which are grossly painted the objects which the scene is about to represent. At the back of the enclosure hangs a great curtain, painted in like manner and nearly always pierced and torn that it may represent at a little distance gulfs on the earth or holes in the sky. . . . The sky is made of certain blueish rays suspended from poles and from cords. . . . The sun . . . is a lighted torch in a lantern. . . .

Mozart's stage settings were merely decorations; Weber aimed at complete illusion, as did the showman Berlioz. With Verdi the settings were of less importance, for he took over the decorative element into the music and he made his characters and action so important that eyes were focused on them. Wagner proposed stage settings that were both realistic and imaginative, in a number of instances impossible even for the largest and wealthiest theaters. Fortunately his drama and his music make his operas effective even though the scenery itself be unconvincing and the action that he indicated can be only symbolized. Few later composers have required anything in stage setting and costume that is more than conventional.

COSTUMES AND MAKE-UP

What has been said about stage scenery and properties applies equally to costumes and to make-up, both of which may properly be considered a part of the setting of opera.

They help compose a picture which creates an atmosphere conducive to the mood of the play.

Costumes should be appropriate to this atmosphere and in the best opera houses they are usually reasonably accurate with regard to the time and place of the action. Such "worn scenery" also contributes to the stage picture and not infrequently is "practical," in the sense that some part of it has a utility in the play—a cloak to conceal a face, a pocket in which to hide a letter, a train over which to trip, and the like. Costumes are also used to characterize a person: Basilio can be nothing but comic in the garb that he wears, a black robe and a long shovel hat, nor can Lakmé or Salomé or Beckmesser in their costumes get far out of character. Costumes also are a convenient means to help us in distinguishing two characters who at their first appearance are more or less alike; for example the Bohemian artists. Fafner and Fasolt would be alike as two peas if one were not made dark and the other light. In costumes the general effect and the silhouette are most important, but color and to a less extent detail are contributory. All costumes should of course be in harmony with the background. Too much credit cannot be given to the artist who designs for a large chorus costumes in many colors and tints that make a harmonious ensemble. Modern dyes and the marvelous techniques of lighting make possible effects that previous generations could not enjoy.

The task of dressing the characters in an opera is far greater than the amateur usually understands. The Metropolitan Opera Company has a total of some 7000 costumes, only a few of which can be used in more than one opera. *Siegfried* requires only 7 costumes, *Die Walküre* only 15; but for *Aïda* there must be 420, and for *Carmen, Die Meistersinger, Il Trovatore, Lohengrin,* and *Manon* well over 200 each.

Make-up is an art too full of tricks for us to consider them here.* Indeed, the amateur at opera is not concerned with the

* Anyone interested may consult Serge Shrenkouesky's *The Art of Make-up* (Dutton).

techniques used by actors to make themselves look their parts. He should accept with appreciation what they accomplish, and he should supplement their efforts with sympathetic imagination. If costume and make-up do not make Juliet look sufficiently young or Violetta sufficiently emaciated, the spectator must imagine that they are what they are intended to be, or he will miss a part of the pleasure that he has come to enjoy. The blind Samson is sometimes made up so that one is inclined to smile at the absurdity, but what gain can there be in that? However he may actually look, one should accept the symbol of the blinded hero tricked and despoiled by his enemies, but patient and powerful with the aid of his God to bring about their destruction. The absurdity of Basilio is emphasized by his false chin and nose, and many a heroine is made more beautiful on the stage than she ever was in real life. Whatever its shortcomings and however imperfectly it is used, make-up contributes much to the effectiveness of opera.

STAGE BUSINESS

The stage business in opera, what the actors do and how they do it, is in large part traditional, especially for the minor characters. This is justifiable because for the first production the director and his aides, including the actors and the composer, very carefully work out what seem to be the best ways of producing the effects desired; in later performances proposed changes that prove to be improvements are adopted, until gradually there is built up a tradition which all follow closely. This is particularly true in the Wagnerian operas.* A well-trained singer who has had experience in one company can fit into the performance of another almost without rehearsal. A novelty in "business" proposed by one actor may be good in itself, but it cannot be accepted if it interferes with what the others do to make up a cooperative effect. The

* Wagner wrote an exhaustive treatise on the performance of *Tännhauser*, giving the stage director and the singers the most minute instructions.

placing and the movements of the ensembles and the choruses are strictly determined by the stage director. It is no small accomplishment to have these groups compose an artistic picture and then to move about and get off the stage in a seemingly natural manner.

Not all great singers are great actors, but there are some notable exceptions. Only by seeing an opera over and over can an audience know what "business" has been determined by tradition or what has been invented by an ingenious director or by the actor himself. Usually the novelties are in small details, which only by experience will the audience notice and appreciate. It is amazing what effects are achieved by subtle differences in the way of doing what on the whole is the same thing. For instance, as Brünnhilde watches Siegfried ride away on Grane for new adventures she waves her arm five times in farewell. All Brünnhildes do this, but Flagstad conveyed what was in her heart by raising her arm less high each time, until the last is scarcely more than a gesture of grief and resignation.

Great singing actors "create" a role, even in operas that have been performed many times. But for the most part genius manifests itself in details.

Laufkoetter by his inventions vastly improved the conventional Mime, especially in *Siegfried*. Every Carmen has flung a flower in José's face, but one clever actress began a persisting tradition by pausing for a moment by the door of the cigarette factory to observe the effect. After José's flower aria he throws himself across Carmen's lap, but to evidence her changing mood ingenuity determined that she neither caresses nor touches him. In the new Metropolitan production of *Aïda*, Amneris brings a bracelet to the Princess instead of entering for no apparent reason.

Olive Fremstad's Isolde was very far from traditional. Her very costume of deep green was a flaunt in the face of Wagner's conventionally white-robed heroine. In the first act, after taking the love-potion, she did not indulge in any of the swimming movements usually employed by sopranos to pass the time away until the occasion came to sing again. She stood as a woman dazed, passing her hands futilely before her eyes. In *Parsifal*, Flagstad with utmost simplicity and restraint manifested her histrionic art largely by what as Kundry she does *not* do, while Varnay, many think a better actress, expresses her role by movement. Parsifal himself, and Ortrud in *Lohengrin*, have long periods on the stage in which they must act by not acting.

Stage business is more easily seen in comedy, perhaps, than in serious opera, and there the actors are usually given somewhat more freedom. In the Metropolitan presentation of *The Barber*, Figaro repeatedly turns Bartolo's chair and splashes lather generously into his eyes so that he cannot see the lovers. He replaces Rosina in the impromptu dance, to the embarrassment of Bartolo when he turns for an embrace. When singing "La Calunnia" Basilio stamps on Bartolo's foot; after his "good night" he returns for his red umbrella, and finding it he slams it on the piano, giving the lovers a start and the spectators a laugh; and he rises repeatedly in exaggerated politeness when Almaviva disguised as a music master, sings "Peace and blessing." Rosina pretends that her shoe is untied, and when Bartolo stoops to tie it she slyly extends her hand for Almaviva to kiss, and later under the very eyes of her guardian is handed a letter which she conceals by dropping her handkerchief over it. Most of this business is traditional and all of it is in character, adding much to the effectiveness of the scenes.

Small details in stage business make a great difference in the effect, as illustrated in the following incident related by George Middleton and quoted by Gorelik.

Too strict an adherence to the stark economy of the stage directions in the French script evoked the lesson Belasco gave me. "You don't dramatize each situation enough, George," he used to say. The curtain rose on the second act, with the audience knowing the lawyer had worked all night preparing his defense on a murder charge brought against the woman he loved. . . . I had followed the French script, telling Sothern merely to walk up and down to express his agitation. Belasco rushed to the stage. He clapped his hands for "Matty," his amazing assistant, who could have produced in a few minutes, if suddenly asked, a live elephant from his property room. Authentic French law books began suddenly to appear. Large strips of paper were torn up dramatically and hectically placed between the pages to mark citations the lawyer had discovered. Cushions were thrown upon the floor and a myriad of crumpled paper scattered about, to reveal his mental confusion. A lamp was left lighted in the early sunlight, a curtain half opened, and the French window widened to catch the morning air. And, as a crowning touch, the head cushion on the couch was pushed in to indicate where his head had rested in his futile efforts to relax. "This is how the room should look. Anyone can see now what he had been through," Belasco said.[8]

Good production of opera requires complete planning for consistency, unity, and effectiveness. In too many instances there has been no over-all direction that coordinated the acting of the singers, the soloist as well as the ensemble and the choruses. Sometimes in years past they were allowed merely to "stand around," especially when others were vocalizing. A soloist would step out of character to the footlights, sing, moving arms with gestures meaningless to the audience, and after applause return to acting or retire. The choruses might be placed and moved without regard to contribution to dramatic progress. Such laissez faire has of course been less in the better opera houses, but even there direction has often led to a serious lack of unity in the production as a whole and a failure to achieve in opera the effects that are common in the spoken drama and in the cinema. To improve the coordination of all the parts—scenery, costumes, movements, and acting—the Metropolitan Opera Company under Director Bing began the planning of each production as a whole by a single expert experienced in theater. The result is that opera is better drama.

Amateurs who are especially interested in stage settings and

8 Gorelik, *op. cit.*, p. 171.

effects may profitably consult H. K. Moderwell's *The Theater of Today*, Kenneth Macgowan's *The Theater of Tomorrow*, Sheldon Cheney's *Stage Decoration*, Herbert Bittner's *Theatrical Designs*, Lee Simonson's *The Stage Is Set*, Mordecai Gorelik's *New Theaters for Old*, Donald Oenslager's *Scenery Then and Now*, Adolphe Appia's *Die Music und die Inscenierung*, d'Amico's *Theater Art*, and Theodore Fuchs's *Stage Lighting*.

Pictorial illustrations of stage settings old and new can be found in a number of books and magazines, for example, in Lee Simonson's *The Stage is Set*, in Komisarjevsky and Simonson's *Settings and Costumes of the Modern Stage*, and in *The Studio* (London). The most convenient source of illustrations of scenery, especially of that used in New York, is *The Opera News*, published by the Metropolitan Opera Guild.

SUMMARY

The amateur at the opera should take the scenery, costumes, make-up, and acting as they are intended, settings for the drama—settings that facilitate creation of the appropriate atmosphere which makes reasonable the emotions developed in the characters of the play and to be shared by him if he achieves the enjoyment that he seeks. Understanding of the means used by the creating artists of scenery and costumes often satisfies an intellectual curiosity, but it should take second place to appreciation of what is intended. Enjoyment of opera is dependent not merely on the cooperative efforts of librettist, composer, scene and costume designers, singers and actors, and performers on the instruments of the orchestra but also on the active efforts of those who see and hear to fuse everything on the stage and in the pit into one appeal to such appreciation as arouses the emotions that are intended.

Chapter Fourteen

DANCE AND BALLET IN OPERA

FROM earliest times dancing and song have been intimately associated. Some of the best music that we have is an outgrowth of the formal union of music and dancing—the minuets, gigues, sarabandes, chaconnes, gavottes, waltzes, bourreés, and the like. And it was spectacular pageants in which there were dances and singing that made an important contribution to the beginnings of opera. In the seventeenth century the English were producing the masque, which was a dramatic entertainment, usually with a mythological or an allegorical subject, combining poetry, vocal and instrumental music, dancing, usually by members of the nobility in splendid costumes, with decorative scenery and spectacular machinery. Sometimes there was a comic antimasque, performed by professional dancers. These entertainments were very nearly operas.

In 1573, when Polish ambassadors came to offer their country's crown to Henri Duc d'Anjou, Catherine de' Medici had presented for their entertainment *Le Ballet des Polonais.*

And all about was an infinity of torches; she (Catherine) presented the most beautiful ballet that was ever on earth, . . . which was composed of sixteen ladies and young girls . . . they were set upon

227

a great silvered rock in niches . . . representing the sixteen provinces of France, with the most melodious music imaginable, and after the rock had made a parade tour of the room . . . all came to set down from the rock and being formed into a little battalion of bizarre invention, viols to the number of some thirty sounding pleasantly forth an *air de danse*, they came forward to step to the tune of the viols and in perfect time, without ever getting out of step, approached unto and stopped themselves a little before their majesties, and then danced their ballet, so fantastically conceived, and by so many turnings, contours and detours, interlacings and confusing, encounters and arrests, in which not one lady ever failed to turn in her place nor in her rank, so well that every one was amazed by such confusion and such a disorder never ceasing from a superior order, for these ladies had solid judgment and good memory and had been so well rehearsed; and this bizarre ballet went on for less than an hour, which being finished, all the ladies, representing the said provinces, were presented to the king, to the Queen, to the King of Poland, to Monsieur, his brother, to the King and Queen of Navarre and other lords of France and Poland each gave to the other a golden plaque, big as the palm of one's hand, well enameled and nicely worked upon which were engraved the fruits and specialties of each province, in which each was fertile: Provence, lemons and oranges; Champagne, wheat (not yet the wine); Burgundy, wines; Guyenne, warriors . . . and mark you well that all these inventions came from no other shop nor other wit than the Queen's (Catherine).[1]

And in 1581 to celebrate the marriage of the Duke of Joyeuse there was presented in Paris perhaps the most famous of all the spectacular dances ever given, the *Ballet Comique de la Royne*. For the first time there was a harmonious integration of familiar elements: music, verse, tableau, and scenery were fused into artistic unity by a coherent plot given in spoken dialogue. The presentation of this ballet is reported to have cost 3,600,000 francs. Increase the emphasis on the plot and music and you have essentially opera.

About the time when opera was beginning in Italy the great composer Monteverdi wrote music for the new type of entertainment which was given in Mantua and Florence. His *Ballo della Ingrata* required three hours for presentation; and

[1] Quoted by Lincoln Kirstein, *Dance* (Putnam's), pp. 148–49.

later ballets are reported to have run six hours or more. The Italian poet who worked with Monteverdi directed the architects in the development of marvelous spectacles, especially featuring clouds, the approach and passage of Night, and transformations. Following is a description of a scene in the spectacle presented at the marriage of Francesco Gonzaga, Duke of Mantua, and the Infanta Margherita of Savoy.

At the end of the third act, the main scene of the comedy displayed a prospect of shadowy grottos full of dread nocturnal creatures. Out of this gloomy place, Night, summoned by Mercury, arose on a starry chariot, while behind her there issued out of the cave Dreams and Phantasms on little clouds resembling a dense smoke. On the cloud nearest to the chariot of Night were Morfeo Forbetore and Fantaso, who sang. Still Night soared upwards, the sky darkening and the moon and stars appearing as she rose, the Fates appeared riding on a cloud, Jove entered on his chariot, and Aurora dawned gradually and the air was lit up by a sudden comet.

In Italy the influence of Monteverdi, Scarlatti, and other composers resulted in the supremacy of the music element in opera, while the French, lacking Italian voices and the tradition that their excellence had justified, continued to emphasize the spectacle and the ballet. To a lesser degree they have always done so since then. In the operas of Lully and of Rameau from one fourth to one third of the time was given to dancing; and ever since, in the opera as presented in France, the ballet has been given more importance than anywhere else in the world unless, perhaps, in Russia.

The early French dance entertainments were of three types: the *ballet comique*, in which the story was presented in speech; the ballet in princely houses, which led to a form of popular entertainment that stressed dancing and spectacle at the expense of dramatic interest; and the *ballet melodramatique*, with pastoral or romantic subjects, which used recitative and had a dominantly musical interest. This last type led easily to opera.

At this point it should be noted that the comic intermezzi

in Italy frequently included dancing, sometimes grotesque, sometimes merely humorous. Scarlatti wrote music for this kind of ballet, which was not an integral part of his operas; but ballet music, like ballet masters, was usually imported from France. As late as 1700 the ballet was still regarded in Italy as necessarily grotesque.

Dance has been defined as the art of steps employing graceful movements and beautiful attitudes of the whole body. But the conception of dance can easily be widened to include interpretative movements of the entire body or of any part of it. Gestures are as truly expressive as movements of the legs. In reviewing a performance of *Salomé*, Walter Terry wrote:

Ljuba Welitsch does not limit her dance expression to the Dance of the Seven Veils. She dances throughout the opera. From the tumultuous entrance when the figure with racing feet and propulsively motivated body shatters the stillness of the courtyard to the final scene when Salome crouches in half prayerful, half amorous ritual over the gruesome head of the Prophet, Miss Welitsch employs the expressional powers of dance to trace the tortuous paths of Salome's emotional adventure.

Gesturely the soprano is often magnificent. She tosses her mercurochrome-colored hair in defiance, runs her fingers through it in sensual fashion, she clutches it in the frenzy of a tantrum. Her arms thrown wide, her body held high to entice the Prophet; the clenching of fists, the contraction of the torso, the twist of the shoulders as she is spurned and the nervous plucking of the cape and the skirt are but a few of the gestural patterns which mirror the heart of Salome. In the way of large-scale movements Miss Welitsch makes use of crashing falls, of vibratory movements which make the entire body tremble with anger or lust, of full-body contractions and releases which tell of Salome's shifting impulses, of percussive motion which characterizes the imperious Princess, of sinuous action which suggests the passionate woman.

A case of laryngitis should never cause Miss Welitsch to cancel a performance of this work. The results would not be opera, but it still would be an engrossing, if soundless, dramatic study of a passionate woman, for where some other opera singers appear to be propelled into various degrees of action merely by the gusts of air which govern the intensity of their notes. Ljuba Welitsch seems to be propelled into rhythmic, dynamic, and patterned action by the inner compulsions of the character she is portraying. In this sense in *Salome* at least she is dancing.[2]

Ballet, of which dance is an adornment, consists of design in related figures. It is, as Chujoy says, "a very definite art form based on the classic technique and tradition, and its underlying principle is the reduction of human gesture to bare essentials, heightened and developed into meaningful patterns." The *ballet d'action* is dance to music with gesture and pantomime to interpret a mood or a plot. The *ballet divertissement* differs chiefly in that it has greater variety, intricacy, and expressiveness in its movements.

Walter Terry says, "Ballet is an art exhibit, a symphonic concert, a beauty contest, a drama, and a track meet all rolled into one big, spectacular event. . . . There is always something going on at the ballet to keep one attentive and interested." And Perugini gives a more helpful characterization. He says,

[The ballet is] an orchestra of dancers who are also mimes, who represent—one should rather say, realize—the imaginative creations of an author, or a number of authors, working harmoniously together, in terms of rhythmic movement and dramatic expression, with the aid of color and movement and sound. Every step of every dancer, every gesture, every phase of music, is composed and selected to express particular ideas or series of ideas; every color and each change of tone in the whole symphony of hues has been appraised. Not a thing that happens is haphazard.[3]

The ballet as we know it in opera makes demands on the cooperative contributions of the dramatist, who creates a situation in which dance has significance, the choreographer, the scenic artist, the costume designer, the composer of music, and the dancers. Each adds something to the effectiveness of the whole. To appreciate the several contributions, consider a

[2] Walter Terry, *Invitation to the Dance* (New York: A. S. Barnes, 1942).
[3] Mark E. Perugini, *Art of the Ballet* (London: Jarrolds, 1935).

ballet presented without costumes or scenery, the tempo being given only by the clacking of castanets. It is far more difficult for the ballet to be successful, even with the aid of the elements just mentioned, when it has to create its own atmosphere and tell its own story. Contrast the best independent ballet that you have ever seen with the Dance of the Blessed Spirits in *Orfeo ed Euridice,* where the drama has already developed a situation that explains the ballet and invites its contribution to heighten the effect. The spectator should always attempt to fuse all the observed elements into one aesthetically effective whole, but he can at the same time appreciate the contribution that each one makes.

The common bond between dance and music is, of course, rhythm. Both attempt as a rule to express human emotions.

The dance rhythm is carried out not only as far as the musical measure, or group of measures, is concerned, but much deeper; the rhythmic justification in choreographic terms of the musical composition as a whole, of its theme and mood. The musical themes are bound with the choreographic, and unity of form is achieved. The emotional rises in the dance coincide with the emotional rises in the music, and the curve of the movements. Every change of key in the musical composition is paralleled by a change of key in the choreographic, every musical major and minor finds its equivalent in the choreographic. The instrumentalizations of the musical composition are reflected on the stage: every group of instruments in the orchestra has its counterpart on the stage.[4]

The ballet has always been more pleasing to some operagoers than the music itself. In the early days, especially in France, it was demanded, and it needed to have only the slightest connection with the plot. Frequently a successful ballet in one opera was lifted and inserted in another, not because it contributed to the development of the music drama, but because the audience liked it. This was, of course, frankly a *divertissement.* When opera was introduced into Russia the ballet could always be counted on as a drawing card when

[4] Anatole Chujoy, *The Symphonic Ballet* (New York: Kamin Publishers, 1932), pp. 20, 23.

the music and action failed. In 1773 the English traveler
Burney wrote from Paris that everyone who goes to the opera
"either yawns or laughs, except when roused or amused by the
dances or decorations." However popular the ballet was in
Paris, the French public did not like sustained dance. They
preferred their ballets to be short, with simple plots having
little or no logical sequence, and inserted into the operas.
Though many were to our modern notion absurd intrusions,
they were in France the most pleasing aesthetic expression
during the first half of the eighteenth century.

The greatest influence in forming and in modifying French
taste was Lully (1633–1687), an Italian dancer who became
the first great opera composer and director in France. As a
dancer he understood the problems of ballet music, which he
composed with a free-flowing melody sustained by simple
counterpoint. He incorporated into his ballets passages of
recitative that gave them meaning, and he developed the importance of symphonic music so that dance became not wholly
an end in itself but to a large extent an inherent part of the
opera. He insisted on a unified coherence—one poet, one
composer, one designer of decor, and one director. Yet
he never wholly got away from the idea that the ballet was
a *divertissement*. He merely attempted to integrate the ballet
with the opera by writing music which gave to its movements
a character harmonious with the musical drama. Unlike the
Italian ballets of his time, Lully's were not merely intermezzi
between the acts.

At the time of Lully, ballet problems were complicated by
a narrow stage and the necessity of the dancers' facing an
audience. Previously, when ballets were a part of masque or
of a spectacle given in the great hall of some nobleman, with
the spectators ranged all around on the same level, the problems of the choreographer were vastly different. Lully realized
that when the dancers were elevated on a stage they had to
face the spectators as much as possible, to make pleasing
silhouettes for them, and to add pleasing vertical movements

to those that had previously been on a horizontal plane. Thus began an increased use of the arms and greater activity of the whole body, but to no such extent as later. The ballet of the seventeenth century was, to our modern way of thinking, stiff, relying for its effect, mostly on feet and legs.

After Lully, France came to supply dance music for the continent. Though the Italians were developing the musical side of opera, both the vocal and the instrumental, the French continued their devotion to the ballet. In the first half of the eighteenth century they developed a new form, the opera-ballet, a sort of opera in which dancing and orchestral music predominated. Each act was on a different subject, each a little opera in itself, with the dramatic action and the vocal music reduced to a minimum. Gradually the opera-ballet "suffered the crystallization of formula and academic inertia." Long books were written still further to fix the tradition of efficiently presenting a movement, or a series of movements, which had already got far from portraying natural feeling. When the formalized ballet was so dominant that the poet, the composer of the music, and the scenic artist were not expected to cooperate with the *maître de ballet*, the time was ripe for reform.

Reform came with Jean Georges Noverre (1727–1810), though he was long denied a post in his native Paris. Sympathizing with Gluck's contention for the unity of all the arts, he sought first to make the dance a living unity in itself. In his celebrated *Lettres sur la Danse* Noverre wrote, "A well-composed ballet is a living picture of the passions, manners, habits, ceremonies, and customs. . . . If it is devoid of expression, of striking pictures or strong situations, it becomes a cold and dreary spectacle." He wished the ballet to mask illusion from the spectator and to transport him in a moment to the spot where the action has taken place and to fill him with the same thoughts that he would have were he in reality to share in the experiences of the drama. Holding that mere technical mastery of steps was no longer enough, Noverre contended that all dance action should emanate from deep emotion, and that the *corps de ballet*, instead of being a mere decorative background, should participate in the action of the drama. He wanted the pantomime to appeal to the intellect as well as to the eye.

His arguments and his vigor not only gave actual life to the ballet, but forced composers to write dance music that expressed the feelings in the dramatic situation. That the dancers might be more effective, Noverre had them remove the facial masks that were traditional, and he brought about reform in the costumes that they wore, a reform that had already been advocated by others.

The ballet dancers of the preceding period had worn heavy costumes, dresses with panniers, frameworks to enlarge a woman's skirts at the hips, wigs, shoes with high heels, and other impediments to free body movements. Male dancers, when not costumed in accord with the assumed style of the scene of the drama or when they did not wear court costume, had long sleeves, a velvet bodice and trunks, with long tights. The dances were of course necessarily stiff and formal.

In the early part of the eighteenth century all sorts of anachronisms were committed with costume. Warriors of different nations appeared and danced *pas seuls* wearing laced tunics and wigs with pigtails a yard long, two in front and two behind, neatly plaited and richly powdered so that when they shook their heads or became animated, clouds of hair powder were seen. The wigs were surmounted by helmets, and the manly breasts of the much-beribboned warriors were encased in a cuirass.

In 1734 Sallé, a female dancer, created a sensation in London by appearing in a muslin costume without head dress; and a few years later Camargo almost caused a scandal by wearing a skirt that reached just below the knees.* Those who are especially interested in the evolving costumes of ballet dancers

---

* Boys, who had earlier taken women's parts in ballets, had gradually been replaced, beginning about fifty years before this time.

may find illustrations in Paul Magriel's *Ballet* and similar books.

Other great contributors to the development of the dance are Vigano, who about the beginning of the nineteenth century popularized a naturalistic rhythmic pantomime subordinated to music; Taglioni, who a few years later introduced toe dancing, "the speech of the inexpressible"; and others, especially Russians, of whom only Fokine will be mentioned.

In a letter to the London *Times* in 1910 Fokine stated his principles of ballet, which may be taken broadly to express the general ideals of the present time. They are:

To invent in each case a new form of movement, corresponding to the subject and character of the music, instead of merely giving combinations of ready-made steps.

Dancing and gesture in ballet have no meaning unless they serve as an expression of dramatic action.

To admit the use of conventional gesture only when it is required by the style of the ballet, and in all other cases to replace the gestures of the hands by movements of the whole body. Man can and should be expressive from head to foot.

The group is not merely an ornament. The new ballet advances from the expressiveness of the face or the hands to that of the whole body, and from that of the individual body to groups of bodies and the expressiveness of the combined dancing of a crowd.

The alliance of dancing on equal terms with the other arts. The new ballet does not demand "ballet music" from the composer, nor "tutus" and pink satin slippers from the designer; it gives complete liberty to their creative powers.[5]

BALLET IN OPERA

The immediately preceding notes concern primarily the independent ballet, but what was happening in it also was happening in the ballet that was associated with opera.

In its association with opera, dance is often an inherent part, but often it also is introduced as an interlude, either for beauty or for humor. Gluck established the tradition that there should be a ballet in the second and the fourth acts of

[5] Paul Magriel, *Ballet, An Illustrated Outline* (New York: Kamin Publishers, 1938), pp. 42–45.

operas, a tradition that became so strong in Paris that the members of the Jockey Club practically booed *Tannhäuser* off the stage when Wagner, who had little liking for the ballet, so far yielded to advice of the management as to introduce into the *first* act a dance to the Venusberg music. The opera habituées asserted with hoots their right to come late and yet see the ballet.

Opera composers between Gluck and Wagner made much of the ballet, chiefly no doubt because it was a popular tradition which they saw no reason to abandon. Also, when skillfully used, it was a valuable means of securing aesthetic and dramatic effects, and it afforded opportunity for writing a type of music that was a challenge to creative genius. Naturally opera composers varied in the use that they made of ballet and in the emphasis that they gave to it, partly because of their interest and technical knowledge, and partly because of appropriateness to the plot to be developed. Such showmen as Meyerbeer made much of the ballet in pageantry and spectacle. Gradually it was more and more incorporated into the plot and became not merely decorative but also an integral part of structural development.

Committed to his theory that the opera should be a complete unity, Wagner was interested in the dance only as the mimicry by the whole body contributed to a harmonious development of the dramatic story being conveyed by music and song. And yet Wagner often gets the essential effects of dance by a simple gesture, the brandishing of a sword, the lifting of a cup, the trembling of a veil, Mime's scowl, and the like, and the dance of the flower maidens in *Parsifal* is well known. Although Verdi was never completely at home with dance effects, one of the most magnificent ballets in opera is found in the triumphal scene in *Aïda*. Puccini used no ballets at all.

A twin of the ballet is the social or folk dance. In *Traviata*, *Romeo and Juliet*, and *Rigoletto* we see the characters whirling in dances which furnish harmonious background but do nothing to forward the dramatic action. Similar is the stately Spanish dance at the end of the third act of *The Marriage of Figaro*. And in *The Bartered Bride* and *Die Meistersinger* are characteristic folk dances exemplifying the spirit of the scene. In contrast the solo dances in *Salomé* and *Carmen* are dramatically essential.

THREE TYPES OF BALLET IN OPERA

In the opera that we see and hear today there are three distinct types of dance or ballet. First there is that which is an integral part of the dramatic movement. In *Carmen* the ballet of the gypsies is decorative, but the solo dance of Carmen herself is an essential part of the drama. So are solo dances of Electra and of Salome. The dance in *Coq d' Or* could be omitted only with grave loss. In *Aïda* the ballet is a natural part of the pageant of victory. For this type of dance or ballet the composer of course writes the music just as he does for the songs.

Second, there is the dance which, though not essential to the dramatic movement, furnishes an appropriate background for the music and the action. The dance in the first scene of *Rigoletto* is a good example. Though it is not necessary to the advancement of the plot, the dancing by the courtiers while the Duke sings of his amorous adventures is just as harmonious a contribution as the setting of the room in the palace. In *Don Giovanni* the dances accompanied by three orchestras on different balconies of the ballroom are mere background for the action, as is the Kermesse in *Faust*. The dance in *Thaïs* emphasizes the contrast between the gaiety of the court and the poverty of the Cenobite monk Athanaël. For this type of dance also the composer provides music.

Third is the *divertissement*, a ballet introduced at any point in the opera, between the scenes or even during a suspension of the action, for the pleasure that it can give. In no sense is it necessary to the development of the plot; in fact, it usually causes an interruption which some opera lovers resent, but in which others delight. Usually there is an attempt to make the ballet as harmonious as possible with setting and plot.

The dances in the second act of *The Bartered Bride* and in Menotti's *Amahl* are mostly *divertissements*. The music may be provided by the composer, but not infrequently it has been drawn from some other composition of his or even written in a similar style by someone else. Berlioz adapted Weber's "Invitation à la Valse" for the dance in *Der Freischütz* when it was presented in Paris, and later he expressed his indignation when music by another composer was used. An orchestration of Mozart's "Rondo alla Turca," from the piano Sonata in A, is commonly used for his *Entführung aus dem Serail;* Bizet's *Jolie Fille de Perth* music has frequently been used for a ballet in *Carmen.*

On the other hand, ballets originally provided by the composer are sometimes omitted when the opera is given outside of France. A notable instance is the frequent omission of the ballet and its music in Gounod's *Faust.* This is due sometimes to a lack elsewhere of the passion for the ballet that is still strong in Paris, sometimes to a desire to shorten the performance, and sometimes to inability to muster a corps of competent dancers.

In *Alcestis* the first ballet, though not necessary to the drama, is a pleasing insertion. The second ballet (in Act III), on the other hand, is an integral part of the drama, a celebration of the safe return of Admetus from the gates of hell. It is unique in that it closes the opera, the subsequent chorus in the text usually being omitted.

In *Orfeo ed Euridice* the dance of the Blessed Spirits, though beautiful and harmonious, is not dramatically functional; but the spectacle of the Furies is. In the best performances it is not a mere waving of green scarfs, but a horrifying mass of the damned crawling toward Orfeo and threatening to tear him limb from limb. The half prostrate figures sweep upward, with arms waving and mingling tumultuously, wavering like lurid flames from the underworld. There are pauses of movement, sudden stiffenings and convulsions as the damned spirits repeatedly thunder "No!" to Orfeo's pleading.

FORM IN BALLET

A good ballet is said to have a form of composition comparable to that in the other arts: a unity to which a hierarchy of parts all contribute. But this form is often difficult, if not impossible, for the amateur to discover; so difficult, in fact, that there is a reasonable doubt that in many cases it exists. There seem to be two theories held by choreographers.

On the one hand, there are those who work on the basis of "self-expression," making the desire to dance the only requisite for the making of dances and never doubting that audiences will consider it a privilege to watch the physical venting of emotional overcharges. At the other extreme are those who treat composition as an entirely objective process, consisting of the putting together of "steps" and movements, either so that they conform to some predetermined pattern recognized as a good form, or so that they build in climactic values. Good art somehow never merely superimposes form on its materials, or vice versa, but rather, through a combination of knowledge, perspective, and hard labor compels its material to evolve its own forms.

The medium of the dance is movement, and not only movement, but a continuum of movement, so to speak. Merely stringing together isolated postures, pantomimic or pictorial, arbitrary arrangements or disarrangements of the members, nervous fidgetings, or virtuoso acrobatics, is not dance composition, any more than putting together a collection of interesting noises is musical composition.[6]

The amateur operagoer should note the purpose for which a ballet is introduced into opera. If it is an essential part of the development, he should appreciate it as such. If it is merely decorative, like scenery or costumes, he should not look for any more vital contribution. And if it is frankly a *divertissement*, he should enjoy it as beautiful dancing and at its conclusion be ready to pick up the thread of the opera where it was broken by the interruption.

[6] John Martin, "Dance." *New York Times*, December 18, 1938.

Appendix A

BOOKS ABOUT OPERA AND OPERA
COMPOSERS: A SELECTED LIST

WILLIAM F. APTHORP, *The Opera Past and Present.* Scribner's.

PAUL BEKKER, *The Changing Opera.* Norton.

—— *The Story of Music.* Norton.

ALLEN M. BERNSTEIN, *The Do-Re-Mi of the Niebelung Ring.* Greenberg.

WALLACE BROCKWAY and ROBERT WEINSTOCK, *The Opera: A History of Its Creation and Performance.* Simon & Schuster.

EDWARD J. DENT, *Opera.* Penguin Books.

—— *Mozart's Operas.* Chatto & Windus.

DAVIS EWEN, *Encyclopedia of Opera.* A. A. Wyn.

LAWRENCE GILMAN, *Strauss's Salomé, a Guide to the Opera.* Lane.

—— *Wagner's Operas.* Farrar & Rinehart.

—— *Aspects of Modern Opera.* Dodd, Mead.

BORIS GOLDOVSKY and MARY ELLIS PELTZ, *Accents on Opera* (Goldovsky's talks on radio broadcasts of opera). Farrar, Strauss and Young.

ROSE HEYLBUT and AIMÉ GERBER, *Backstage at the Opera.* Scribner's.

ERNEST G. HUTCHINSON, *Electra, a Guide to the Opera.* Schirmer.

—— *A Musical Guide to Wagner's Ring of the Niebelungs.* Simon & Schuster.

JOSEPH KERMAN, *Opera as Drama.* Knopf.

ALBERT LAVIGNAC, *The Music Dramas of Richard Wagner and His Festival Theater in Bayreuth.* Dodd, Mead.

ROBERT LAWRENCE, *The World of Opera.* Thomas Nelson.

GEORGE E. MAREK, *World's Treasury of Grand Opera.* Harper's.

ERNEST NEWMAN, *Gluck and His Opera*. Bertram Dobell.
—— *Richard Strauss*. Lane.
—— *Wagner as Man and Artist*. Knopf.
—— *The Wagner Operas*. Knopf.
G. BERNARD SHAW, *The Perfect Wagnerite, A Commentary on the Ring of the Niebelungs*. Brentano.
RICHARD SPECHT, *Giacomo Puccini*. Knopf.
RICHARD A. STREATFEILD, *The Opera*. Routledge.
G. HOWARD TAUBMAN, *Opera Front and Back*. Scribner's.
FRANCIS TOYE, *Giuseppe Verdi: His Life and Works*. Knopf.
—— *Rossini, A Study in Tragi-Comedy*. Knopf.
W. J. TURNER, *Mozart—The Man and His Works*. Knopf.

Appendix B

STORIES OF OPERAS:
A SELECTED LIST

LOUIS BIANCOLLI, *The Opera Reader*. McGraw-Hill.
LOUIS BIANCOLLI and ROBERT BAGAR, *Victor Book of Opera*. Simon & Schuster.
MILTON CROSS, *Complete Stories of the Great Operas*. Doubleday.
OLIN DOWNES, *Ten Operatic Masterpieces*. Scribner's.
RUDOLPH FELLNER, *Opera Themes and Plots*. Simon & Schuster.
JOHN TASKER HOWARD, *The World's Great Operas*. Random House.
GUSTAV KOBBÉ, *Kobbé's Complete Opera Book*, edited and revised by Lord Harewood. Putnam.
FREDERICK H. MARTENS, *1001 Nights of Opera*. Appleton.
HAROLD VINCENT MULLIGAN, *Stories of Famous Operas*. Signet Key Books.
ERNEST NEWMAN, *Stories of the Great Operas and Their Composers*. Alfred A. Knopf, Inc. 3 volumes in one.
—— *More Stories of Famous Operas*. Knopf.
MARY ELLIS PELTZ and ROBERT LAWRENCE, *The Metropolitan Opera Guide*. The Modern Library.
HENRY W. SIMON, *A Festival of Opera*. Hanover House.
HENRY W. SIMON and ABRAHAM VINUS, *Pocket Book of Great Operas*. Pocket Books.
Opera News, published by the Metropolitan Opera Guild, 654 Madison Avenue, is indispensable for those who listen to opera broadcasts. Besides containing articles of general interest, it presents the casts that will sing, a brief outline of the story, a description of costumes and scenery, and discriminating criticism of phonograph recordings of operas.